Barbara Sato

The New Japanese Woman

MODERNITY, MEDIA, AND WOMEN IN INTERWAR JAPAN

Duke University Press   Durham and London   2003

© 2003 Duke University Press

All rights reserved

Printed in the United States of America

on acid-free paper ∞

Designed by C. H. Westmoreland

Typeset in Palatino by Tseng Information Systems, Inc.

Library of Congress Cataloging-in-Publication

Data appear on the last printed

page of this book.

The New Japanese Woman

ASIA-PACIFIC: CULTURE, POLITICS, AND SOCIETY

Editors: Rey Chow, H. D. Harootunian, and Masao Miyoshi

賜台覧

婦人世界

十月特輯
安産と難産號

FOR KAZI AND SHO

Contents

List of Illustrations

PLATES (between pages 82–83)

Acknowledgments

I finally am able to thank those people whose advice and guidance saw me through what sometimes seemed like an obscurely lighted tunnel. It is impossible to properly acknowledge everyone, but each of you helped in a special way to bring this book to completion.

At Columbia University, my mentor, Carol Gluck, imparted the fine points of Japanese history and the desire to strive for the academic excellence apparent in her own work. She guided me through every stage of the dissertation process, reading and rereading numerous drafts, always offering insightful criticism. Special thanks to my teachers: the late Herschel Webb, Arthur Tiedemann, and Paul Varley. Thanks also go to Gina Bookhout and the Department of East Asian Languages and Cultures; to Madge Huntington and the East Asian Institute; and to Amy Heinrich, Ken Harlin, and John McClure of the C. V. Starr Library.

Without the support of Harry Harootunian the dissertation could not have become a book. Harry's meticulous comments made the task of rewriting an exercise for which no words of thanks can suffice. Harry introduced me to an exciting world of critical scholarship, of which his work forms an integral part. Louise Young helped me shape and reshape my ideas, read innumerable versions of the manuscript, and offered criticism and encouragment. Harry and Louise invited me to participate in the Japan Seminar hosted by New York University in 1995, as well as their graduate seminar in 1998. The suggestions I received on both occasions were invaluable.

During my days in the doctoral program at the Institute of Journalism and Communication Studies at Tokyo University, Uchikawa Yoshimi spent endless hours sharing his vast knowledge of newspapers and magazines with me and debating the complexities of my research project. Arase Yutaka, Kōchi Saburō, and Kōchi Nobuko contributed greatly to my understanding of the 1920s.

I wish to thank Seikei University, where I am affiliated, for providing a generous grant to help offset publishing costs. Special thanks to Aono Kōko, Katō Takashi, Yanai Michio, and all my colleagues at Seikei for their support and for creating a stimulating atmosphere for work. The Center for Asian and Pacific Studies at Seikei offered encouragement and funding. Thanks are due to Kōmura Chikara, Suzuki Kenji, Takeshi Tomita, and staff members Hiroshi Hasebe, Satoko Uno, and Oi Toshiaki.

To the Seikei University library staff for your patience and the facilities that made my research possible, to the folks at Tokyo University, Waseda University, Musashino Bijutsu Daigaku Bitjutsu Shiryō Toshokan, Nihon Manga Shiryōkan, Kokusai Nihon Bunka Kenkyū Center, the archives at Mainichi Shinbun, Shufu no tomo, and the Fujin kōron—sincere appreciation.

Deep gratitude to the late Minami Hiroshi and to the members of the Shōwa bunka kenkyūkai (Ishikawa Hiroyoshi, Sakata Minoru, Orihashi Tetsuhiko, Ueda Yasuo, Takeyama Akiko, Ichikawa Kōichi, Yanagi Yōko, Chiba Nobuo, Ikari Seiya, and the late Satō Takeshi and Shibuya Shigemitsu) for friendship and the opportunity to explore the possibilities of Japanese *modanizumu* as part of cooperative research projects. Thanks also are due to Azuma Emiko and Yamaguchi Tomoko.

To Don Roden—whose friendship and scholarship I hold in high esteem—for his thoughtful readings of the manuscript and his invaluable suggestions. To Jim Fujii for always making time to read one more chapter and including provocative comments in the margins. To Kathy Uno for perceptive readings and advice. To Paddi Tsurumi, Sandra Wilson, David Wells, Ulrike Wöhr, Furuyama Nobutaka for their advice and encouragement.

To Suzuki Sadami, thank you for your friendship and intellectual support, and for charting a new course in interdisciplinary studies. To Sonoda Hidehiro, for being there and helping clarify my arguments. To Arai Noriko, Araya Shigehiko, Arima Hideko, Asaoka Kunio, Egami Wataru, Eto Fumio, Fujita Keisuke, Haga Tōru, Hama Yuki, Hayashi Hirotchika, Ibi Takashi, Ikegami Hiroko, Inoue Ken, Inoue Shōichi, Inoue Teruko, Jinno Yuki, Kadoguchi Mitsunori, Kakegawa Tomiko, Kamibiyashi Chieko, Kimura Ryōko, Kenjo Takehide, Mizukoshi Shin, Liu Jinhui, Muta Kazue, Nakae Keiko, Nakagawa Shigemi, Nakai Takeshi, Nakazato Akihiko, Naramoto Akiko. To Narita Ryūichi, Narita

Tamiko, Nishizaki Fumiko, Ochiai Emiko, Ōkubo Yōko, Okuno Masa-hiro, Omuka Toshiharu, Ōno Harumi, Ōshima Hisako, Makino Ma-moru, Sasaki Ayao, Senda Yuki, Shimada Atsushi, Shimokobe Mitsuko, Shinohara Hajime, Sugiyama Mitsunobu, Sung Hae-Kyung, Suzuki Kenji, Suzuki Yasuko, Takata Akihiko, Takeuchi Keiko, Takemura Tamio, Yamaguchi Masao, Yamazaki Takayasu, Yoshimi Shun'ya. To the members of WINC and the Tokyo Modern Japanese History Workshop, my thanks.

To John Dower, Julie Rousseau, and Wendy Spinks for invaluable help in the early stages of this project. To David Ambaras, Robert Angel, Jan Bardsley, Mary Baron, Milton Baron, Margaret Beetham, Kim Brandt, Mike Brownstein, Geoffrey Chambers, John Clark, Sandra Col-lins, Elyssa Faison, Josh Fogel, Atina Grossmann, Ellen Hammond, Yu-kiko Haniwa, Robin Harris, Amy Heinrich, Joke Hermes. To Keiko Ikeda, Mark Jones, Joan Judge, Roz Kalb, Ayako Kano, Jeff Kingston, Earl Kinmonth, Dina Lowy, Barbara Molony, Carol Morley, Kate Nakai, Kathleen Nelson, Lucy North, Peter O'Connor, Ken Oshima, Linda Penkower, Gregory Pflugfelder, Ellen Radovic, Giles Richter, Betsy Roadman, Larry Roadman, Alan Rubens, Joanne Rubens, Louisa Rubin-fein, Jordan Sand, Robin Sears, Fred Shane, Bonnie Simon, Steve Simon, Henry Smith, Judith Snodgrass, Michiko Suzuki, Elise Tipton, Ron Toby, Julia Thomas, Gennifer Weisenfeld, Leila Wice, Jack Wool, Jenny Wool, Verna Wool, my appreciation.

How do I thank Reynolds Smith for taking on this project and see-ing it through to the finish? And Pam Morrison for guiding me through the editorial and production process and for her endless patience. And Katie Courtland, Christine Kealy Jensen, Sharon Torian, and the entire staff at Duke. And Cherie Westmoreland for the superb cover design. Mindy Conner's careful job of editing saved me from many miscommu-nications, as did Nancy Zibman's creative work on the index. Indeed, I am fortunate to be included in the Duke University Press Asia-Pacific Series.

To my parents the late Moses Shapiro and Elizabeth Shapiro, my dear soul mate. To the late Kazuma Sato and Noriko Sato and to my family in Japan. To Brenda Lewis, Herbert Lewis, Joshua Goldberg, Erika Goldberg-Murray, Sam Murray, thanks is not enough.

And finally, to Kazuki Sato and my son Sho, who never took a family vacation without books and the computer. Thank you both. Kazi, the numerous discussions we shared infinitely broadened my historical perceptions. Your criticisms, though not always easy to accept, always were on target.

Factual and interpretive errors are solely my own.

Chapter 2 is a reworked and expanded version of my article "The *Moga* Sensation: Perceptions of the *Modan Gāru* in Japanese Intellectual Circles during the 1920s," *Gender and History* 5, no. 3 (1993): 361–81, Blackwell Publishers. Chapter 4 is a reworked and extended version of chapter 8 in *Being Modern in Japan: Culture and Society from the 1910s to the 1930s,* ed. Elise K. Tipton and John Clark (Singapore: Australian Humanities Research Foundation, 2000).

Prologue

WOMEN AND THE REALITY OF THE EVERYDAY

Identity is actually something formed through unconscious
processes over time, rather than being innate in consciousness at birth. There is always something "imaginary" or fanta-
sized about its unity. It always remains incomplete, is always
"in process," always "being formed."—Stuart Hall[1]

In interwar Japan as well as in Western countries, technological growth,
industrial expansion, and the acceleration of urbanization redefined the
practices of everyday life. This process of social change produced an
explosion of new images of dynamic women. In the media, women appeared in the guises of café waitress, housewife, dancer, and shop girl.
In magazines, books, and movies, women became prominent icons of
the modern city, strolling through bustling shopping districts and becoming a presence on crowded buses and streetcars. These images of
women were notable for their mutability as well as their novelty: the
persona of the shopper changed as quickly as fashions in clothing; the
middle-class housewife remade herself as she moved from one hobby
to another. Such images defined the modern woman as both multifaceted and ceaselessly changing.

These new images of the feminine challenged a previously existing widespread mythology of a monolithic Japanese woman. Feminine stereotypes had always placed women within a family setting,
stressing their gentleness and meekness: it was this particularly docile
and family-oriented quality that came to identify them as "Japanese" women. The endorsement in 1891 of Prussian adviser Herman

Techow's plan for the Meiji Civil Code that sanctioned a legal system in keeping with Japanese values supported that image. In the 1920s, the representations that circulated of independent working women and decadent, outspoken flappers began to loosen the hold of this mythology.

The myth did not yield to change immediately. Aspects of it were still present in postwar Japan. Director Ozu Yasujirō's most famous film, *Tokyo Story* (*Tokyo monogatari*, 1953), explores the disjunction between a stereotyped "traditional" Japanese woman and the complex identities that constituted the "modern" Japanese woman in the early 1950s.[2] Certainly, the themes addressed in *Tokyo Story* cannot be divided into clear binaries. Nevertheless, the breakdown of the family brought about by postwar urbanization, the main theme of the movie, highlights how these phenomena shape the behavior of the female characters that dominate the film. Ozu's women are almost bewildering in their complex mix of the old and the new, Western and Japanese, rational and emotional, independent and self-effacing. In making these characters a mélange of qualities that draw on images of both "traditional" and "modern" women, Ozu directs viewers' attention to the contradictions inherent in the concept of the Japanese feminine. Ozu's vivid depictions of multidimensional women belie the authenticity of stereotypical Japanese female images.

Shige, the brash wife and eldest daughter of the family portrayed in *Tokyo Story*, provides one example of this complex notion of the feminine. While in some ways Shige fits the stereotype, in others she does not. She works in her home on the outskirts of Tokyo as a hairdresser. This portrayal captures her within a purely domestic space and identifies her with work performed by women since premodern times. And yet her cavalier treatment of her parents evinces the cool and calculating behavior often associated with modern womanhood. The scene in which Shige discusses preparations with her brother, Kōichi, about an impending visit to their ailing mother in Hiroshima epitomizes this motif. Shige, still uncertain of the seriousness of their mother's condition, calmly poses the question of whether to pack mourning clothes or not. When Kōichi's surprise at her callousness causes him to hesitate before voicing a tepid acquiescence, Shige quickly retorts: "Settled. Let's pack them just in case. If we don't end up wearing them, all the better."[3] Shige's assessment of the situation, despite her professed filial piety, upsets the commonly articulated conception of Japanese women.

For both Japanese and Western audiences, Shige's thinking reflects the shifting demands of her age exemplified in behavior that eludes a simple Western/non-Western dichotomy. Her matter-of-fact subordination of family claims to the demands of her work makes Shige a disquieting image of domesticity. Nevertheless, even Shige, on occasion embodying a mixture of "old" and "new," engages in a struggle to situate herself within broader social practices; in this case, those of urban professional women, first represented by the working woman of the 1920s. It is not Shige, however, but the widowed daughter-in-law Noriko who outwardly exhibits the qualities of a working woman active in a wider society. And yet, Noriko conforms to female behavior appropriate within the family. While Shige and Kōichi are too caught up in their personal lives to do anything for their parents, Noriko remains a paragon of filial piety. She leaves work without complaint to entertain her parents-in-law during their visit to Tokyo, and later remains with the father to ease his adjustment to his wife's death long after the others have paid their perfunctory respects and departed. This behavior is at odds with Noriko's image, the prevailing stereotype of the modern single woman. For it is Noriko who lives alone, independent of her family in a modern apartment complex (*danchi*), and commutes daily to her white-collar job as a clerk in a modern office. She clings stubbornly to the past, however, reluctant to embrace views that might alter her private life.

Noriko's mother-in-law, Tomi, is another hybrid character. In a poignant dialogue, the aging Tomi addresses the dutiful Noriko:

Tomi: Ahhhh, Jōji has been dead for over eight years, but the thought of your displaying his picture and other mementos makes my heart ache for you. Thinking about it, I realize the injustice our family has inflicted on you. . . . Should there be a good person, please feel free to marry.

Noriko: This is my wish. I am satisfied with my life as it is.

For a moment the viewer is caught off guard as the seemingly "traditional," *yukata*-clad Tomi, always deferential to her own husband, logically implores Noriko to begin anew, to forget old family customs and remarry. It is precisely such unexpected twists that account for the popularity of Ozu's movies and the appeal of his heroines.[4]

The tensions in the figure of the feminine depicted in Ozu's women remained the central problematic of discourse on the Japanese woman long into the postwar period. Its origins go back to the 1900s, when the destabilizing images of the modern woman first appeared. In this book I take up the irruption of these images of urban modern women onto the social scene in Japan during the interwar years. Central to the story is the role of mass women's magazines in the social and cultural construction of a new set of possibilities for middle-class women to act and to imagine themselves within the context of consumerism.

Capturing Women's History

The historiography of modern women in Japan reflects many of the dilemmas depicted in Ozu's movie. With the "liberation" of women as an important priority of the postwar Occupation reforms, books offering guidance on how to live in a "democratic" (*minshū*) society and books devoted to women's history enjoyed wide popularity.[5]

Probably no book was more important in constructing a master narrative of Japanese women than Marxist historian Inoue Kiyoshi's classic study, *A History of Japanese Women* (*Nihon joseishi*). Published in 1948, just a few years before *Tokyo Story* was released, Inoue's book concentrated on the mechanisms of the oppression of Japanese women, unwittingly reinforcing the stereotype of abjection and passivity that Ozu's film would challenge. Inoue's history linked the suppression of Japanese women to the Emperor System (*tennōsei*) through an analysis that blamed their plight on the peculiarities of the state and placed women's suffering in a class by itself.[6] Such histories painted a picture of a downtrodden female population awaiting enlightenment, modernization, and liberation.

The first postwar histories and guidebooks demonstrated how the process of liberation, and hence the very inception of the "modern woman," began with the reduction of the emperor and his family to a largely symbolic role in the wake of Japan's defeat in World War II. Inoue and later authors who studied educated women and feminists, such as women historians Tanaka Sumiko, Ide Fumiko, and Horiba Kiyoko, took less interest in women who fell outside that category. In this sense their work shared the perspective of research in the fields of general political and intellectual history that focused on upper-class members of the bureaucracy and intellectuals.[7]

From the late 1940s onward, Inoue's work was echoed even by so-called liberal intellectuals like Maruyama Masao and Ōtsuka Hisao, who were enjoying newfound academic freedom with the end of the wartime regime. Critical assessménts of Japan's modern age helped popularize the view that the thought patterns embedded in the Japanese political and social systems were directed toward preserving "traditional" values.[8] From the standpoint of women, however, the overturning of the Tokugawa regime in 1868 did not bring about a fundamental reordering of gender relationships. Conversely, the enactment of the Meiji Civil Code legalized women's social status and place within the patriarchal family system.

In 1970, writer and independent scholar Murakami Nobuhiko posited a new approach to women's history. Murakami insisted that "because women's history is a 'history of women,' from the outset it is not a history of special women. To select women on the basis of their being famous does not constitute history."[9] Criticizing Inoue for the narrowness of his perspective, Murakami gained the support of historians Irokawa Daikichi and Kanō Masanao, both champions of people's history (minshūshi).[10] Though the majority of historians still sided with Inoue's political approach, Murakami's arguments encouraged a broader methodology. He attempted to observe the everyday lives of women from outside the domain of the state, viewing women as a social group driven by independent rhythms.

Studies published in the 1980s followed Murakami and no longer accentuated the role of privileged women. While women's history continued to be viewed as a process of self-liberation, the category was extended to include women who participated in small, regional labor and civic movements. This line of argument departed from earlier narratives, which attributed women's inferior status and liberation primarily to the effects of powerful outside forces. In their quest to uncover moments of self-liberation, historians moved the spotlight away from national politics and elite movements, and highlighted women distant from the political and economic center—women who worked in spinning mills, tuberculosis-ridden factories, and farm villages.[11] Moreover, other topics like the "good wife and wise mother" (ryōsai kenbo) ideology, home, and family, which since the late nineteenth century had been concerns for scholars and government officials, were not subsumed under the rubric of "traditional" feudal concepts. Particularly valuable was the research on the "good wife and wise mother" as an ideological construct that formed the basis of the Meiji (1868–1912) government's educational system for women.[12]

Thus, by the 1990s, a new window on everyday life had opened. Areas untouched by historians, such as child care, housing, and hygiene, unveiled a set of issues that reconceptualized both the identity of women and the nation. Constructing a social and cultural narrative that situates the questions of agency, power, and politics within the context of everyday life took on special meaning to those working to revise the project of women's history. Historian Wakita Haruko said: "Our aim is to trace how women lived and what kind of role they played in their daily lives from the empress all the way down. . . . We believe that it is extremely important to consider living conditions in every era, and within that context, to examine the 'life-cycle' of women."[13]

This book participates in these efforts to shift the focus of Japanese women's history toward the social and cultural history of the commodification of the everyday.[14] By exploring new images of the feminine that emerged in the 1920s, it provides a narrative that runs across class lines and counters the notion that female identity fitted a single mold in Japanese women's history. While this conceptual elasticity has come later to Japanese women's history than to other fields, as elsewhere, the process of constructing identities—class, ethnic, national, or gender—is contingent on mutable cultural practices, images, and narratives. The myth of a fixed identity was challenged by contradictory and diverse representations of Japanese women. The multiplicity of feminine identities disrupted established views of gender relations, but it also implied the possibility that women who lived within the confines of the state might intervene in the struggle to reject the closure imposed on them from above.

A Place for Women in the Everyday

Judith Butler has pointed out that the "presumed universality and unity of the subject of feminism is effectively undermined by the constraints of the representational discourse in which it functions."[15] Reflective of the myth that "a sharp break at the end of the war [World War II] made continuity a troubling concern" is the belief that Japanese women were reborn as a consequence of the war.[16] As was true of other segments of Japanese society, World War II may have made breaks in continuity more conspicuous, but the conditions that promoted the transformation in urban women's lives and produced complex feminine images were already in progress before the war. More than attributing shifts in women's attitudes and behavior patterns to a radical division that marked Japan's pre- and postwar periods, the changing context of urban women's roles should be examined within a larger framework, one that takes into account contemporary interrelated trends like the mass media that helped shape women's lives in industrializing societies not only in Japan but also in other parts of the world in the 1920s.

This book examines three new types of urban women: the bobbed-haired, short-skirted modern girl (*modan gāru*); the self-motivated housewife (*shufu*); and the rational, extroverted professional working woman (*shokugyō fujin*), each of whom offered Japanese women new identities in the 1920s. While the disparate discourses and lively debates that surrounded their existence constitute the main subject of my discussion, I also want to highlight the issues that moved and captured the interest of the women themselves. These interests were reflected especially in the expanding consumerism that encompassed a broad range of social changes. All three types of women came under the sway of new media, especially mass women's magazines. But a reciprocal relationship evolved whereby women could assume an active role in their interaction with the media.

All three types of women came to the fore in the 1920s against the backdrop of consumerism, referred to by intellectuals at the time as *modanizumu* (modernism), a neologism that combined the English *modern* with *ism*. Distinct from modern in the definition of Meiji-period industrialization (*kindai*), it was written as a proper noun in the *katakana* transliteration of the English word. In journalistic circles from approximately 1924 until the late 1930s, this "modernism" became identified with the latest "lowbrow" fads and fashions that were representative of the everyday. To be modern in Japan during the interwar years connoted being in the social vanguard of the age.[17] Consumerism in 1920s Japan was identified as a major trend in the popular culture of the time. But it was not a movement with a structured ideological framework or representative luminaries. If the changes, which some praised and others damned, were not lauded by all, few of our three types of women protagonists could have been oblivious to them.

I do not mean to suggest that the commodification of everyday life had its grounding in Western modernism, which indeed remained on the plane of "high" art.[18] Soon after World War I, some Japanese artists who had been exposed to the modernist art that was flourishing in Europe saw modernism as socially symbolic of an end to the elite domination of art trends that thrived in Japan in the early twentieth century. In the wake of the social and political upheavals that followed the Great Kantō Earthquake (Kantō daishinsai) of 1923, writers such as Yokomitsu Riichi, Kataoka Teppei, Ryūtanji Shizuo, Yoshiyuki Eisuke, and Kawabata Yasunari referred to their works depicting the lifestyle and trends popular in Japan at the time as "modernism" literature. In light of recent dialogues on modernity, the art, literature, and even the lifestyles that flourished in Japan in the 1920s seem to have resonated with some aspects of Western modernism. The temptation to link *modanizumu* and modernism beckons. But because modernism has a specific ideological and cultural meaning, I will restrict myself to the story of how indigenous changes in the commodification of everyday life acted as a progressive force in the self-identification of middle-class women in Japan in the 1920s.[19]

The development of a communications industry in the form of newspapers, magazines, movies, radio, and records coupled with the increasing numbers of readers, viewers, and listening audiences became a major component of this expanding consumerism. Certainly, the modern girl, the new type of middle-class housewife, and the professional working woman were not solely representative of all urban women, much less of Japanese women as a whole. Nevertheless, they revealed the temper of an age symbolized by changing women's identities in which a consumer culture marked by the consumption of ideas and fueled by the media reached beyond Japan's borders. Although the media clearly provided a critical force for the construction of these female identities, media formulations were shaped by the actions of women themselves. Moreover, these three figures of the modern struck fear into the hearts of most male intellectuals, government officials, and the public at large.

None of the three modern women participated in organized political movements as a means of gaining prominence. For the most part their concerns centered on the realm of everyday life. What role, if any, did these urban women's own actions have in determining their identities? In what ways did the autonomous aspects of women's changing behavior act to map out the more radical changes reshaping Japanese society — changes that spilled over to women like Shige and Tomi decades later in *Tokyo Story* and established the range of women's images still apparent today? Was there not room within the confines of the nation-state for urban women to find agency—be it in the form of changing fashions; attitudes toward work, love, and sexuality; marriage and the family; communication; or personal self-fulfillment?[20] Such issues were of pivotal concern to the women themselves: they were situated in areas women considered their own, and thus were realms in which women could contemplate alternative opportunities. How did the link between these women and the media allow historians and intellectuals of the period to denigrate the newly emerging women's culture, leaving many of the exciting questions unasked? It is these kinds of concerns, which grew out of the ambivalence and complexity surrounding the image and reality of women and consumerism, that form the nucleus of this study.

Chapter 1 articulates the position of Japanese women in urban space in the 1920s, the period that marked a definitive turning point in the construction of the idea of a female identity. Why did new images of the feminine emerge in the wake of World War I? In contrast to the model woman symbolized by the "good wife and wise mother" ideology, the turning point for urban women in the 1920s emerged with images of a consumer society.[21] While the embrace of consumerism called into question the existing social mores, many prewar intellectuals pointed out that the changes brought by consumerism were superficial and were restricted in at least one very important way: from the standpoint of class. Because affordable commodities for "mass" consumption still remained limited, more than anything else consumerism reflected the *fantasies* identified with consumerism. Modern production and consumption habits and the installment plan, which speeded up the electrification of the modern American home in the late 1920s and prepared the way for washing machines, mechanical refrigerators, and vacuums, were not widespread in 1920s Japan. It was not until the 1960s that such items began to make an appreciable impact on the average woman's lifestyle.[22]

Chapter 2 deals with the media's portrayal of the modern girl—one of the most visible products of the consumer dream—and examines various intellectual discourses voiced in response to the early changes in gender relations that accompanied the development of a consumer society. Irrespective of ideological differences, their analyses of the modern girl led intellectuals to create a new idealization of women best suited to the changing age. Indeed, the media, and especially women's mass magazines, molded the image of the modern girl. As one of the few commodities actually to reach mass proportions in the 1920s, mass women's magazines positioned the modern girl in two variant narratives. On the one hand, she came to symbolize the sexual and social decadence typified by the café hostess, the prostitute, and the unfaithful wife. On the other hand, she projected an image that overlapped with that of the professional working woman, and thus became a sign of a fundamental change in the tenor of everyday life. This was the juncture where fantasy gave way to alternative behavioral codes among urban women. While most intellectuals saw little value in consumerism, the transformation in daily life wrought by widespread social change carried the promise of a new lifestyle that presented potentially profound social ramifications because of the figure of the modern girl.

Chapter 3 challenges the assertion that women's magazines failed to mirror the actual changes taking place in urban women's lives. One has only to point to the many magazine articles aimed at the self-motivated middle-class housewife to see that journalism provided a focus for the upheaval then in progress, an upheaval that went beyond the representational imagery reflected by the modern girl.[23] Articles that offered useful information about upper-class women and the home and family took on a new and different meaning in the 1920s. Moreover, the addition of confessional articles written by the readers themselves provided an emotional outlet for both housewives and working women. The sensational reporting of scandals involving famous personalities revealed that some women were determined to be true to their emotions in matters of love and marriage. Conversely, that readers throughout Japan assiduously followed the movements of the modern girl, the professional working woman, and the housewife is confirmation of the rapid expansion of commercial journalism.

Reading magazines, a process that involved the actual purchase of consumer goods, allowed women to define their identities and to evaluate the directions in which their own lives were moving. Reading and writing to women's magazines, considered one way to improve oneself or achieve self-cultivation, offered the possibility of social fluidity for middle, and to a lesser extent lower, classes in urban and rural Japan. True, few women could stand on the marble floors of department stores and choose from the commodities on display. But as chapter 4 demonstrates, many women did subscribe to the new mass women's magazines and in them found space to debate and explore alternative lifestyles. In the early twentieth century, women's higher-school graduates began to fill the jobs that opened up for women. These middle-class young women were not driven to become professional working women solely for economic reasons. Work served as a vehicle for self-cultivation. The link between the modern girl, the housewife, the professional working woman, and consumerism during the 1920s validates the prominent role played by mass women's magazines in the increasing feminization of self-cultivation. Even so, the mechanism of "mass" consumption still rested on relatively fragile material conditions. Thus, without exaggerating the scope of the changes that these Japanese urban women were experiencing in this period, it may be said that they were searching for a language and symbols to differentiate themselves and to express their desires. Underlying the interest in new ways of thinking was a questioning of existing constraints and mores. This process might be described as adding yet another layer to the already multilayered identities that Japanese women consciously and unconsciously adopted. By buying into ideas, even if they could not afford the actual commodities, urban women were redefining the modern, encoded in figures like the modern girl, self-motivated middle-class housewife, and professional working woman. Now to the task of re-creating the dreams and hopes of these three urban women in an age that seemed to each to be filled with previously unimagined possibilities.

1

The Emergence of Agency

WOMEN AND CONSUMERISM

The adage "consumption, thy name is woman" resonates with
such venerable authority that one might expect to find it cited
in *Bartlett's Familiar Quotations,* attributed to some Victorian
Savant or to an eminent critic of modern frippery.

If women figure not only as the proverbial shoppers, the
Un-decorators, the perennial custodians of the bric-a-brac
of daily life but also as objects of exchange and consumption, what then can be inferred about the relationship of
man, males, and masculinity to the world of commodities?
—Victoria de Grazia[1]

The conditions that set the stage for the modern girl, the self-motivated
middle-class housewife, and the professional working woman in the
1920s had in fact germinated in Japan in the 1910s. It was at this time
that the notorious "new woman" (*atarashii onna*), a woman who trans-
gressed social boundaries and questioned her dependence on men,
started to pose a threat to gender relations. Contemporaneous with her
coming were the first intimations of consumerism. This nascent con-

sumerism reflected the development of an industrialized state taking root after the Russo-Japanese War (1904–5) and came to shape the desires of an ever-widening segment of society. Growing intellectual concerns centering on ascetic and spiritual practices thus co-occurred with growing materialistic desires.

From the early twentieth century, the term *new woman* in Japan connoted a progressive group of educated young intellectual women who found solace in self-cultivation through reading, writing, and meditation.[2] The liberation these women sought, which included a demand for social equality, overturned the common notion of femininity. In May 1902, the newspaper *Yomiuri*, anxious to capitalize on the "Woman Question," as the Victorians called it, went so far as to add a special column titled "New Woman" to its daily features.[3] Japan's *new woman* waxed less vocal about the monthly hormonal changes affecting her sexual feelings than did her sisters Olive Schriener and Eleanor Marx in Britain; nor was she as embroiled in the suffrage campaign as some of her American counterparts.[4] Yet, she too aimed to situate herself within the intellectual and cultural practices of society in search of creative fulfillment. She engaged in activities that encompassed only a small number of women with literary aspirations, however, with the result that the scope of her interests remained circumscribed.

Hiratsuka Raichō, the principal founder of the Bluestocking Society (Seitōsha) and its literary magazine, *Bluestockings* (*Seitō*), asserted: "I am a *new woman*. As *new women* we have always insisted that women are also human beings. It is common knowledge that we have opposed the existing morality, and have maintained that women have the right to express themselves as individuals and to be respected as individuals."[5] Raichō articulated her position with pride in a January 1913 special issue of *Chūō kōron* (Central Review), a general interest magazine for intellectuals devoted to the new women.

From the time that Henrik Ibsen's play *A Doll's House* debuted on the stage of Oslo's Christiana Theater in Norway in 1879, the fictional image of Nora and the new woman were synonymous.[6] By forsaking her position as bourgeois wife and mother, Nora portended the changes that were soon to affect intellectual women in far-reaching parts of the world.[7] The dissatisfaction expressed in the play with the prescribed gender roles that defined Nora's marriage led to a celebration of the individual that resonated with feminine intellectual discourse in Japan.

"Bluestocking." By Hattori Ryōhei, in *Ketsuketsu Manga,* 1914. Reprinted with permission of Nihon Manga Shiryōkan.

The acclaim that actress Matsui Sumako received for her rendering of Nora in Shimamura Hōgetsu's 1911 Japanese production of the play stemmed more from the emotional response generated by Nora's boldness in female audiences than to Matsui's artistic talents. The play's impact on its Japanese audience acted as an interface between the newly emerging agenda and the public, of which middle-class women formed a significant proportion.

On the surface, consumerism and the new woman in Japan appeared antithetical. In fact, however, they shared a close bond in the context of twentieth-century Japanese women's history. The new woman reflected a departure from state-imposed values. She lashed out against the "good wife and wise mother" morality that served as the ideological legitimization of the legal status of married women institutionalized in the Meiji Civil Code (1898), which determined women's legal and social status and place in the family. Although legal scholars in recent years have argued that aspects of the Civil Code were beneficial in the legalization of human rights, the Meiji Civil Code provided only limited protection for women in the domestic and social arenas. In everything from its articulation of divorce procedures to property rights, the code worked in favor of men.[8] Hidden within the "benefits" of the code were an increasing number of middle-class women relegated to a way of life defined by home and family.

In the early 1890s, the home was idealized in Sakai Toshihiko's socialist journal *Katei zasshi* (Home Journal), and in the family column of the mammoth publisher Hakubunkan's more conservative intellectual journal *Taiyō* (The Sun), as a space where husbands and wives shared responsibilities.[9] But by the late 1890s the home had come under the purview of the state.[10] Women, made the cornerstone for implementing a new national identity, were assigned specific gender roles as wives and mothers. Emphasis on "hard work and simple living" expressed a quintessential virtue for all Japan's citizens.[11] The "good wife" positioned at the core of this morality epitomized these traits. The dawning of the cultural and social aspects of a consumer society in the early twentieth century threatened to undermine that ideology. Consumerism—buying for the sake of buying—posed a challenge to the state's call for frugality and struck a discordant note in its rhetoric.

Early-twentieth-century consumerism in Japan may be described as a form of visual representation. Although it as yet bore only the merest hint of the complexities that would be wrought by postwar mass culture, the products it made available nevertheless titillated women's imagination. While the exposure of women to commodities for personal and household use probably incited and played on their anxieties, it also very likely offered simultaneously the hope/opportunity for a satisfactory form of release from the desire for material goods, which had previously been largely repressed. Photographs of women browsing in department stores suggest a form of escapism. No doubt escape was what some women longed for.

Whether or not women had the wherewithal to purchase new products is of secondary importance. More significant was the empowerment that consumerism, as an expression of decision making, offered to them. Women figured as active role players weighing the positive and negative consequences of the commodification of the everyday. Paul Glennie observes that "department stores were pivotal sites of cultural appropriation and identity construction, through their ability to create the meanings of commodities and consumers."[12] In writing about early-twentieth-century America, Richard Ohmann notes that "products and their auras resided not only in proper social space but in the system of symbols," through which people perceived "their affinities, their place in the world, and their historical agency."[13] Ohmann cautions, however, that "to grasp consumption as the same activity with the same meanings across class lines is to falsify the reality of the time."[14] In Japan, too, cumulative social changes were disrupting life in city and country alike. On the one hand, there was a pull to maintain the ties of family; on the other hand, signs of instability sent tremors through the domestic community and through society as a whole.

Another link between consumerism and the new woman in Japan is evident in the media that developed rapidly late in the nineteenth century. The media, with consumerism as its intermediary, was social testimony of women's cerebral development and material wants. By 1890, almost every family subscribed to at least one newspaper. Advertisements for cosmetics and medicine excited women's interest in commodities for their everyday use and accounted for the biggest percentage of all advertisements in the early twentieth century.[15] The media demonstrated the enormous allure of goods promised through the conduit of newspapers and magazines. The early use of the media as an instrument of consumer capitalism brought changes both in women's consciousness and in the concept of gender. Thus, the media served not only as a forum for the assertion of new political and social rights for women, starting with the new woman, but also as a vehicle for the spread of consumerism and the desire for new things and the lifestyle they embodied.

Yellow journalism was a mainstay of many Western-language newspapers in the United States from the time California publishing mogul William Randolph Hearst purchased the *New York Morning Journal* in 1895. In Japanese society, where an obsession with "proper" appearances ran deep, media coverage also promoted scandalous news stories. The visit by members of the Bluestocking Society to the pleasure quarters in Tokyo's Yoshiwara district and the "five-colored cocktail" incident, reports of which castigated the group of women for their brazen drinking in public, disrupted assumptions surrounding appropriate behavior for genteel women. While the sensational accounts of their actions brought untoward social recognition to these self-proclaimed "new women," the reportage favored by the press raised many eyebrows and complicated the problematic placement of the new woman.[16] The hullabaloo that reinforced her "deviant" behavior further enhanced the media's power. It also affirmed the determination of some

"Longing to Be a New Woman." By Hattori Ryōhei, in *Ketsuketsu Manga*, 1914. Reprinted with permission of Nihon Manga Shiryōkan.

intellectual women in the early twentieth century not to subjugate their desires. The autonomy sought by these women was not entirely beyond their reach. Although their yearnings emerged within the structure of the nation-state, they were amplified by the allure of commercial forces.

In the aftermath of the Russo-Japanese War, the state's emphasis on nation building leveled off and shifted to include, if only slightly, the gratification of individual desires. Journalist Tokutomi Sohō, in examining the cultural formations that propelled young men in the Meiji period to act, commented that they "differed from their predecessors in having developed an individual awareness," and they lacked "all, or at least a major portion of the national awareness."[17] For middle-class women, the implications of the shift coupled with the challenges that resulted from the maturation of the industrialized state after World War I took concrete form following the Great Kantō Earthquake. By the mid-1920s the commodification of the everyday that was embraced by middle-class urban women—a broad term used here to refer to women, most of whom lived in Tokyo, with at least an elementary-school education and a basic level of literacy—was closely linked to the conspicuous aspects of a rising consumer society.

The rebelliousness simmering among these women found expression in popular culture through the mass media: women's magazines, movies, radio programs, popular music, and jazz. A cultural shift that affected middle-class women directly was required for them to incorporate and formulate the experiences that were to transform the parameters of their existence. The time was right for them to utilize resources like mass magazines whose editors and publishers now had women as their targets, women who yearned to recognize their own voices in print. The information made available by the media was not disinterested, and as consumers, women were no mere passive receivers. The media afforded women a way to forge a relationship with a broader segment of society. Women perceived the possibility of creating their own social relations using techniques such as self-cultivation, or *shūyō*, that would give special meaning to their lives. For many of these women, consumerism created a new set of images by which they could better understand who they were, or at least who they might be.

Women Challenge the Modern

In the early twentieth century a group of young literary feminists conveyed dissatisfaction with existing gender relationships as they were configured by the nation-state and courageously attempted to disengage themselves from the rhetoric endorsed by the national interest. That is not to say that the promotion of women's freedom from long-standing social restraints was unknown before the formalization of the "good wife and wise mother" ideology and the advent of the "new woman." Debates on the status of women had existed before. For the most part, however, intellectuals, regardless of their ideological leanings, stressed two avenues through which women could override conventional images. The first included enlightenment through education and reading. Iwamoto Yoshiharu's *Jogaku zasshi* (Magazine for Women's Learning, 1885–1904) was one of the earliest women's magazines to hail the attainment of equal rights.[18] Fukuzawa Yukichi, a major contributor to the narratives addressing the awakening of women, lamented women's lack of social awareness. In his 1885 treatise *On Japanese Women* (*Onna no Nihonjinron*), Fukuzawa proposed that husbands and wives share responsibility for educating their children. To prepare women for this task, Fukuzawa recommended a school curriculum that placed economics and science above calligraphy and simple math. Insistent on marital fidelity (though he himself was known to have dallied), he urged couples to combine their family names after marriage to create a new family name. For Fukuzawa, a harmonious marriage accorded women equal property rights and free rein over their emotions both spiritually and sexually, which implied the right to divorce.[19] Although Fukuzawa directed his treatise to women whose everyday lives were informed by domesticity, and presumably hoped his proposals would have an effect on unmarried young women as well as housewives, his views did not find practical application during his lifetime.

In private schools, educators including Shimoda Utako, Tsuda Umeko, Hatoyama Haruko, and Naruse Jinzō worked to consolidate and expand educational opportunities for women limited by the 1899 edict that clamped down on Christian mission schools and exerted state control over girls' secondary education. But like Iwamoto and intellectuals such as Fukuzawa and Nakamura Masanao, the measures these educators advanced were not antagonistic to the ideals of the state. Further, Japanese-style Confucian ethics contained the prescription for the "good wife and wise mother" philosophy that Shimoda, Hatoyama, and others endorsed.[20] With male education the priority and women's education an afterthought, gender divisions evolved in accordance with plans for the nation-state. Marked gender differentiation was apparent in the reading materials and curricula of both private and state-run institutions.

Nevertheless, by the late nineteenth century the spread of education had brought with it the concomitant growth of an intellectual class that included a small number of socially attuned women. Welfare organizations like the Women's Reform Society (Fujin kyōfukai), established by Yajima Kajiko, Sasaki Toyosu, and others in 1886 and recognized as the Japanese chapter of the Women's Christian Temperance Union (Nihon kirisutokyō fujin kyōfūkai) in 1893, reached out to the downtrodden. Young women's working conditions in factories and the prostitution that proliferated both in Japan and abroad informed the tone of their crusades.[21] Representative of this breed of outspoken young women in the early twentieth century was the poet Yosano Akiko, whose powerful poems protesting the Russo-Japanese War received wide acclaim, and Hiratsuka Raichō, the main force behind the Bluestockings.[22]

Another way in which intellectuals believed women could obliquely challenge conventional roles involved their organization into social movements: one example was the women's division of the labor movement. Some women intellectuals in their teens and twenties saw socialism and Marxism as the only solution to the day's economic and spiritual crises, which they viewed as rooted in capitalism. A few members of this group, such as the woman socialist Yamakawa Kikue and male socialist Sakai Toshihiko, were cognizant of the more basic inequities within the home. But they, too, advocated a social revolution that pitted capital against labor and would pave the way to gender equality.[23] Yamakawa saw marriage as an obsolete institution:

The institution of marriage began with the subjugation of women by men during battle. Women were taken possession of and became the personal property of men, being bought as objects of labor. . . . Even today the archaic features of the marriage system in which a woman exists as a man's slave (outwardly they have changed) still tend to be preserved. Marriage kills love. As long as bourgeois societies continue to exist, I am afraid that most men and women—but particularly women—will dig their own graves. As soon as lovers become husband and wife, instead of living as two people, only one remains. That person is generally the man. It cannot be understood logically. It is a habit, a pledge between a husband and wife that a woman will submit unconditionally. In most cases, women flatter men and repress their own egos. Only when everything they do, from work to hobbies, benefits their husbands are they considered suitable companions and thus qualify as good wives [ryōsai].[24]

Yamakawa's effort to expose the discrimination women suffered at the hands of their employers was predicated on her intent to raise women's awareness. Commenting on the incongruities of the factory/social system, she remarked that "the longing for economic independence lures many young women into the labor market, which results in their competing with men." But "it is the capitalists," she continued, "who end up reaping the benefits."[25] On the one hand, Yamakawa's perspective is reminiscent of Marx's call for "autonomous social relations."[26] On the other hand, she saw women as being excluded from the process of producing concrete images through which their thought could be expressed. No doubt Yamakawa feared that women occupied a position in the workplace different in type and location from that of their male co-workers.

Yamakawa was not the only woman socialist to champion the cause of women. Fukuda Hideko, an activist in the People's Rights Movement (Jiyū minken undō) before she turned to socialism, drew intellectual inspiration from German socialist August Bebel's 1883 treatise on women and the new family.[27] When Fukuda's article "A Solution to the Woman Problem" (Fujin mondai no kaiketsu) appeared in Seitō, the magazine was placed under a temporary restraining order.[28] Yamakawa's decision to single out women's issues was prompted less by women like Fukuda, however, than by the social milieu she shared with leftist members of the intellectual community.[29]

Marxist literary and social critic Hirabayashi Hatsunosuke, well schooled in the ideas of Sakai Toshihiko and Katayama Sen and later a founding member of the Japanese Communist Party, initially joined Yamakawa in demanding the reorganization of society. Hirabayashi, an early advocate of gender equality, argued that

> inequality between men and women is not a result of inferior biological differences—rather it is a gradual process that begins at birth because of our social system and ingrained customs. . . . Women should rebel against despotic fathers and husbands. Since individuals no longer have the right to bear arms, they must rise up as a group. In today's society women and workers comprise a class of slaves, both of whom are miserably oppressed. . . . In our society rights mean the right to inherit, and only men have inheritance rights. In our society rights mean the right to run the country, and only men have the right to become high government officials and sit in the Diet.[30]

Here Hirabayashi was singling out the Meiji Civil Code, which, he contended, exacerbated the despair and isolation of women. Hirabayashi railed against the patriarchal family system, the underpinning of the Civil Code. From a young girl's formative years in her parent's home, through her student years, and as a young bride and mother under the control of her husband and parents-in-law, the Civil Code defined a woman's options. Nature did not will the loss of a woman's creativity; the Civil Code did. As long as the code remained intact, Hirabayashi argued, the emancipation of women was but an illusory dream. Hirabayashi maintained that "the patriarchal family system together with the private ownership of property forms the basis of today's social system. Herein lies the root of discrimination against women."[31]

Hirabayashi and Yamakawa were contemptuous both of "conservative" educators like Shimoda and of "progressives" like Raichō and Yosano, who called themselves the "new women" of their time. In Yamakawa's estimation, the feminist Bluestockings professed but another bourgeois view of women, an extension of Fukuzawa's 1880s rhetoric. Before the Great Kantō Earthquake, and at approximately the same time that French Marxists like Georg Lukács (*History and Class Consciousness*, 1923) were challenging the question of human subjectivity, Hirabayashi's stance, though more flexible than Yamakawa's, rested on a deterministic explanation of historical materialism. Hirabayashi believed in determined stages of historical development. Until the early 1920s, he, like Yamakawa, saw socialism as the empowerment behind women's liberation. "At the heart of gender inequality," he observed,

is the extreme differentiation of labor that separates the two sexes and accounts for the differences in their earning power. Because women are not involved in the usual economic and social activities and are consumed by housework and child care, they have become mentally and physically inferior. As long as a woman's household tasks and the time spent in caring for the children are not reduced, and unless she becomes socially active, she will not be able to raise her position in society. . . . Talking about the attainment of women's rights and women's liberation is meaningless. The socialization of labor in the home can only be accomplished through socialism.[32]

With World War I ravaging Europe, domesticity—or as Ruth Whittaker labels it, "devotional glamour"—became a public issue in Japan as it did in the United States.[33] The "protection of motherhood debate," or *bosei hogo ronsō*, a narrative that had occupied a significant position in intellectual circles, surfaced in women's magazines and provides a barometer for measuring changes in middle-class women's consciousness.[34] The debate, which initially involved Yosano and Raichō, made headlines in the January 1918 issue of *Jogaku sekai* (Women's Higher-School World).[35] Yosano, whose perceptions of education, women's suffrage, and economic independence were inspired by the writings of Mary Wollstonecraft, John Stuart Mill, and Olive Schreiner, wrestled with women's issues within the context of economic independence.[36] Yosano attributed the ubiquitous pattern of economic dependence to the authoritative position of husbands. Since marriage roles were gender-differentiated, she argued, the construction of equal status for housewives was flawed from the outset. The sanctification of subservient relationships in the home stymied women's emotional and intellectual growth. Similarly, women who accepted financial assistance from the state forfeited their autonomy and became pawns of the establishment. The mother of eleven children, Yosano believed that bearing children required forethought on the part of the individuals concerned, not the state.[37]

Raichō, a devotee of Swedish feminist Ellen Key, countered with a sharp rebuttal in the May 1918 issue of *Fujin kōron* (Woman's Review). Key proposed an economic partnership in the home entitling a wife and mother to half of her husband's holdings, advocated state subsidies for unwed mothers, and claimed that "the transformation of society begins with the unborn child."[38] Raichō articulated Key's logic, as did some German, Norwegian, American, and other feminists from the early twentieth century, and ignored the issue of total equality with men invoked by Yosano. The constraints imposed by marriage laws did not give wives the legal right to a designated share of the household's income. Raichō felt safer arguing for a guarantee from the state that motherhood would be valued and protected.[39] This exchange marked the beginning of a yearlong protective legislation debate, which spoke to a growing number of women readers. Yamakawa also joined the fray, insisting that rather than "economic independence" (Yosano) or a "glossed-over" policy like the call for the protection of motherhood (Raichō), "the present economic structure, which is the source of the evil," must be eradicated.[40]

Raichō's prescription included reservations about a woman's ability to engage in outside employment and still perform her job as wife and mother. Even so, Raichō attached equal importance to men's and women's work. By accepting conventional divisions of labor—or, in today's parlance, by not questioning gender as a historical construct—Raichō's approach clearly differed from Yosano's. Yet, women's historian Kōchi Nobuko has pointed out that the two shared "a kind of commonality," vituperative as their debate may have sounded at times, that opposed Yamakawa's views.[41] For Kōchi, Raichō's and Yosano's interpretations reflected the expectations experienced by young, intellectually inclined women in conjunction with the building of the Meiji state. In spite of both women's earlier anticipations, the contradictions inherent in a system that promoted a stereotypical image of the ideal woman meant actually extricating themselves from the "good wife and wise mother" rhetoric advanced by mainstream educators. Their ability at least to conceptualize a life for women apart from that formulated by the state attests to their tenacity.

In contrast, Yamakawa's stance was colored by socialist tenets and her denunciation of a capitalist culture that devalued women. In her later writings, she continued to affirm that socialism provided the only proper basis for understanding social change.[42] It is worth noting, however, that Yamakawa's views, like those of most of her leftist contemporaries, involved no significant gender analysis. The Marxists' gender-blindness clearly affected their reaction to the advent of the phenomenon of consumerism and its particular relationship to women. Neither the Marxists—with the exception of a few intellectuals like Hirabayashi—nor the socialists heeded the new historical forces that were in the process of transforming modernity. Ironically, it was the discourse on women's everyday life, particularly in the mass women's magazines of the 1920s, that constructed a new notion of gender that most Marxists were unable to see or deal with.

With renewed concern over women's education, the establishment of women's higher schools (*jogakkō*) accelerated. As of 1907, after completing the six years of compulsory schooling, girls wishing to continue their education had two options. One was to enter a higher elementary school (*kōtō shogakkō*). These provided an additional two or three years of study and rendered the young women graduates eligible for admission to "normal" schools (*shihan gakkō*), which offered a five-year teacher-training program. The other choice was enrollment in the more prestigious women's higher schools (*kōtō jogakkō*), where the period of study was between four and five years.[43] By 1911, 250 women's higher schools (*jogakkō*) were in operation, 44 of which had opened that same year.[44] Approximately 72,000 young women were attending women's higher schools, in comparison with approximately 3.5 million girls enrolled in elementary schools throughout Japan for the same year.[45]

In the 1920s, more than 20 percent of the graduates of women's higher schools anxious to further their education enrolled at one of

Women's higher-school students, early 1920s.

the two government-sponsored women's higher normal schools: Tokyo Women's Higher Normal School (Tōkyō joshi kōto shihan gakkō, 1884) and Nara Women's Higher Normal School (Nara joshi kōtō shihan gakkō, 1908). Others attended private women's colleges such as Tsuda Umeko's Joshi eigaku juku (1900, now Tsuda College) and Naruse Jinzō's Japan Women's University (Nihon joshi daigaku, 1901).[46] Both of these schools received the designation "special school" (*senmon gakkō*) following the promulgation of the Special School Act (Senmon gakkō rei) in 1903. Nevertheless, women's colleges remained separate from men's universities until after World War II.[47]

In spite of an educational program inspired by Japanese-styled Confucian precepts, the seeds for a modern woman's identity were being sown against the backdrop of consumer culture.[48] In the early twentieth century, the new woman in Japan—often ridiculed and blamed, and only sometimes the object of praise—consciously tried to circumvent the restrictions placed on her by society. One might say that the ideas and ideology that symbolized Japan's new woman, though constantly undercut by conventional forces working within the state, constituted the beginnings of a new gender awareness. By moving outside the existing structures, the new woman endeavored to create a new subject position for women. What began with the new woman's embrace of *The Doll's House* narrative, her scandalous behavior, and later her public visibility because of claims on social space through a degree of social activism, gathered force with the consumer boom of the 1920s. The new woman's changing views of love and sex, education and work were among her most important bequests to the modern woman of the 1920s. No doubt the rapid and major shifts that followed filled the new woman with anxiety and disappointment. But the alacrity with which the modern woman used her legacy to grasp the implications of the changes consumerism offered should also have been a source of pride. Consumerism furnished new resources for redefining the lives of urban middle-class women. In the process, it laid the groundwork for trends that continue today. In the 1920s, intellectually inclined women like Hiratsuka Raichō and urban middle-class women like the modern girl, the housewife, and the professional working woman were claiming identification with the modern.

Women Come of Age: The Desire for Consumption

The catchphrase "Today, the Imperial Theater, tomorrow, Mitsukoshi" (*kyō wa teigeki, ashita Mitsukoshi*) resounded throughout the years 1910–19, a harbinger of the coming decade. Coined in 1911 for Mitsukoshi, Japan's first department store, the phrase predicted a decade defined by leisure and consumption. The store effected its transformation in 1904, when the Mitsui Apparel Store (*gofukuten*) refurbished itself and took the name Mitsukoshi. Years later, Hamada Shirō, a former Mitsukoshi advertising executive and the person who created the popular phrase, reflected, "If women of leisure could really have made theatergoing and shopping a daily practice, women and their maids [who customarily accompanied their mistresses on outings] would have found the path to heaven."[49]

No longer mere purveyors of material goods, department stores, like plays, offered a visual outlet and the promise to satisfy people's desires. At that time, Hamada's slogan reflected a different spirit of the times. "Anyone who comes to Tokyo goes to the international exhibition [*hakurankai*]. And anyone who goes to the exhibition stops off at Mitsukoshi."[50] Hamada's "anyone" referred to a class of men who traveled to Tokyo from the provinces and certainly would have included a visit to the exhibition in their itinerary. Women would have had prior knowledge of Mitsukoshi's offerings through the store's magazine and direct mailings. For most countrywomen, a trip to Tokyo was likely to happen only in their dreams. Nevertheless, the media had already recognized women as a lucrative target for advertising campaigns. Theaters and upper levels of department stores were havens of delight for upper-class or upper-middle-class wives and daughters. The majority of women, however, had to wait for the short-lived economic boom after World War I to contemplate Hamada's musings.

The period following the Great War has long been a repository of popular nostalgia. Some called it the Golden Age or the Roaring Twenties. Others saw its darker side, characterized by unemployment and class antagonisms. British historian Eric Hobsbawm wrote about the general impact of World War I "in terms of the social transformations which affect[ed] the ordinary men and women of the world." Hobsbawm saw the effects of the war as the "most revolutionary ever experienced by the human race."[51] In Japan, Kuwabara Takeo stood out as one of the first postwar intellectuals to dismiss the identification of the early twentieth century as a "cold," "sunless" age. Although Kuwabara did not focus on a gendered change per se, he applauded the move toward an alternate lifestyle perceived as taking root after the war: "In the Meiji period a tremendous gap existed between Japanese and Western lifestyles, and it was difficult to directly import new ways of thinking and culture. In the Taishō [1912–26] period, however, because the standard of living of the ordinary people had risen, we could even see farmers drinking beer and cider. Following World War I the borrowing really became obvious."[52]

For politicians, particularly members of Ōkuma Shigenobu's cabi-

Mitsukoshi Department Store in downtown Tokyo, early 1920s (Libroport).

The Ginza Main Street, Tokyo. 近附店貨百屋松と街大座銀 (所名京東)

Matsuya Department Store on the Ginza in Tokyo, early 1920s.

net (1914–16), faced with the problem of severe economic recession and social unrest, World War I came at an opportune time. In Europe, confusion over the exchange rate coupled with the precarious state of overseas shipping virtually crippled trade and sent orders pouring into Japan from the Allied countries for military armaments. From late 1915 until early 1916, stock prices soared. Japanese exports reached an all-time high, creating an unprecedented economic boom. Although the prosperity was fleeting, Japanese capitalism gained considerable ground at this time.

The economic growth that Japan achieved through its indirect involvement in World War I had ended by 1920. During the period from 1919 to 1922, however, the standard of living rose, as did the level of consumption.[53] Cultural historian Wakamori Tarō, writing in the 1960s, defined the features of "Taishō mass culture" that distinguished Japan's interwar "period of massification" (*taishū no jidai*). First, Westernization gradually was incorporated into the average person's lifestyle and the term *massification* (*taishūka*) began to be heard in the vernacular. Material goods, once the property only of affluent people, became identified with "mass" production (*tairyō seisan*) and "mass" consumption (*tairyō shōhi*).[54] Although caution is necessary when analyzing the extent of the development of Japan's prewar mass society, data available from national income tax records indicate that in 1903, approximately 2.3 percent of the total population fitted the category of "middle class" with an annual income between five hundred and five thousand yen. In 1918, the percentage rose to 6.5 percent; and in 1921, to 10 percent.[55] White-collar workers were beginning to find themselves with extra money to purchase available consumer goods like clothing and housewares. Kuwabara mused that even the unskilled laborer enjoyed newfound leisure time, albeit in varying amounts. For some urban women, the taste of this honey would render the transformation of everyday practices irreversible.

World War I affirmed the sociohistorical context bolstering a consumer culture in Japan. With women as a significant coefficient, the war stimulated new patterns of consumption. While the 1918 Rice Riots stand out as a sign of women's frustration and rage in the economic and political realms, capitalism, which made great leaps during the war, changed the face of urban life: the commodification of the everyday, characterized by women, represented the new in the now.

America and women became the symbols of the social and cultural changes of the postwar period. Both were troubling figures of modernity, modernity's Other. By the war's end, America had reached a high level of development among the emerging consumer societies. America took the lead in the production of a machine culture. That many aspects of consumerism in Japan were conveyed at the time by the terms *Americanism* (*amerikanizumu*) and *Americanization* (*amerikan-aizeishon*) was natural. America and the American way of life cast a long shadow, a symbol of the ultimate in "modernity."

America took pride in flaunting the epithet "top runner in the modern world."[56] German intellectual Rudolf Kayser, who wrote at the same time as Hirabayashi, emphatically disagreed with this label: "In fact, Americanism is a new European method. The extent to which this method was itself influenced by America seems to me quite unimportant. It is a method of concrete and of energy, and is completely attuned to spiritual and material reality."[57] In considering the goal of modernity and the sequence modernity follows, America might have claimed the title "top runner," but *Americanism* and *Americanization* did not necessarily reflect the so-called essential character of America. Hirabayashi attributed Americanism's pull to its connection with mechanization: " 'Americanism' [*amerikanizumu*] demonstrates man's efficiency to the highest degree, and there is just no getting around this fact. As long as man continues to make advances in civilization, this is something we cannot escape. 'Americanism' is affecting the direction of all the civilizations in the world. Even Russia is not beyond the reach of American culture."[58] Hirabayashi called Americanism a major element in the modernization process for women in Japan. In his evaluation, America's breakthroughs in the field of industrial development indirectly gave women a more pluralist vision. For him, the questions of which elements appeared earlier, where, and under whose influence became moot.

Life changed in many parts of the world after the war. World War I dismantled the European paradigm. The standards set by Europe for the previous generation were now of the Old World. Rather than the substitution of America in Europe's place as a model, however, in Japan the postwar shift unleashed a reexamination of basic values. The transformations altering the social fabric of society accentuated the extent to which gender definitions were being reconfigured. Using America as an example, Frederick Lewis Allen's 1930s best-seller *Only Yester-day* referred to the war as a "revolution." Allen assumed that diverse forces were working in tandem "to make this revolution inevitable," and that the "woman question" was one of them.[59] "The growing independence of the American woman" figured as an accelerating factor of this "revolution."[60] No sooner did the war end than adolescent boys and girls "were making mincemeat" out of an ethical code that characterized women as "the guardians of morality," a morality that proclaimed "women were made of finer stuff than men and were expected to act accordingly."[61] But it was not only American women for whom the Great War established new boundaries for potential change. Much the same can be said for the European women who lived through those turbulent days, and for Japanese women.

Women, the Earthquake, and the Commodification of the Everyday

Following the Great Earthquake, consumerism became a way of representing and judging the new urban-centered culture. In its most visible form, consumerism was incarnated in the media, popular music, and jazz. It was symbolized by the neon lights, the cafés and dance halls, Western fashions, and the bobbed hair of the modern girl. Most intellectuals at the time, who were absorbed in ideological debates, repudiated consumerism by using the appellation *modanizumu* interchangeably with the terms *amerikanizumu* and *amerikanaizeishon*. The intellectuals' out-and-out rejection of consumerism, which they labeled a by-product of American bourgeois culture, laid bare their arrogance and downplayed the transformation taking place in urban middle-class women's lives. Marxists tended to see Japan's social structure as dominated by feudalistic relationships that existed between landowners and peasants. They thus looked askance at the civic society emerging with the rise of consumerism, which for them was emblematic of a "superficial" urban culture that remained outside the realm of social reality.[62] Nevertheless, until the late 1930s, before consumerism was effaced by the resurgence of national military priorities, the commodification of the everyday denoted a redefinition of predominantly urban social mores.

Hirabayashi, whose discourse grew out of the same socialist discourse as that of Yamakawa, was the first intellectual to link the attainment of women's rights with technological development, or "mechanization" (*kikaika*), after the earthquake. Hirabayashi suggested that a symbiotic, rather than contradictory, relationship existed between the machine, science, and his vision of the commodification of the everyday. He concluded that "only the fin de siècle person fears and damns the machine."[63] The machine, a product of scientific technology, became the embodiment of scientific rationale and progress. As life in the city underwent a metamorphosis, Hirabayashi was ready to reevaluate his position on women. He no longer advocated a proletarian revolution as a criterion for women's independence. Hirabayashi analyzed the emerging social phenomenon in the following way: "From Meiji through early Taishō, Japan feverishly adopted Western civilization on an institutional level. . . . But from late Taishō and on into Shōwa, Western civilization put its stamp in a more direct way on everyday life, reaching into every nook and cranny, and permeating tastes and interests. We call this period the universalization of Japan by Western civilization."[64] In the process, consumerism marked a new stage in the self-conceptualization of urban women. Artist and essayist Kimura Shōhachi detailed, in both his pictures and his essays, the transformation taking place in Tokyo lifestyles, taking special pains to illuminate the changes that distinguished Taishō and Shōwa women. "The foundation," Kimura declared, "was laid in Taishō. There followed development and growth beyond description. Having experienced (Taishō) myself, in comparison with (Meiji), the things that underwent a dramatic restructuring were the physical appearance of the city (Tokyo), and women's manners and customs. This was because the earthquake, a natural disaster that occurred midway through the period, brought changes (no one) could have imagined. When these (changes) actually materialized for the eye to see, we were no longer in Taishō, but had moved on to Shōwa." (Parentheses in the quote reflect Kimura's original punctuation.)[65]

The earthquake struck two years and three months before the Taishō emperor died and the era came to a close. In the public's mind, however, the earthquake marked the end of the era. Tokyo and its surrounding areas had been physically destroyed. Cultural life, centered in the capital city, came to a temporary standstill. That the entire country was "paralyzed" helps account for the general sense of apocalypse.[66] The destructive force of the earthquake did not alter the basic pattern of Tokyo culture, but it served as a catalyst for the entry of new customs—most conspicuously, aspects of American consumer culture, which were assiduously taken up by mass women's magazines.[67]

Modern Japanese history often describes these years in terms that imply that the earthquake was a watershed.[68] To be sure, the streets of Tokyo assumed a different appearance, a fitting transformation that matched changes in everyday modes of life and women's fashions. But in spite of the emphasis placed on the earthquake as a turning point, the rationale for the gradual erosion of daily customs can, in fact, be traced back to before 1923.[69] The move toward a new way of life for urban middle-class women began in the early twentieth century.[70] It was only after the disaster, however, that the contours of social life changed. When Meiji period writer Natsume Sōseki lamented the exogenous (*gaihatsu-teki*) nature of the modernization that had occurred since the Meiji Restoration (1868), he was expressing doubt that the motivation for cultural change had come from within (*naiatsu-teki*) and fear that it thus lacked sufficient vitality for Japan to create its own cultural identity.[71] Sōseki relied on words like *superficial* (*hisō de uwasuberi*) and *imitative* (*mohō*) to describe the so-called opening of Japan. Intellectuals writing fifteen years later, when consumerism was in full flower, employed similarly derogatory language.[72] While the intensity of their criticism echoed that of Sōseki, however, the dissatisfaction they experienced was of a different nature.

The intellectuals' voluble critiques of consumerism sometimes reflected an inability to accept their own alienation from the new process of constructing culture. Women, for example, because of their participation in consumerism, could now initiate their own cultural tastes without having to rely on the mediating role of intellectuals. Not only did the changes wrought by consumerism in the popular customs of women seem radical and unprecedented in scope, but intellectuals were playing only a small role in effecting them.[73] The intellectuals criticized their generation of urban middle-class women and consumerism as a static American construct, but to take their views at face value would be naive.

True, many of the features of the new culture originated outside Japan. In the field of entertainment, the overwhelmingly popular reception accorded American movies cannot be denied.[74] And department stores and rush hours were representations of urbanization and consumer culture not only in Tokyo, but also in New York, Berlin, Paris, and other metropolises.[75] The construction of Berlin's largest department store, the Wertheim, brought shopping to unprecedented heights in Germany, and in so doing sold a dream to German urbanites for whom shopping and restaurant dining became a mark of middle-class identity.[76] Similarly, the realization of Osaka entrepreneur Kobayashi Ichizō's plan in 1929 for a department store located in the Osaka terminal sold a similar dream to urban dwellers. It combined rationalized shopping with features like a family restaurant and a rooftop amusement area that provided leisure activities for the entire family.[77] One need not assume that Kobayashi received the stimulus for his own undertaking from the Berlin construction. More likely, the two projects were independent responses to similar urban conditions.

One only had to frequent the nearest dance hall and gaze at the dress and hairstyles of urban young women imitating the Hollywood stars — like Naomi, the protagonist in Tanizaki Junichirō's novel *Naomi* (*Chijin no ai*, 1924–25) — or listen to the intermingling of foreign words like *dancer, jazz,* and *liqueur* in the 1928 hit tune "Tokyo Marching Song" (Tokyo kōshinkyoku) to realize the extent to which popular culture from abroad was being incorporated into the quotidian vocabulary.[78] As previously mentioned, these aspects were formulations of urbanization and consumer culture in many areas of the world.[79] One would be hard-pressed to prove that either or both arose in Japan solely because of foreign influence. Give or take a slight difference in timing, urban-centered consumer culture had become a widespread phenomenon by the late 1920s in America, Europe, and Japan.[80] Within this changing context, new female identities were being negotiated.

An examination of the media, which played a crucial role in forming the tie between urban middle-class women and consumerism, illustrates the limitations of viewing the commodification of the everyday in terms of Westernization or Americanization.[81] While the introduction from abroad of the latest in printing technology (the *Asahi shinbun* [a newspaper] purchased the world's fastest rotary press from an American company in 1927) made large-scale printing and publishing possible, ambitious industrial development in the 1870s had already allowed the purchase of such sophisticated equipment.[82] The new broad-based reading public, which included women, sustained the publication of Japanese mass women's magazines, some of which claimed readerships exceeding 100,000 by the mid-1920s.[83] For these women, then, the media, with its capacity to appropriate trends, patterns, and practices from Europe and America, represented the articulation of a rising modern mass society.

To understand how female consumers of media culture increased at such an astonishing rate, three preconditions must be considered. First, compared with Japan's rate of industrial growth, literacy was high. According to R. H. Dore's classic study *Education in Tokugawa Japan*, approximately 10 percent of the female population possessed basic literacy at the beginning of the Meiji period. Although recent research offers room for skepticism, the enactment of the 1872 Education Code (*Gakusei rei*) and the establishment of compulsory education did augment literacy among women.[84] Second, as economic conditions on an individual level improved, subscribers to newspapers and magazines grew. So-called middle-class families—those with an income of approximately 70 yen per month (14,000 yen in today's currency), or 800 yen annually (1,600,000 yen in today's currency) in 1925—routinely subscribed to one newspaper and at least two monthly magazines.[85] Third, Japan had long been accustomed to a sensational style of news reporting—the *kawaraban* (tile-block printing)—dating back to the Edo (1603–1868) period. Printed handbills hawked on city streets recounted racy stories about goings-on in the pleasure quarters, news of natural disasters, and current events. The so-called small, Western-style newspapers (*ko shinbun*) that took off in the late 1880s combined local news with human interest stories and light fiction and were printed in easy-to-read language. Women were among the readers.[86]

Thus, rising literacy for women and a degree of economic latitude combined with the demand for reading material precipitated the spread of books, magazines, newspapers, and other publications. Although Japan's development fell short of the economic expansion in the United States, the proliferation of a consumer culture and the establishment of the media materialized at approximately the same time, or were separated at most by only a few years.[87] To speak of the emerging urban culture as devoid of originality is to overlook a significant part of Japan's social history and the position this culture assumed in the identification of urban middle-class women. Indeed, from today's vantage point, it is easier to recognize the gap between the alarmist discourse of Japanese intellectuals—or for that matter of recent Western scholars of Japan—who assign the dimensions of urban capitalist Japanese life to Western models and the constitution of a vigorous, home-grown consumerism that clearly exceeded the boundaries of simple Western influence.

Intellectuals Speak Out

Kurahara Korehito, a leading theorist of the proletarian literature movement, was one of several leftist intellectuals to voice anticapitalist sentiment and antipathy toward the symbiotic relationship between women and consumerism:

> Modernism [*modanizumu*], as a so-called social phenomenon, is an outgrowth of the ideology, mentality, and customs of the leisure class [*yūkan kaikyū*] and the ordinary petty bourgeois types who emulate their lifestyles. I am referring particularly to members of the salaried class, all of whom are now antiproductive [i.e., consumers]. If that is what modernism is all about, then we are talking about a culture designed to fit the needs of parasites. . . .
>
> The special features of modernism are (1) that it reflects the position of the socially elite, and (2) that it has no productive power. In short, it is consumer-oriented and hedonistic.[88]

Other intellectuals on the left also feared the shift to consumerism in this "new" salaried class (*shin chūkan sō*).[89] They, too, decried the trend as antiworker, unproductive, and hedonistic, and in the late 1920s characterized it by the catchphrase "erotic, grotesque nonsense" (*ero guro nansensu*). An essay by Ōya Sōichi, a journalist and prewar critic with Marxist leanings, titled "Modern Social Strata and Modern Social Trends" (Modan sō to modan sō) is the source of an oft-quoted critique of consumerism. In this article, first published in the February 1929 issue of the general interest magazine *Chūō kōron* (Central Review), Ōya declared that "modernism [*modanizumu*] is nothing more than consumer-oriented hedonism. To be modern [*modan*] means to lead the lifestyle and culture of the age. And yet, modernism is not only essentially unproductive, it is superficial and based on spending."[90] Among the intellectuals and critics who shared a similar antipathy toward consumerism, some at least recognized its newness. Movie critic Sawamura Torajirō, writing in 1926, announced: "Ah, the threat of 'Americanism' [amerikanizumu]. America is inundating the whole world. In Japan the influence is particularly apparent. In this small country of Japan, the huge American automobile, so out of place here, speeds along."[91]

Generally, Japanese intellectuals in the interwar and postwar years, irrespective of their political agendas, echoed the opinions of the European intelligentsia.[92] Like members of the Frankfurt school, they abhorred the threat of cultural imperialism that consumerism epitomized for them.[93] Although the German philosopher Walter Benjamin contemplated the nature of the new technology and its effect on political change with ambivalence, he left little to the imagination when he spoke of women and media culture: "The reactionary attitude toward a Picasso painting changes into the progressive reaction toward a Chaplin movie. . . . With regard to the screen, the critical and the receptive attitudes of the public coincide. Who could deny the impact of women on the cultural scene, in the media, movies, fashion, or literature?"[94] A gnawing fear persisted that Japan's social upheaval would follow the same trajectory as that in America—the ultimate in bourgeois decadence. Most Marxists, socialists, and conservatives perceived consumerism as an ersatz culture invading Japanese society. Takasu Yoshijirō, founder of the ultranationalist New Oriental Society (Shin tōhō kyōkai) in 1928, argued that Japanese consumerism imitated American and European styles, in which women and men "lost themselves to jazz and dance."[95] In describing the spread of American culture, the intelligentsia envisaged a scenario in which television programs relayed via satellites and other state-of-the-art technologies helped extend the boundaries of American culture to other countries, "impacting lifestyles, religion, language, and every other component of culture."[96]

The term *speed* (*speedo/sokudo*) conveys the tempo of 1920s culture. Fredrick Lewis Allen has labeled the lightning-like upheaval in women's dress in the United States as "the most conspicuous sign of what was taking place," but the changes were also visible in "prohibition, the automobile, confession and sex magazines, and the movies." In combination with other forms of mechanization, they expressed a different aesthetic based on speed.[97] Hirabayashi, one of the less ambivalent intellectual debaters of consumerism in Japan, dreamed of the view from the window of a moving train or airplane, the motion of traveling on a paved superhighway, and the thrill of working in a high-rise building equipped with a gleaming elevator. All epitomized a new concept of beauty with speed as its underpinning. Hirabayashi correlated speed with efficiency, and in doing so promoted a site for women in the discourse.

The benefits derived from speed and efficiency provided radical changes in the commodification of the everyday, and thus in the discourse surrounding women. The first benefit involved domestic rationalization. "Speed" would release women, especially housewives, from the drudgery that precluded their involvement in society. Hirabayashi supported "the socialization of the family." Society should bear the burden for household tasks—from washing to sewing—hitherto characterized as women's work. He anticipated the impact of natural gas, running water, and electricity in daily routines, and he saw the growth of mass production as a major factor in alleviating the housewife's travail. Foodstuffs formerly made by women in individual households would be manufactured in the factory. Inexpensive restaurants and cafeterias would present an economical way out of the kitchen.[98] The changes in women's clothing and hairstyles, both of which caused a furor, would streamline the lives of urban women especially.[99] In the process, society would become more complex.

Hirabayashi's idea of a complex society was premised on time and space being compressed by improvements in communications and transportation facilities. When mechanization facilitated women's social involvement, they would naturally fill the labor gap, an inevitable result of the shortage of manpower. Hirabayashi's ability to redefine gender roles within the context of the emerging mass society offers an explanation for his positive response to mechanization.[100] With mechanization seen as an integral proponent in forging a social identity for women, women's emotional and spiritual independence also came up for consideration. So it was that leisure, as a by-product of the rationalization of everyday life, became a factor in the promotion of Hirabayashi's vision for the "feminization of culture."[101]

If love is premised on freedom from the bonds of a conventional marriage, then a monogamous union imposes as many restraints on a woman's personal freedom as on a man's. Indeed, a second benefit inherent in Hirabayashi's vision for women incorporated sexual relationships based on free love. Hirabayashi insisted that "inequality is most apparent in marriage laws, which John Stuart Mill has likened to slave laws, and in inheritance laws, which perpetuate male superiority."[102] Hirabayashi's ideal relationship was one without legal and moral restraints. That obviously was not feasible as long as gender-related economic and political inequalities existed. The Meiji Civil Code, which perpetuated an outdated family system, must be revised or eliminated to alleviate women's anxieties, Hirabayashi argued. Hirabayashi's comments on women's education express his disdain for the system as a whole:

> When a woman graduates from a women's higher school [*jogakkō*] it is believed that she no longer needs any formal education. In fact, schooling available for a woman beyond that point is almost nonexistent. The reason is that a woman is not even regarded as a social entity. . . . Sooner or later a woman must leave her father's home; she is forced into a new family where the despot this time is the husband. Of course, she does not go as an equal, but as an appendage of the husband. . . . The male takes over his father's family, or else he becomes independent and starts his own family. The same is not true for the woman. She has nothing to call her own. The woman, who is inferior in terms of education, skill, and physical endurance, cannot become independent even if she so desires.[103]

The waning of patriarchal authority in the 1920s seemed to promise some liberation for women. Established authority figures unable to adapt to changing circumstances were slowly losing the power to exert unquestioned domination over women. A father's or husband's declining control over a daughter or wife demonstrated his unwillingness to keep up with new revitalizing trends, shifting values, and the consequences of innovative technology. Hirabayashi's recognition of the key role of mechanization in the future attainment of women's rights registers this awareness. The machine epitomized scientific rationale and progress. "Only the 'fin de siècle man,' " he wrote, "fears and damns the machine."[104]

The founding of Hani Motoko's Jiyū gakuen (Free Academy) and Nishimura Isaku's Bunka gakuin (Culture Academy) in 1921 were acknowledgment that the desire for agency among some women was being heard. Neither school conformed to the standards set down by the Ministry of Education for government-approved women's higher schools, which automatically excluded both from the official system. Nevertheless, a number of bold parents favored such schools for their children, proof that an alternative form of education was desired. School uniforms were cast aside; a low student-to-teacher ratio maintained good scholarship; teachers rather than the state decided on textbooks and curriculum; and above all, subservience, the cornerstone of a conventional education and regarded as a paramount virtue for women, was rejected. Despite these similarities, each school adhered to distinctive educational philosophies that reflected its founder's principles.[105]

Architect Nishimura Isaku traced his lineage to a wealthy liberal family in Wakayama. More than a keenly developed critical sensitivity toward social inequality, his love for the arts made him detest any kind of spiritual repression. The avant-garde educational policies he adopted mirrored his attitude toward art, which he considered a representation of an individual's total freedom.[106] Gender differentiation violated the laws of nature and was unnatural and intolerable. Whether a woman could work up to her potential and develop her individual talents was the issue. Nishimura's fancy rhetoric aside, his motivation for founding Bunka gakuin rested more on his own child's educational needs than on an altruistic desire to augment the social position of women.[107]

Hani's "holy mission" in establishing her school, Jiyū gakuen, emanated from a desire to create an intellectual milieu where children could think for themselves. Creative writing offered a way for young women to express their innermost thoughts. Students, who eventually would join the ranks of the housewives, actively participated in running the school, from calculating a balanced budget to planning menus and preparing meals.[108] Hani's resolve to help housewives lead rational lives at home by teaching them to eliminate waste and to budget effectively rested on the same Christian ethics that governed the founding of her magazine, *Katei no tomo* (Home Companion). The education received at Jiyū gakuen prepared young women for married life, and thus conformed to the standard requirements of a women's higher school, but Hani's conception of a "good" wife meant a "clever" (*sōmei*) housewife, for whom "there was nothing she could not do for herself."[109] An independent, self-confident young woman became a prerequisite for the *shufu* in an emerging consumer age. Moreover, it advanced an objective not fostered by most women's schools.

Conclusion

Since mass consumption is commonly associated with the manipulation of people's desires, one might ask whether the spread of consumerism posed an obstacle to Nishimura's and Hani's "ideal" for the cultivation of independent, liberated young women. Consumerism in 1920s Japan, with its various pejorative labels, remained a vision for the future rather than a *fait accompli*. An important dimension of mass culture emerged in Europe back in the fifteenth century, when Johann Gutenberg used interchangeable parts to construct a printing press in Germany. In the eighteenth century, a limited supply of guns manufactured with standardized parts appeared on the U.S. market. And by the nineteenth century, a few of Chicago's meatpacking plants had installed conveyor systems. The production of bicycles in Paris underwent a comparable mechanization. The Ford Motor Company's success with the moving assembly line in the early twentieth century was followed by technological innovations never dreamt of before. Japan was next in line to enter the age of consumerism.

Cultural historian Wakamori Tarō called this period "the age of massification" not so much because of the actual advent of mass production and consumption, but rather because the hegemony that controlled social change was moving away from the state and elitist intellectuals in the direction of the "masses," among whom women inevitably figured prominently. Changes conspicuous in the startling demeanor of women in the 1920s reached maturity only with the consumer-oriented mass culture that developed in the postwar years.[110]

Nevertheless, a few interwar intellectuals like Nii Itaru, Chiba Kameo, and especially Hirabayashi ventured to explore consumerism's appeal for women. Other feminists did not share Hirabayashi's optimistic analysis of mechanization. Indeed, Hirabayashi's views are still largely unchronicled in the social history of Japanese women. One history describes post–World War I developments in industrialization and the relationship to women in the following manner: "Industrialization in the modern period strengthened gender discrimination and intensified sexual distinctions based on the division of labor. On the other hand, because of the universalization of modern human values such as 'equality,' 'human rights' and the 'individual,' women gained a perception of discrimination and oppression, which resulted in a desire to become emancipated."[111] Certainly not all women were victims of ideological precepts they swallowed whole. Technological advancements did encourage women to examine their circumstances. But unless women uncovered a new set of values by and for themselves, any restructuring of daily life and its intertwinement with technological innovation bore no relationship to the potential for alternatives. The changes involving urban middle-class women and consumerism were considered meaningless. The most visible aspects of urban culture continued to be labeled a short-lived fad. More important, this urban culture was contrasted with "Taishō democracy," which was said to have "developed by linking the direct and indirect needs of the people with an awakening of the ego and the autonomy of the individual."[112]

Today, the connection between technology and political and social change is taken for granted. No one would deny the possibility that changes in lifestyle owing to industrial development directly influence thought patterns. Jean Baudrillard, in rethinking his views on media and the masses, once said: "I would no longer interpret in the same way the forced silence of the masses in the mass media. I would no longer see it as a sign of passivity and alienation, but to the contrary an original strategy, an original response in the form of a challenge."[113] Rather than relying on Baudrillard to belabor the trajectory of the rise in women's consciousness during the years of nation-state building, it is more pertinent to map out the often circuitous routes followed by urban middle-class women in the 1920s. To get a picture of the situation of urban middle-class women who had no stake in government, we must examine their position using contradictory gender discourses or cultural representation that helps fill in the gap between the idea and the reality.

The new consumer culture was linked with the social and cultural redefinition of women and the construction of a new gendered subject of modernity in complex ways. It involved a tension between ways that women were seen and represented as icons of the new consumerism, and it centered on ways that women sought to appropriate the new consumer culture for their own ends. To what extent did the media-related transformation in women like the modern girl, the housewife, and the professional working woman reveal these shifts in the reconstruction of female identities in the interwar period? Did the new middle-class women's culture emerging within the context of consumerism reflect any concerted attempt for autonomy, contradictory though the fruits may have been? The following chapter examines a wide range of discourses surrounding the modern girl, who, like the housewife and the professional working woman, did not come under the sway of any organized movement.

2

The Modern Girl as a

Representation of Consumer Culture

A new way of understanding oneself in relation to society
was emerging. Linked to matters of personal decoration, it
broke from a past in which *who* you were in society was a matter of social and economic class. —Stewart Ewen and Elizabeth Ewen[1]

Not quite one year had passed since the Great Earthquake of 1923
struck Tokyo and its environs. Life in the city had resumed its normal
pace, and a sense of calm had gradually returned to the quake-stricken
areas. The modern girl, a quintessential icon of consumerism, added
a new dimension to the city streets. At first, she seemed to represent
just another change in women's fashion and hairstyles. Within a matter
of months after her "debut," however, she had assumed the attributes
of someone associated with self-indulgence and loose morals. This was
the image that the press, happy to capitalize on the more scandalous
side of her nature, furthered. Whether the media created the image of
the modern girl or merely reported the phenomenon is a mutually constitutive question. But without a doubt the rapidly developing consumerism—especially the popularity of mass magazines for women and

the impact of American movies—helped to reciprocally construct a so-cial backdrop for the modern girl.

The way social factors are read is not what determines the individual. But the conspicuous dress and the habits that separated the modern girl from the home were a reflection of the image she portrayed in the pub-lic mind-set. The complex representations of the modern girl not only suggested the need to readdress the relationship of women to moder-nity, but also pointed to shifts in the understanding of femininity and masculinity that spelled the disruption of gender codes. From the early years of the 1920s, the image of the modern girl, constructed and recon-structed, was accompanied by values commensurate with the budding of consumer culture.

In department stores, the modern girl appeared in the guise of a floor model. Referred to as a "mannequin girl" in Japan, she captivated shop-pers with her trendy fashions. On posters, she was the young woman with bobbed hair who advertised Sapporo beer, Suntory wine, and even the soft drink called Calpis that boasted the healthful properties of calcium. The cosmetic company Shiseido chose her to illustrate its latest cosmetics and toiletries. In 1929, when the Tokyo subway linked the Ginza with Asakusa, the visage of a woman distinguished by a cloche hat and stylish Western dress heralded the event. The Ginza, re-nowned for its nightlife and transient delights, figured as the perfect playground for the modern girl, while Asakusa, Tokyo's oldest enter-tainment district and home to its first cinema, provided a public form of consumer-generated leisure that presaged the looming transformation in lifestyles.

The writer Tanizaki Junichirō's interpretation of the modern girl in his novel *Naomi* emphasizes the progression from a virginal child-woman to a seductive temptress.[2] In naming his protagonist Naomi, Tanizaki ingeniously combined a name with biblical resonance spelled out in Japanese characters to cross East-West boundaries. Songwriter Saijō Yaso portrayed the modern girl as an ineffectual, lovestruck office lady in his million-selling record "Tokyo Marching Song." Both Tani-zaki and Saijō broke the taboo that said "normal" women should remain silent about issues related to sexuality. Much like a pastiche, the com-modification of the modern girl bespoke both fancy and imagination.

Because of the images that undermined the modern girl's formation into a figure with coherent unity, she lacked scholarly consensus in aca-

The height of fashion for modern girls, circa 1925 (Hakubunkan Shinsha).

Modern girls on the
Ginza, circa 1928
(Hakubunkan Shinsha).

demic circles. The inability of most intellectuals to perceive her as an imaginary by-product of modernization left the modern girl devoid of a birthright that would lend reality to the predominant representations of her. In meaning and status, she existed more as an object than as a self-defining subject.

Unlike the professional working woman and the housewife, the modern girl made no verbal pronouncements about her position in urban culture. Hers was a voiceless existence surrounded by ambivalence—the ambivalence of class and occupation, ambivalence presented and represented through the media. In the absence of a clear social referent, the uproar over the modern girl exacerbated intellectuals' inability to see her as the phantasmagoric figure that she was within the context of the changes being wrought in the social and cultural order.

The task of providing the modern girl, or *moga,* as her name became abbreviated, with a social and historical raison d'être fell to the intellectuals, whatever their particular ideological stance. The political views of women intellectuals Hiratsuka Raichō, Yosano Akiko, and Yamakawa Kikue varied, but all three women envisioned women's subjectivity within the context of awakening, be it through learning, awareness to women's causes, or a belief in activism. Male intellectuals like Hirabayashi Hatsunosuke and Chiba Kameo, on the other hand, recognized that without sensitivity to the dynamics of the time, the modern girl would be seen outside history and would be ignored or distorted. Multiple discourses, most of which conceived of the modern girl as something fragmentary, played a formative role in articulating her identity. The derivative views of the modern girl daunted the hopes of the "new woman" and those intellectuals who had imagined her as someone who would devote her energies to public activities and would duplicate those values historically associated with men. When some intellectuals said that in fact, she was not "modern" at all, they were alluding to her failure to make choices in keeping with their set of norms. The negative critiques that formed the bulk of the commentary about the modern girl were mainly responsible for fanning the flames of the *moga* sensation.

We begin, therefore, with the publicly defined images of the modern girl as a site for exploring the responses of Japanese intellectuals to the social and cultural gender transformations that characterized the 1920s. The "modern" that identified the modern girl clearly was inconsistent with prevalent female norms. The modern girl may best be understood as a phantasm rather than as a social reality. Nevertheless, that phantasm was a marked feature of an urban society in flux, a powerful symbol of Taishō modernity.

Positioning the Modern Girl: Modern Girls in Print

Intellectuals tended to idealize the modern girl in ways they considered appropriate to the changing age.[3] Many regarded her as an ephemeral craze especially prevalent among young Tokyo women who strutted the stage of the Ginza and Marunouchi. One of the first intellectuals to embark on a statistical study of changing fashions and lifestyles after the earthquake was Kon Wajirō, a professor of architecture at Waseda University. Kon's meticulously detailed survey compared the way of life in Tokyo with that in a number of farming villages. In the summer of 1925, Kon surveyed more than one thousand men and women. He found that 99 percent of the women he observed on the Ginza wore traditional Japanese dress, while 33 percent of the men were wearing kimono.[4] Where was the modern girl? By 1925 the fashionable aspects of consumerism were said to be everywhere visible, but the imaginary multiplication of the modern girl is revealed by the discrepancy. What made the modern girl such a powerful symbol was not that she represented a small percentage of "real women," but that she represented the possibilities for what all women could become. She also symbolized consumption and mass culture, phenomena identified with women after the Great War.

The Ginza was home to many of the defining elements of consumerism: the department store, the café, the dance hall, and the modern girl.[5] Taking into account the place and the number of people in Kon's survey, one would have expected a sizable number of the women there to be in Western dress. Yet the few he found were primarily a few modern types and the wives and daughters of peers or government officials. (Schoolgirls dressed in Western-style uniforms were considered separately.) It is perhaps no wonder, then, that the modern girl outwardly resembling the American flapper, only one in a hundred, stood out from the crowd and became an immediate object of public attention. By boldly focusing people's attention on her daring Western attire, one of the few

Images of modern girls, circa 1928. Reprinted with permission of Mainichi shinbun.

A view of the Ginza in the 1920s (Hakubunkan Shinsha).

clues used to identify her, she epitomized a shift in the history of Japanese women's fashion. More significant, she was associated in the public mind with defiance—defiance of a lifestyle many women presumed impossible to transcend.

The modern girl's strength, as Kon's survey substantiated, lay not in statistics that might have determined her presence numerically, but in the possibilities that her radical break with convention offered a growing spectrum of women. The challenge that representations of the modern girl posed for the nation became a yardstick for measuring real changes in the social status of women. Such representations situated the relation of women and consumerism within a broader discourse, making it possible to debunk the myth that all women were dependent. By example, the professional working woman was crossing boundaries into urban public space just as the new image of the woman as a modern housewife was surfacing.

Indeed, the representation of the modern girl as a purveyor of bourgeois consumerism, the first image of her to capture the public eye, was fraught with anxiety. It featured a vapid young woman clad in a brightly colored one-piece dress reaching only to the knees or a little below, favoring high-heeled shoes and sheer stockings that showed off her legs. A wide-brimmed floppy hat or cloche made of a soft material partially concealed her short hair, or *danpatsu*, which had been bobbed in the style of Hollywood idols Clara Bow, Pola Negri, Mary Pickford, and Gloria Swanson. In the Swanson tradition, she often penciled in a thin line over her shaved eyebrows. Over her shoulder she casually slung a pouch bag.[6] This mindless, fashion-addicted young woman certainly did not denote the evolution of a new political force. Rather, she represented the object of male desire much like the Naomi-dominatrix in Tanizaki's novel.

Like her mode of dress, the modern girl's hairstyle also symbolized transition. In Edo times it had been the custom among men and women to pull the hair into a topknot (*chonmage*). But in early Meiji, a move to end the practice of applying camellia oil to the hair known as *yuigami* gained momentum. Like cutting off the queue in China, cutting off the topknot bespoke a break with long-established mores. Short haircuts (*danpatsu* or *sanpatsu*) became early signs of the state's efforts to inculcate Western thought and "suitable" daily practices. The changeover from the Japanese to the Western style of hairdressing ostensibly sug-

"A Modern Girl's Belongings." By Kobayashi Kiyoshi, in *Manga Mangun*, 1928. Reprinted with permission of Nihon Manga Shiryōkan.

gested support for the new reforms for civilization and enlightenment (*bunmei kaika*).

In 1871, an official announcement accorded the people the freedom to cut their hair, and in 1873, news spread that the emperor himself was wearing a short cut. According to a survey taken in Shiga prefecture in 1873, almost all the men had short cuts; those who did not were fined.[7] But this so-called sign of civilization, which had been encouraged in the name of "modernity," was limited to men. Women abided by a different set of social rules. Officially, women were encouraged to adopt a "Western" hairstyle, but the recommended styles (*yōhatsu* and *sokuhatsu*) were really just variations of the conventional style.[8] During the early 1870s, when the social impact of the "civilization and enlightenment" reforms was greatest, it appeared that women too would stop dressing their hair in the old style. But in 1872, the year after men received official sanction to cut their hair as they wished, a state ordinance prohibiting women from having a *danpatsu* was enacted because in cutting her hair, "the essence of a woman's beauty would be destroyed."[9] In spite of its initial requirements for "modernity," the state affirmed the masculine and negated the feminine. The social pressures to preserve the ways of the past were far greater on women than men, at least when it came to setting new norms that would effect changes in women's lifestyles.

Until the image of the modern girl surfaced, women's hairstyles had several variations. But the "new" style (*sokuhatsu*), much like the conventional style of oiling the hair and pulling it back in some form of a bun, continued as the proper hairdo worn by girls as young as thirteen years of age.[10] Thus, the modern girl's short cut marked a definite departure. Although the word *danpatsu* remained in use, it connoted something quite different in the early twentieth century than it had for the Meiji woman. The Meiji *danpatsu* referred to hair that had been pulled into a bun; the *danpatsu* that identified the modern girl fell into the category of the most up-to-date American hairstyle, the bob. The *moga*'s short cut mirrored a style that was current throughout the world. By the 1920s, women who had been largely excluded from such symbols of change were acknowledging a desire to question the old aesthetic. The alteration of a woman's physical appearance suggested behavioral disruptions that could not help but result in social tensions.[11]

Past and present observers of the modern girl have often failed to recognize that her impact was based on representations that went beyond the issues of clothing and hairstyles. Best understood as an ideal type, the modern girl portrayed the social transformation in progress. The curious sense of freedom her image exuded did not result from a calculated effort to improve her lot or to join in social movements. It was more the result of a fascination with a fashionable new lifestyle triggered by World War I and the Great Earthquake. The modern girl represented a different type from the earlier new woman, whose name suggested the feminism that propelled members of the Bluestocking Society.

The style associated with the modern girl entered Japan from Europe via the United States following the war, although only a few young women at the time had enough courage to cut off their hair and defy the ensuing criticism and outright ostracism. An aspiring young novelist named Mochizuki Yuriko, who returned to Japan from Europe shortly after the war, stood out as one of that brave minority. In later years, Mochizuki reminisced about the bob she had decided to have.

> The long kimono was beautiful, but it was no longer in keeping with the age. Long Japanese hair was also beautiful, but that, too, had become anachronistic. Those were the feelings I had when I decided to cut my hair. . . .
> You cannot imagine the shock it gave to the people around me. My mother took one look at me and cried out in indignation, "You must be crazy! If you go out, everyone will call you one of those new women" — the term *modern girl* was not in use yet. . . .
> I remember another instance after I returned to my family home in the country. I ran into two girls, fifteen and sixteen, living in the neighborhood who had had a short cut [*danpatsu*]. Ours was an extremely provincial, tradition-bound village, and it caused a great sensation. The girls were punished severely and their mothers sobbed and wailed, carrying on as if they were lunatics. My own mother confronted me and said, "It is your fault that this dreadful thing has happened. You have lost face with everyone in the neighborhood. I wish that you would just go right back to Tokyo." In no time I packed my bag and returned to Tokyo feeling as if I was escaping. . . . It has been almost ten years since I got a short cut. During that time there have been a string of tragicomedies.
> On another occasion I was on my way back to Kansai [western Japan] and an elderly woman on the train kept staring at me. "You are so young and you had to cut off your hair. When did you lose your husband?" I managed to give a strained smile.
> When I think back [to 1918], the painful experiences far outnumbered the comic situations. Even today, it is appalling how many idiots jeer and hiss at me and are ignorant enough to label me a *modern girl*.[12]

Mochizuki prided herself on recognizing the liberating aspects of the short cut. She boldly asserted that women who wished to compete in society on a level comparable with men would have to rid themselves of any encumbering entrapments. Long hair and kimono, although elegant, physically impeded a woman's social development. Being a woman and a self-proclaimed intellectual, Mochizuki resented being singled out by her gender as a modern girl, whom she equated with the superficial aspects of the modern.

The lead article in the January 1927 issue of the women's magazine

Fujin kōron, "Random Views on the Modern Girl" (Modan gāru zak-kan), presented the general consensus on the modern girl. One woman intellectual remarked:

> Whenever I hear the popular word *modern girl,* I recall the time people were interested in the word *new woman.* Although I was quite disappointed with the new woman's behavior, at least I thought of them as kindred spirits because of their fresh way of thinking. But I wonder if there is anything to be discovered in the modern girl's thinking? I suppose that in these uncertain times, their way of expressing themselves is inevitable, but is it possible for anyone not to notice how vapid their lifestyles are? [13]

Another woman, obviously of the same generation, expressed a similar view:

> I think it is interesting to compare today's *modern girl* with the so-called new woman who appeared more than ten years ago. The *new woman* was an enlightened woman. Her way of thinking was intellectually sound, and she was able to understand innermost problems. She was in her late twenties or early thirties. The modern girl, however, has no intellectual basis for her way of thinking, tends to be concerned only with outward appearances, and is in her late teens or early twenties. She is nothing more than a fad.[14]

Yet, another woman intellectual, whose viewpoint resembled Mochizuki's, wrote:

> I do not think that *modern girls* are particularly modern in their way of thinking; they just look modern. You see them wearing flashy clothes — a shiny purple and green dress with a big sash tied under the bosom. If that is the criterion for being modern, it is pitiful. It is an insult to the real *modern girl* even to use a word like *modern girl,* which has such derogatory connotations. For me, the word connotes someone who is a total fake, heavily made-up, and who is satisfied with just having something that is new.[15]

Writer Suzuki Bunshirō warned that if the criteria for modern girls were based on bobbed hair and Western-style skirts reaching to the knee, young women working at fruit shops and greengrocers in the United States also deserved the appellation.[16] Suzuki's image of the modern girl was not a young woman who belonged to a higher socioeconomic class than salesclerks in the United States, but rather someone who would rise to the challenge of meeting new social demands. Even so, the older generation of progressive women intellectuals generally joined their male counterparts in expressing disappointment and anger when the modern girl quashed their expectations for a deeper engagement with modernity. Poet Yosano Akiko, a fervent advocate of equal rights, was struck by the old-fashioned mentality associated with the modern girl:

> Even the prostitutes frequenting the bars and cafés in Paris would never be seen in the type of Western clothing that young women [in Japan] are wearing these days. These girls in their Western dress and short haircuts just copy whatever comes from abroad. The reason that girls who could be mistaken for prostitutes in their crazy get-ups have emerged is not due to the influence of women's liberation. It is because there are certain "new types" among the men who like what is decadent and want young women to look like that.[17]

Almost all the intellectual discourses converge on one point: the modern girl embraced modernity in its most superficial form through such genres as Western clothing, hairstyles, magazines, and movies. The most negative criticism of her came from liberal intellectuals who were struggling with the internalization of Western culture and civilization themselves. Marxist and socialist intellectuals shared the belief that consumerism was a bourgeois ploy to distract modern women from the more pressing issues of politics and class. But the political marginalization of women was really part of a larger marginalization in which women were excluded from the public world.

Indeed, the modern girl's flamboyant style stirred up anxieties among intellectuals and the public at large about the direction in which society was moving. This complemented the hostility to the new currents of thought that were emerging and exacerbated the belief that the commodification of everyday life did not address pressing issues related to the inner spirit, productivity, and the value of restraint.

Contradictory Expectations of the Modern Girl

Hiratsuka Raichō envisioned an ideal modern girl who was a continuation of the new woman of the years 1910–19: "The true *modern girl* is the daughter of the new woman. She was born from her womb." When asked who best fit that ideal, without hesitation Hiratsuka answered Takamure Itsue, the noted anarchist and pioneer in women's history. The media's modern girl hardly fit that description. Hiratsuka castigated the trendy modern girl as an aberration who deserved neither the appellation "modern" nor the public attention she received. Hiratsuka preferred rather to ignore her existence and asserted: "It is beyond me why anyone in the world would call this type of girl a *modern girl*."[18] Nevertheless, Hiratsuka's choice of the word *true* when speaking about the modern girl was not entirely unfounded. The term *modern girl* surfaced in Japan for the first time in its phonetic spelling in an article written by Kitazawa Chōgo. Entitled "The Emergence of the Modern Girl—A Letter to My Sister in Japan" (Modan gāru no hyōgen—Nihon no imōto ni okuru tegami), it appeared in the April 1923 issue of *Josei kaizō* (Women's Reform).[19]

The following year, "Modern Girl" (Modan gāru), which dealt primarily with the modern girl in England, was published in the August 1924 issue of *Josei* (Women), a popular women's magazine.[20] The author, essayist Kitazawa Shūichi, who also used the pen name Chōgo, had spent a number of years in London. Although Kitazawa attributed universal qualities to the English modern girl that he believed eventually would become manifest in a Japanese counterpart, when he first used the term, it was to explain the social trend that had emerged among English women. He did not intend it as an appellation for Japanese women. In Japan at that time, the modern girl was an almost nonexistent type.[21] Kitazawa was certain that situation was about to change. "If I were pressed to answer whether or not the modern girl exists in any great number in Japan, I would have to hesitate before replying. But if I answered with a flat 'no,' I would also feel hesitant. Suffice it to say that quite a few girls in Japan possess the potential for being modern. There is little doubt in my mind that if the modern girl has not already appeared in Japanese society, she soon will."[22]

Kitazawa alluded to two special features intrinsic to the modern girl in England. First, she exuded a new sense of self, evident in the desire for self-expression and individual fulfillment. Because she believed herself equal to men, ingrained customs and conventional concepts of morality posed no constraints for her. Second, her openness was not the result of a conscious effort to achieve intellectual awakening. It occurred spontaneously within her. By following her own feelings, she unconsciously surmounted existing behavioral patterns. Kitazawa suggested that being modern generated a degree of economic independence and a liberated ego—both attributes that men would find appealing.

> If I were to take a survey of the younger generation's likes and dislikes in girls, we would find that young men prefer girls who walk side by side and are in step with them rather than girls who trail behind like sheep. Young men are enamored of girls who speak their minds instead of always being humble and never voicing their opinions. They seek out girls without a lot of shortcomings whom they can enjoy life with.
>
> My analysis does not even deal with things like beauty, intelligence, or taste. But it is clear that members of the young generation respect those girls who do not use their feminine wiles and pretend to be like docile cats with bells tied around their necks. They admire girls who perceive things as human beings and are on the same wavelength as men. They dislike girls who try to get the upper hand when they are in a fix by insisting that they are the weaker sex. If my observations are correct and today's young generation really want girls of this type, they have no choice but to look to the modern girl.[23]

Kitazawa's article on the English modern girl opened Pandora's box. Within months, articles like "The Modern Girl: Sudden Transformation by Mutation" (Modan gāru totsuzen hen'i, *Josei,* December 1925), "The Originator of the Modern Girl" (Modan gāru no honke honmoto, *Josei,* February 1927), and "What Is Modern?" (Nani ga modan ka, *Josei,* June 1927) were filling the pages of monthly magazines. The widely read popular journal *Bungei shunjū* (Literary Chronicle) gave top billing to the modern girl in its January 1928 issue on modern life. Even editors of journals like *Chūō kōron* and *Kaizō* (Reform), both supported by intellectuals, commissioned articles on this spreading social phenomenon. In 1930, *Bungei shunjū,* swept along by the tide, published a new magazine entitled *Modan Nippon* (Modern Japan). Its purpose was to keep abreast of the latest modern trends in Japan. When woman intellectual Kodera Kikuko was asked to render a definition of the modern girl for the second issue (November 1930), she thought for a moment before venturing an answer. "I have never met a real modern girl or modern boy, so I don't know who they are. But in order to be called modern, it is not enough to just look modern. They have to have some substance to them." Kodera's reply is reminiscent of the early discussions of the *moga,* which stressed qualities such as individuality. Like other intellectuals, Kodera was struggling to define what it meant to be modern. Most articles, however, were not concerned with whether or not the modern girl reflected a larger social change that accounted for her emergence. Instead, a preoccupation with what she should be like led to a spate of emotional reactions that dealt with the interiority of the modern girl, revealing the contradictory aspects of the discussions. Intellectuals conflated the modern girl with someone of Takamure Itsue's ilk while other observers zeroed in on a group of empty-headed, sexually permissive young women prone to pleasure. The question of the conflicting loyalties that faced the professional working woman and housewife and centered on the necessity for them to define their own needs was left to others to assess.

Soon, books devoted to the modern girl appeared. Former journalist turned social critic Nii Itaru, an avid follower of women's trends, wrote one of the earliest, *A Dissection of the Modern Mind* (*Kindaishin no kaibō,* 1925).[24] Unlike Kitazawa, Nii had never traveled abroad. His analysis derived solely from his knowledge of Japanese society. Nii distinguished the modern girl from the "social girl" (*shakai josei*). The modern girl challenged prevailing ideals, but no doubt unknowingly. Nii labeled her a present-day Don Quixote. Without the support of an organized movement, she aimed to better herself, not society. Had she had political aspirations, Nii said, she would have been an anarchist. Her essence lay in an awakened sense of self. The "social girl," in contrast, worked within the system. Dominated by her intellect, she would speak out for women's rights and demand suffrage. She would act as a member of a group. Nii probably had in mind Bluestockings like Hiratsuka and Itō Noe when he wrote about the "social girl."[25]

As the term *modern girl* gained popular currency, the monthly women's journal *Fujin no kuni* (Woman's Land) sponsored a roundtable discussion in May 1926 to debate her pros and cons. The panelists were Nii; Chiba Kameo, the author of several books and articles on women who also preferred the sobriquet social critic; and Kume Masao, a writer who favored the so-called mass literature of the 1920s. Women writers Miyake Yasuko, a regular contributor to the general interest journal *Taiyō* as well as mass women's magazines; Yamada Waka, a reformed prostitute turned Bluestocking whose advice column was a fixture of the *Tokyo Asahi shinbun* throughout the late 1920s and early 1930s; and novelist Sasaki Fusa, often listed as a modern girl herself, also joined the discussion.

The discussants entertained mixed opinions. Most spoke out harshly, calling the *moga* sensation symptomatic of a general social malaise that had been plaguing the country since the signing of the Portsmouth Treaty after the Russo-Japanese War. Those more tolerant of the *moga* were in the minority. Nii, for example, disagreed with Kume's assessment of the modern girl as a "flower that blooms in the midst of rubble, where there is little chance for survival." "Why is it [that] as soon as we see someone with 'high-collar' [an older Meiji term used to refer to someone enamored of Western] tastes who keeps up with trendy fashions," he countered, "we pin the pejorative label *modern girl* on her?" Chiba concurred: "If the modern girl seems to be someone preoccupied with clothes and having fun, it is only natural in a bourgeois society that has developed to the extent that ours has."[26]

Miyake agreed with Nii and Chiba in principle, but added that only fifteen- to eighteen-year-olds qualified for the epithet "modern girl." The young held no preconceived images of good or bad, right and wrong. Oblivious to what people around them said, they followed their hearts and not the dictates of society. Miyake felt that even if women in their twenties had the "outward" makings of the modern girl, "inwardly" they were bound by conventional images.[27] She envied the self-assurance of teenage girls, something she said was unknown, even among women like Yamakawa, in her own generation.

Miyake's statement recalls a comment by Yamakawa, with whom she had participated in a panel discussion shortly after the earthquake. When Yamakawa was questioned about Western clothing, she replied: "From the standpoint of convenience, personally, I think it [Western dress] is great. But since we, my cohorts and I, come in contact with many old-guard types, if we are labeled *new women*, we are in trouble." Miyake and Moriya Azuma, another woman writer on that panel, chided Yamakawa for her contradictory statement, berating one of the most prominent so-called progressives of the day for her unbefitting lack of resolve.[28]

While most female intellectuals focused on inner changes that affected the psyche, the image they fostered of the modern girl focused on more cosmetic changes. Their disdain for the modern girl stemmed both from what they labeled a lack of common commitment and from the opinion, shared by their male counterparts, that media-inspired changes were superficial. The consensus depicted consumerism as the manipulator rather than, in Mary Ellen Brown's terms, "as political insofar as women nominate, value, and regulate their own pleasure." Since both conservative and more progressive intellectuals imagined the modern girl as an extension of the new woman, they expected her to give voice to women's emerging consciousness and to actively vent her social dissatisfaction.

Only a few intellectuals like Chiba, Nii, and especially Hirabayashi visualized a positive connection between the modern girl and consumerism. In the aftermath of the earthquake, Hirabayashi moved away from his fellow Marxists. He linked the image of the modern girl to industrial advancement and a modern way of getting things done that would help define a new vision of progress. Unlike most intellectuals, who were impeded by an inability to separate facts from values in dealing with this modern construct, Hirabayashi, and to a lesser extent Chiba and Nii, envisioned an assertive, individualistic woman of the future—a product of consumerism who demonstrated a previously unknown degree of agency. This was in marked contrast to the image of the insipid, superficial young vamp who epitomized the most deleterious aspects of bourgeois society.

Expectations and Extravagances:
The Modern Girl and Promiscuity

The thrilling romantic episodes that became synonymous with the image of the modern girl positioned her as a sex object similar to the professional working woman.[29] Ōya, who had referred to the changing social trends as "nothing more than consumer-oriented hedonism," singled out actress Ōi Sachiko as a typical modern girl because of her outlandish escapades: "Jealousy just does not exist in their marriage—not in the slightest. It goes without saying that Sachiko and her husband both come and go as they please. If either of them wants to stay out overnight, they do so without compunction. She invited one of her friends—a man, of course—to her home, and the three of them, her husband included, slept together and had a good time. I don't know how

Dance-hall dancers waiting for customers, circa 1929. Reprinted with permission of Mainichi shinbun.

she keeps her relationships straight and distinguishes between her husband, her lovers, and her friends."[30]

Writers wasted no time in seizing on the negative publicity to sensationalize the sexual depravity of the modern girl. Loose morals like Ōi's signified a lack of morality in all *moga*. The purportedly harmful influence of love scenes commonplace in American movies was enlisted into a narrative proclaiming that all modern girls enjoyed sexual freedom.[31] A series of reports published in the *Tokyo Nichi Nichi shinbun* (Tokyo Daily Newspaper) in May 1927 claimed that promiscuous behavior had prompted the police to investigate modern girls and foreigners who lived in the Tokyo-Yokohama area, the assumption being that foreigners could easily seduce modern girls. The police concentrated their efforts on cafés, dance halls, geisha houses, cinemas, theaters, hotels, and the Ginza, all highly probable places for such liaisons to occur. When an English male and a twenty-three-year-old "beauty with a short haircut, Western clothing, and the voluptuousness much favored by foreigners" were taken into custody, the newspaper used boldface letters to report: "Modern on the outside—empty on the inside—prone to reading trashy magazines." Later testimony by the for-

Sapporo beer hall on the Ginza, circa 1929 (Gakushū Kenkyūsha).

eigner's maid revealed that at least two or three different young women spent the night with the defendant each week. They appeared to be women whom he had charmed during job interviews at the fuel company where he worked. "Usually they wore Japanese kimono and did not have short cuts," the maid reported.[32]

Episodes sprinkled with unfounded gossip that played up sexual misconduct became an underlying theme of the modern girl discourse and enlivened the pages of books, newspapers, and magazines. The Western attire that was the identifying feature of the modern girl called into question her consumption habits and reflected the confusion surrounding the morality of class and dress. Indeed, the sense of unease that challenges to the accepted codes of behavior created demonstrated the difficulty of determining respectability by appearance alone. While earlier sex scandals usually described the woman suffering because of her partner's philandering, now the public was scandalized by the so-called subversion of female behavior. Sex became a powerful catalyst in increasing the momentum with which visual identities were formed and accentuated the public's perception of the modern girl as a temptress.

Author Kataoka Teppei assigned leading roles to the modern girl and

"Lovestruck Customer Drinks Too Much Coffee and Ogles the Café Hostess." By Yoshioka Torihei, in *Tōsei Hyaku Baka*, 1920. Reprinted with permission of Nihon Manga Shiryōkan.

modern boy in two novels and a short story. For Kataoka, dress was the only criterion for a boy's being modern. But Western clothing, no matter how fashionable, was not unusual enough to cause the same sensation when worn by a man that it did for the modern girl. The modern boy was clearly a media construct whose chief justification was to act as a balance for the modern girl.[33] When the magazine *Shinseinen* (New Youth) came out in 1920, the editor boasted that it was designed for a new type of young man who possessed an "international outlook, but also was a loyal and patriotic citizen of Japan." When writer Yokomizo Seishi assumed the editorship in 1927, however, the *moga* boom caused him to rethink the magazine's direction. He claimed that "New Youth" should not be equated with the term "modern boy."[34] The 1930 edition of the *Sentango jiten* (Dictionary of Ultramodern Words) defined the modern boy as a young man who is "flashy and follows the latest fads, sports a silk handkerchief in his breast pocket, wears bell-bottomed trousers, and is a kind of hooligan." A similar definition appeared in the *Modan ingo jiten* (Dictionary of Modern Slang) published that same year: "A young man who combs his hair in the all-back (*ōru bakku*) style, wears baggy bell-bottoms, follows the latest fads, and is prone to debauchery." While fads in men's clothing and hairstyles underwent several modifications between the 1860s and the 1920s, male debauchery was nothing new. The growing feminization of society coupled with the changeover from *kimono* to Western dress and the heightened sense of sexual freedom that described the modern girl, however, were new. Under these circumstances, it was only natural that the modern girl was received with raised eyebrows while the modern boy received only snickers.

A short story written by Kataoka features a young typist who is dating three young men, all modern boys, at the same time. Without compunction she agrees to go for a drive with one of her lovers in a taxi that will go anywhere in central Tokyo for one yen (*entaku*).

> *Boyfriend A to the modern girl:* My philosophy is this: Today is today. Tomorrow is tomorrow. I want to be totally swept away by what I am feeling the very instant that I am feeling it.
> *Modern girl to Boyfriend A:* I'm with you 100 percent.
> *Boyfriend A to the modern girl:* You mean you don't need any guarantees for tomorrow either?

And so they arrive by taxi at an inn on the outskirts of the city. The last scene finds the modern girl engaged in a serious conversation with Boyfriend B. "Let's get married," she practically hollered into his ear. "Promise. We've really done everything married people do, you know."

In the same scene, Boyfriend C, who is not quite as "modern" as his rivals, stands slightly separated from Boyfriend B and the modern girl at the edge of a pond. Gazing out absentmindedly, Boyfriend C winces whenever the modern girl speaks. He turns on his heel ready to make his retreat, but her voice trails after him: "It took a long time to wear you down. We met almost two weeks ago."[35]

Kataoka's portrayal of the modern girl as an impulsive flapper is filled with tongue-in-cheek exaggeration. In fact, his story contains almost all the derogatory terms popular at the time to describe the modern girl: *decadent, hedonistic,* and *superficial.* Kataoka was not unique in taking the generally accepted definition of the modern girl and adapting his stories to fit that definition. Other writers portrayed the modern girl in similarly compromising sexual situations. All became part of the fictionalized *moga* image that the media passed on to the general public.[36] Kiyosawa Rei elaborated on this point in his article "Dissecting the Modern Girl":

A girl from Niigata became so distraught because her friends spoke about her as "that *modern girl*" that she finally committed suicide. In her mind *modern girl* was another name for flapper. It is not only unsophisticated young girls from the country who think like this. Recently, one of the newspapers came out with a special edition attacking the *modern girl*. Another newspaper printed in boldface letters, "Modern Girl Refused Employment at the Ministry of Railways." After carefully looking over the contents of that article, I realized that the reporter and a high-ranking official in the Ministry of Railways agreed that the modern girl was the type of person who met bad boys on the sly and did a lot of fooling around.[37]

The eroticization of the modern girl in literature and the panic over the "decline" in feminine morality were evidence that some young people were exploring their sexuality. Although fiction such as Kataoka's reinforced the negative image of the modern girl by sexualizing her, it also depicted a shift in attitudes toward fraternizing with the opposite sex and ultimately marriage. Few young women in the early years of the twentieth century thought of asking themselves how or with whom they were going to spend their lives.

The reaction to the various "myths" that sprang up around the modern girl can be read in several ways. Certainly the intellectuals' own biases influenced their response to her. Frightened, perhaps, by the implications of the changes symbolized by the modern girl and consumerism, most were unwilling to deal with their internal conflicts and unable to perceive reality. A second reading concerns the documentation of fiction by authors like Kataoka. Clearly, novels and short stories demonstrated the interaction of the author's fantasies with questions of gender. Third, magazine editors performed a kind of balancing act in constructing an acceptable relationship with their readers. Unlike novels or movies, in which young women often were the objects of the adult male's gaze, in order for editors to successfully sell their wares, they had to satisfy young women's tastes. Although the commercial motive was to create loyal subscribers, through a variety of clever strategies the magazines also helped create a vital sense of community among their readers.

Crowds in front of a popular Asakusa movie theater, circa 1927.
Reprinted with permission of Mainichi shinbun.

Intellectual Takamure Itsue's perception of the modern girl reveals
her opposition to the "recent sexual depravity." Takamure challenged
journalist Hasegawa Nyozekan, who had cited economic instability as
the reason for the growing popularity of late marriages among young
people:

> The birthplace of modern hedonism is America, where all the wealth of
> the world is concentrated. The concentration of wealth is the motivat-
> ing force behind amusements and entertainment. In Greece the luxuri-
> ous lifestyle of the upper class and the wealthy townspeople who sur-
> rounded them produced the class of prostitutes known as *hetaira*. The
> same can be said of *modanizumu* in our modern cities, and sex for fun,
> which goes along with *modanizumu*. Without question the ruling class
> and the wealthy citizenry are responsible for creating this situation.[38]

What Takamure referred to as "sex for fun" lent further credence to
the discourses that appeared in books, newspapers, and magazines regarding the unrestrained behavior of the modern girl. The sensational
reportage favored by the media made the modern girl appear to be an
attention seeker. Nii settled on the term *instinctive* (*muishikiteki*) to de-

Asakusa showgirls—a bit of the erotic, circa 1929 (Gakushū Kenkyūsha).

scribe her behavior.[39] Nii added, however, that the guiding force behind her actions was American culture.[40] Compared with the new woman, whose newness was linked to social demonstration and a conscious self-awakening, most intellectuals perceived nothing of import about the modern girl that she could claim as her own. Their elitism mirrored their hostility toward consumerism and their inability to see the modern girl in her role as a modern construct.

Materials from the period include little direct criticism of the modern girl written by conservative intellectuals. But that is not to imply that conservatives approved of the phantasm of the modern girl any more than the younger generation of intellectuals, most of whom had ties to Marxism. More likely, devoting their energies to combating their main adversary, socialist thought, took priority over any discussion of the modern girl and the more relaxed attitudes toward sex.[41] In terms of censorship, the state exhibited a particular sensitivity to left-wing thought and erotica that seemed to incite a breakdown in sexual morals and traditional ethics.[42] Cafés that offered "erotic service" were kept under strict police surveillance from as early as 1923, and the authorities labeled café waitresses the modern counterparts of the geisha.[43] Ironically, the image of the modern girl, associated with amusement and decadence, never became offensive enough to make her/it an object requiring direct intervention like the prostitute. An exception has been noted, however: from 1927, the Ministry of Railways refused to hire modern girls—that is, young women singled out solely on the basis of their dress, makeup, and bobbed hair.[44]

Fictionalized accounts like Murayama Tomoyoshi's play *The Spy and the Dancer* (*Supai to odoriko*) might depict a dancer as a modern girl, but the state did not consider the two synonymous. In the state's view, dancers were young women employed by dance halls for the purpose of prostitution. Although by 1925 customers frequenting dance halls were required to write down their names and addresses before entering, and in 1928 those under eighteen years of age were prohibited, the Casino (*kajino*) Follies opened to much fanfare in 1929 in downtown Tokyo's Asakusa. The government did not actually secure legislation that declared dance halls illegal until 1940. Thus, while the state clamped down on what was deemed sex as an industry, the modern girl, associated with private life, was not regarded as a similar threat that required regulation.

Consumerism—Decadence or Hope?

The movies offered testimony to the modern girl's fascination with American popular customs. Filmmaker Sawamura Torajirō described the attraction as "a reflection of the [American] national character. It is probably America's brightness and energy and the fact that it is not preoccupied with convention and tradition."[45] Hirabayashi also recognized the cinema's role in creating a place for the modern girl.

> The cinema, sports, and Marx: all three and each in a different way symbolize the trends prevalent in today's world. Hollywood, in a sense, controls the world. Even Japan is under Hollywood's yoke. . . . Clara Bow, Rudolph Valentino, and Charlie Chaplin are the most popular names in the world today. It is rare for someone not to know the names of three or four movie stars, but it is not at all unusual not to know the name of the president of Germany, the prime minister of England, or one of the great French painters. Movies are more universal

than anything else is. Movies reach out to people all over the world directly and emotionally just by means of a simple screen. Hollywood has completely changed the Ginza. Without any doubt, the closest relative to the *modern girl* and *modern boy* is the cinema.[46]

Hirabayashi showed a keen interest in the trajectory of the social impact of movies: "No matter what out-of-the-way rural movie theater I happen upon, invariably there is at least one American movie playing. In the cities, the majority of the theaters show only Western films. . . . And most are American. In fact, many fans won't even see a film unless it was made in America. Action films and comedies, the mainstay of American movies, are rapidly changing the lifestyle of the Japanese."[47]

Nii asserted that the arrival of American movies in Japan marked the moment of transition for the modern girl. He acknowledged the impact of the post–World War I influx of American books and magazines on the rhythms of Japanese life. But nothing, in his view, equaled the boost that came from American movies. Movies made visible the Americans' free-and-easy approach to life:

> Without knowledge of the cinema, we will never understand what moves the emotions of our young people and governs their lifestyle. . . . During a lecture tour in the provinces, in one of my talks on Japanese literature, I referred to [Ozaki] Kōyō and [Tokutomi] Roka to illustrate a point, but I elicited only blank stares from the audience. As soon as I mentioned Clara Bow and Louise Brooks, faces lit up in understanding. . . . In Japan, although department stores employ Japanese actresses [as models] to help popularize new fashions, they exert little appreciable influence on what trends will become popular. Hollywood fashion, on the other hand, reaches Tokyo in about one year. . . . It does not take much to imagine how Hollywood has become the Jerusalem of the fashion world and the extent to which American movie stars hold the deciding vote when it comes to creating new trends.[48]

The constant rise in the number of movie theaters during the period from 1912 to 1929 bears out Nii's analysis (see table 1). In 1912, 44 movie theaters operated in Tokyo and its vicinity; by 1929 the figure had risen to 207. Murobuse Takanobu estimated, perhaps too generously, that more than one million people frequented the cinema on a monthly basis.[49] The debate over the immorality of movies crossed ideological lines. Ironically, the demands that society be safeguarded were in effect

TABLE 1   Movie Theaters and Viewers
in Tokyo and Vicinity, 1912–1929

	Number of theaters	Viewers
1912	44	12,772,247
1917	76	13,704,161
1922	112	17,397,817
1926	178	24,870,256
1929	207	36,917,425

Source: Based on figures quoted by Gonda Yasunosuke, *Minshū gorakuron* (1932), reprinted in *Yoka/goraku kenkyū kisō bunkenshū*, vol. 10, ed. Ishikawa Hiroyoshi (Ōzorosha, 1989), p. 208.

affirming the right of the state to pass censorship laws to protect the public from moral dangers.

The interest exhibited by Sawamura, Hirabayashi, Nii, and Murobuse in the complex ways that American cinema was influencing Japanese society set them apart from most Japanese intellectuals, who associated movies with the morally unhealthy side of the modern girl and consumerism. The adverse effect of American movies on young women's morals was also a much-debated topic in the United States in the 1920s. One seventeen-year-old, already addicted to the cinema, explained its appeal: "No wonder girls before the days of movies were so modest and bashful. They never saw Clara Bow and William Haines . . . if we didn't see such examples . . . where would we get the idea of being 'hot'? We wouldn't."[50]

Murayama Tomoyoshi, an ardent supporter of the Japanese modernist art movement and a playwright linked closely to the proletarian theater movement during the 1920s, decried American movies for their "detrimental effect on one's psyche. They try to get to a person at a weak moment."[51] Another woman writer, just as emphatic, remarked that "most of the so-called *modern girl* types are shallow 'bean brains' infatuated with American motion pictures."[52] Such reactions to the emerging urban culture reflect a commonality in the leftist intellectuals' discourse. When Yamakawa defined the modern girl, she chose the term *bourgeois.* Her choice of words articulates the ideological importance of the class struggle in her thought: "The *modern boy* and *modern girl* who are so in vogue today are not necessarily members of the bour-geoisie. Yet, even without the mention of class, their ideals and tastes fit in splendidly with those of the bourgeoisie. For that reason, I feel perfectly justified in calling them the heirs and heiresses of the bour-geois class."[53]

Economist Gonda Yasunosuke, noted for his surveys pertaining to leisure and entertainment, was commissioned by *Kaizō*, a journal for leftist intellectuals, to evaluate the pervasiveness of modern life. His essay, titled "Modern Life and Perverted Tastes" (Modan seikatsu to hentai shikōsei), bespeaks his condemnation of the new trends:

> If I were to define the essence of modern life, I would say that people without ties to labor and production are responsible for creating this society.
>
> In terms of class, they are members of the leisure class, or at least those connected to the petty bourgeoisie. Having no direct connection to labor, their lives are rooted solely in consumerism. In terms of age, they are young men and women for whom the name *modern boy* and *modern girl* is appropriate.[54]

Leftists asserted that girls from ordinary families and those forced to work for a living were not even distantly related to the modern girl. The vehemence with which these critics of consumer culture spoke about the danger to civic morality verged on hysteria. In their eyes, American capitalism promoted the degenerate urban lifestyle of which the mod-ern girl was a direct figure. Indeed, most intellectuals—left and right—envisioned the modern girl as a by-product of the leisure class. By the late 1920s, the neologism *erotic, grotesque nonsense* (*ero guro nansensu*), which consisted of equal parts decadence and depravity, best symbol-ized this "hedonistic" culture.[55]

Murayama lashed out against the modern girl and all forms of "cul-tural hedonism." From the standpoint of a leftist intellectual, any kind of commercialized recreation smacked of dissipation. This included "drinking, sex, going to shows—be it movies, plays, or sporting events—looking at [popular] magazines, eating fancy foods, reading foolish books, and thriving on the warmth of family." Murayama saw "no real value or beauty" in love based on romantic sexuality.[56]

Kurahara Korehito also did not limit his criticism of the modern girl to her heavy makeup and flamboyant dress. The new social and artistic trends in which the modern girl figured, and which he referred to as an appendage of the growing urban culture, entered prominently in his appraisal. The modern girl's trademark Western dress had to go; but more important in his view was the elimination of sensational journalism available in mass women's magazines. Put in a broader context, Kurahara's dismissal of the modern girl reflected his own pessimistic view of consumerism, a worthy cause for hysteria.

Particularly distasteful to Kurahara was the fact that the new consumer culture represented a capitalist endeavor. He envisioned the media as an unfair benefactor of large-scale capital and technology. Furthermore, it exerted a one-sided controlling influence on people's lives. Like Murayama, Kurahara's disdain for leisure-related activities directed toward satisfying individual pleasures mirrored his own stoicism. The modern girl, the symbol of consumerism, epitomized women's susceptibility to their personal whims, with sexual misconduct only one of the consequences. This rationale accounted for the label "hedonistic" being pinned on the modern girl, and for the use of the term *cultural hedonism* to describe the commodification of the everyday. To say that Kurahara was alone in comparing the modern girl to a puppet tied to capitalists' pursestrings would be misleading. His attitude, however, furthers the view that problems involving women were allotted little status in the discourses written by Japanese Marxists of the time. The destruction of the patriarchal family structure, which was tantamount to the abolition of the Meiji Civil Code, was not a major concern, regardless of the views espoused by Hirabayashi.

Although few intellectuals looked favorably on the changes occurring in an increasingly broader spectrum of urban women, Chiba Kameo, who coined the term *new sensationalism* (*shinkankaku*) following World War I, was one who did. The attention he paid to the transformation in attitudes and values, in particular to those regarding gender, affirms Chiba's concern for alternative social trends.[57] Rather than isolating the modern girl as a social anomaly, as many critics did, Chiba imagined her entry into society and the possibilities that awaited her in the labor force. In other words, Chiba equated the modern girl with the professional working woman. By seeking employment and securing some degree of economic independence, women, including the modern girl, would gain the know-how to voice their wants and satisfy them. Moreover, they would learn to define themselves beyond their relation to home and family: "They are so lighthearted. It is as if they are standing stark naked under an open sky calling out: 'We refuse to give in any more, not to you men, or to anyone!' How shall I describe it. Women in the past did not share this kind of carefree attitude. This is a new quality that only belongs to girls today. We see it in many varied forms. Not bound by rules, they think for themselves and are their own masters. According to my definition, they constitute the modern girl."[58] Using England as an example, Chiba emphasized the impact that working outside the home for a salary would have on the modern girl: "The number of young women [in England] who have found paying jobs has suddenly reached seven million. I hear that with the money they are earning they go out freely and enjoy plays and other forms of entertainment."[59] By connecting the modern girl to the increase in the number of professional working women, Chiba's analysis added a different dimension to the argument. True, conditions in Japan and England differed. But the sense of independence and the willingness to challenge accepted codes of behavior that drew Chiba to the modern girl in Japan were also behind his attraction to the English working woman. Chiba realized that any change in the level of consumption had their roots within the context of social, economic, and cultural determinants.

Chiba's ideal modern girl portended the changes he detected taking place in all women, traits he did not wish to exceptionalize. Nowhere in his argument, however, did he touch on the relationship of the *moga* to the commodification of the everyday. As one of the most respected literary critics of his day, Chiba attempted to evaluate the modern girl in terms of a cultural transition.

Only Hirabayashi connected the modern girl to the realities of consumerism.[60] The modern girl represented a sign of social upheaval that was bound to result from Japan's continuing industrialization. Modernists who saw only the surface changes reflected in the modern girl's appearance he accused of sentimentality: "Japan's modernists are still as sentimental as the lyric poets during the Middle Ages were. The modernity that is reflected in their eyes is all in hairdressing, skirts, cinema actresses, the department store mannequin girls and modern girls who stroll on the Ginza and frequent the [famous] movie theater Hōga-za. It is nothing more than flapper modernism. The basis for modernity is modern industry, financial capital, large-scale factories, and the stock exchange. Japan's modernists shiver like the leaves on a tree before these things."[61] Hirabayashi denounced many ideas and attitudes associated with the modern girl and urban culture. But he attributed the problems to the industrialization process, which would eventually lead Japan to a brighter future. Consumerism, in his view, was more than a label attached to a highly visible but ephemeral phenomenon: "Land is tucked away somewhere in a rural area. The factory is off in the suburbs. But on the Ginza we see ultramodern consumerism. The flapper girl and the chic boy are products of modernity, but to grasp only that one aspect of modernism is to grasp modernism in its most superficial form. The flapper girls and the chic boys can be related to our political and economic system, and it is that framework which is the core of modernism."[62] Because he looked at consumerism as a total way of life, Hirabayashi's analysis of the modern girl was more comprehensive than the critiques that centered on her more superficial features. Her debut offered Hirabayashi proof of the machine's effect on the everyday practices and attitudes of the housewife and the professional working woman. He argued that the faster pace of life generated by the machine worked psychologically to diminish the respect that urban women, in particular, demonstrated for elders and authority figures:

All you have to do is pick up a newspaper or magazine, or ask someone on the street for his or her opinion, or look at the people around you to realize that old people are being given less respect than in previous generations. If you mention this to young people, they generally give you a knowing look or a sardonic smile. This is the process by which young women are freeing themselves from the old authority figures. I think that we can find the social basis for the modern girl in this way of thinking.

I see the birth of the modern girl as a special feature in the breakdown of an authoritarian period in which women have had to endure. As the old authority collapses, and from now on that process will probably get more and more intense, I think that the *modern girl* will become more and more modern.[63]

The repositioning of the modern girl in urban society provides a stepping-off point for examining, albeit through varying perspectives, the experiences of the self-motivated middle-class housewife and the professional working woman, two types of women to be reckoned with in the future.

Conclusion

What role did the modern girl, a totally different type of new woman, play within the historical context of the 1920s? Multifaceted and amorphous, even her appellation was used loosely. Representing a relatively small segment of the female population, though she was multiplied in the media, she remained until the end a misunderstood, voiceless image. In their enthusiasm for the modern girl, intellectuals such as Kitazawa Shūichi and Nii Itaru formed constructs that overlapped with their own idealized conceptions of Western women. Marxist Kurahara Korehito and socialist Yamakawa Kikue, on the other hand, related her to the most decadent aspects of capitalism. For Ōya Sōichi, a Marxist sympathizer in the prewar period, and anarchist Takamure Itsue, the *moga* became a wanton sex object. Chiba Kameo, well known for his liberal opinions, observed a connection between the modern girl and the professional working woman and anticipated her incorporation into the labor force. Hirabayashi Hatsunosuke, a supporter of the Marxist theory of social change, attached meaning to societal transitions that resulted from Japan's continuing industrialization—namely, the commodification of the everyday—which for him explained the advent of the modern girl.

Despite the divergence of interpretations, it is significant that within the historical context of the 1920s the *moga* sensation was debated in the media by a wide range of Japanese intellectuals who engaged in serious discourses on alternative conceptions of gender relations. The alacrity with which intellectuals focused on the image of the modern girl demonstrated a certain willingness to accept a redefinition of women's behavioral patterns. Yet their inability to shape the direction of the emerging urban culture caused dismay, skepticism, fear, and disappointment over the ambivalent figure of the modern girl. The turning point that made it possible for society to bypass the intellectuals came in the 1920s with the rapid development of the media, a much more effective conduit for the transmission of new customs than the intellectuals could ever be.

The media projected hope for urban middle-class women to participate actively in the creation of this burgeoning culture, without an intermediary. By going to the movies, for example, women could visually absorb, firsthand, everyday practices different from their own.

Although the modern girl, the professional working woman, and the self-motivated middle-class housewife offered possibilities for a re-fashioning of culture, most intellectuals failed to recognize the special relationship between these women and consumerism. In areas such as gender relationships, family work patterns, and lifestyles the surprisingly influential media began to subvert old ideas. Socially and psychologically, the fight for changes that would alter women's lives in the wake of the post–World War II reforms was already under way.[64] Because the private space of urban middle-class women in the 1920s was defined by a range of social conventions that covered everything from deportment to hairstyles, the image of the modern girl and her daring bob stood out as a graphic illustration of the rise of consumerism.

3

Housewives as Reading Women

What have we women to do with elaborate discourses on the legend of a piece of rusty metal; or the qualities of an unknown animal; the pretended speeches of a stammering senator; or the description of things invisible?—*Lady's Magazine,* February 1772[1]

The appearance of the modern girl, the self-motivated middle-class housewife, and the professional working woman occurred in conjunction with the explosive expansion of women's magazines in the 1920s. The varied and sometimes competing representations that filled the pages of mass women's magazines served as models for all women and played a role in the construction of a new concept of gender. At a time when literacy rates were rising, editors and publishers took advantage of the expanding reading public, of whom women constituted a major share, and targeted them as consumers. The housewife was no exception.

One of the earliest modern references to the housewife, or *shufu,* can be found in the 1876 Japanese adaptation of Isabella Beeton's 1861 *Book of Household Management (Kanai kokoro e egusa)*. But that book was written as a guide for well-to-do, upper-class English women, whose "duties" comprised the supervision of servants and other domestic tasks.[2]

By the 1890s, publications in Japan, put out primarily for women's higher-school graduates, associated well-bred married women (*fujin*), whose family pedigrees determined their destinies, with the housewife. "Skillful" (*kashikoi*) housewives borrowed on their cultural resources to plan frugal menus, deftly train even one domestic, and assist in their children's education.[3] Since many of the older elite families had fallen on hard times by the mid-nineteenth century, abstract qualities like devotion, dignity, and spiritual strength were praised in upper-class women who managed a household on a shoestring budget. In the early twentieth century, women's magazines like *Fujin to Kodomo* (Ladies and Children, 1900) and *Katei* (Home, 1900), both of which focused their energies on women's higher-school graduates, assumed similar lifestyles for privileged young ladies (*fujin*).[4]

When the Meiji-period woman educator Shimoda Utako offered advice to housewives, she made no mention of the transformation of marriage practices as a way to achieve liberation. The voices of women anxious to assert some autonomy over their daily lives were nowhere to be heard. For these ladies, "public" responsibility emerged with the attempt to "feminize" the private sphere but not to change the idea of femininity. In the well-bred upper-class family, just as in society, the husband was clearly the dominant figure.

Mass women's magazines produced a new culture, a "mass" culture that challenged the intellectuals' notion of "pure, high" culture—a category intellectuals themselves had long monopolized. The new culture was a culture of the everyday, and it was labeled a women's culture. By the mid-1920s the elements of a "mass" society, including the expansion of industrial capitalism and the media, had developed sufficiently to alter the shape of society.[5] The new mass culture revolutionized women's status, and in the process destroyed the traditional family, the operational site of the Meiji Civil Code and its ideological apparatus, the "good wife and wise mother" ideology. All three of our urban figures of women were a conspicuous testament to the dislocation brought by that experience. The housewife in the 1920s, whose subjectivity was identified with consumer potential, was remote from her late-nineteenth- and early-twentieth-century namesake.

Magazines were not the only media expanding in the 1920s; the era is also known for newspapers, radio, and movies. The first permanent standing movie theater, or *jōsetsukan,* opened in Tokyo's bustling Asakusa district in 1903, and from the very beginning the crowds clamored for more. In 1922 every prefecture boasted at least one cinema, and the number of Japanese films produced in 1924 and 1925 exceeded the number of foreign films shown in Japan in the same year.

The crackling sound of radio static first startled audiences on March 22, 1925. The words "JOAK is now on the air" soon became a stock phrase among Tokyoites. Within six months the *Yomiuri* newspaper was running a daily radio page. The record business was also booming. As early as 1915 the recording by the actress Matsui Sumako of "Katusha's Song" (Kachūsha no uta), based on Tolstoy's novel *Resurrection,* sold more than 20,000 copies. Thirteen years later, in 1928, Sato Chiyako's recording of "Tokyo Marching Song" broke all records when it topped the 300,000 sales mark. Newspapers, already under pressure to offer local editions in order to remain competitive, spanned the country in their circulation. Both the [Osaka] *Asahi* and the [Osaka] *Mainichi* had amassed circulation figures exceeding one million by January 1924.

Magazines put out to meet the needs of a rapidly diversifying readership were the mainstays of publishing. *Kingu* (King, 1925) became the first mass magazine to achieve a following among men and women in city and country. The brainchild of Kōdansha publishing magnate Noma Seiji, it achieved its circulation goal of one million within one year of its founding. The publication of *Fujin sekai* (Woman's World, 1906), later followed by *Fujokai* (Woman's Sphere, 1910), *Fujin kōron* (Woman's Review, 1916), *Shufu no tomo* (Housewife's Companion, 1917), and *Fujin kurabu* (Woman's Club, 1920), brought to the fore the so-called Big Four women's magazines.[6] A novel media product to which large numbers of women had recourse had been born. Because the predominantly male editors and many of the regular contributors promoted a rhetoric that reflected the objectives of the Meiji Civil Code, the new magazines at first appeared to sanction the precepts set by the state for women in the late 1890s. As editors put efforts into increasing circulation, however, the tone and contents of magazines shifted, and certain ironies, complexities, and contradictions came to the fore.

The admixture of articles published in the mass women's magazines indicates that a dual standard governed editorial policies. It was not simply a question of the new opposing the old, but rather a fusion of old with new. The foundation for the extraordinary growth of women's magazines in the early twentieth century was nothing less than the expanded education given to upper-class women in the Meiji period.[7] From this foundation the mass women's magazines led the way in the production of the new media culture that went beyond existing women's magazines and the place they had long held for a small group of upper-class women.

The shift made by women's magazines to encompass middle-class, and to a lesser extent lower-middle-class, women's needs introduced tensions and contradictions: to what extent were the new opportunities and images of women going to either subvert or lend their support to official ideology?[8] Although mass women's magazines inherited their form and general outline from their predecessors, the continuities and discontinuities that describe the transformation in attitudes and values taking place were hardly static. Firmly embedded in the new mass culture, mass women's magazines were not simply a counterpart to magazines that addressed men. Moreover, to label them mere repositories of established routines and gender conventions downplays the complexities, both ideological and economic, marking their production. In a culture of consumption, mass women's magazines naturally included their own categories of articles. This was evidence that editors and publishers recognized some obligation to women as consumers both in the sense of spenders and in the sense of readers. Just as magazines were in the process of redefining their readers, women were in the process of redefining themselves.

Mass women's magazines catered to a hitherto untapped reading public. Young women who were not in the habit of reading magazines became regular subscribers. Middle-class women provided the model that was to articulate the intimate relationship between mass magazines and women. Through these magazines housewives in rural hamlets had access to information about "modern" lifestyles utterly different from their own lives, a factor that contributed to the diffusion of new female images. Sophisticated family articles (*katei kiji*) and trendy articles (*ryūkō kiji*) allowed urban women, and in a more limited sense some rural women, to become privy to new practices both inside and outside the home. Confessional articles (*kokuhaku kiji*) focused on alternative views of relationships that detailed the lives and love affairs of other women and, even if somewhat obliquely, women's sexuality. Also conspicuous among the features were articles that emphasized a popularized form of self-cultivation, or *shūyō*, which became an important dimension of women's private and public spaces.

Inasmuch as women within a specific social class are not homogeneous, the editors and publishers could not impose their standards on all women. Nor could they deal with the wants and desires of all their readers. Most women were still unaware of the opportunities becoming available that might effect changes in their status within the patriarchal family structure. Removed from the center of political power, their energies were not directed toward challenging the legal constraints that bound them. Mass women's magazines, intent on accommodating a reading public of women who were products of the expanding educational system, sent out determined signals to readers. In the pages of these magazines, efforts were being made to transcend the barriers of status and give young unmarried women, housewives, and professional working women a shared consciousness, a public forum, and an identity that was not limited by class.

The magazines were empowered by the public's equation of "mass" culture with women. With mass magazines as commodities and women as consumers, the magazines assumed their own special place in publishing.[9] The leading role of women's magazines in the massification of publishing partly accounts for the encoding of "mass" culture as feminine. The proliferation of confessional articles, for example, which took the form of letters from readers, drew upon women readers as unpaid sources of revenue. At the same time, these readers' letters created an atmosphere of intimacy among women that encouraged and inspired their active participation. In these articles women assumed a place in which they could give voice to the problematic relationship between their dreams and the realities of their roles. If most confessional articles addressed the mundane, this was, in fact, what formed the core of women's everyday space. The struggles evident in these articles suggest that self-fulfillment had become an ideal for women but was still very hard to attain.

By the 1920s, mass women's magazines were an influential site in the circulation of information. Almost no one credited them, however, with playing a positive role in illuminating those changes in outlook which, figuratively if not literally, had thrust the average woman into the wider society. Women's magazines formed a large portion of the mass magazines of the period, but from the outset they received harsh criticism.

PLATE I Cover of *Fujokai*, January 1924.

PLATE 11 Advertisement for a light bulb, 1927. Reprinted with permission of Musashino Bijutsu Daigaku Bijutsu Shiryō Toshokan.

PLATE III Cover of *Fujokai*, April 1928.

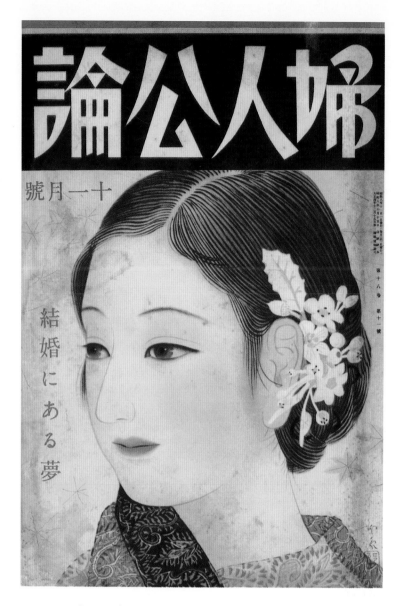

PLATE IV Cover of *Fujin Kōron*, October 1933.

Pejoratively labeled "conservative" and "unscientific" by most intellectuals, they captured the way that urban women were identified in public discourses as well as in private life.[10] Uchida Roan, who wrote a series of essays for *Josei* between August 1922 and May 1928 and was well attuned to the "woman problem," commented that "inasmuch as women's magazines are concerned with a woman's domain, they publish many articles on such things as cooking and sewing. . . . The fact that the opinions and ideas relate to personal experiences is not bad, but experience that is not based on scientific principles, while it may have inspired the writer, is not beneficial for others."[11]

Many contemporary scholars in the field of journalism continue to censure interwar women's magazines for the narrowness of their editorial policies, frivolous tone, and inability to exist independent of the state. Writing in the 1980s, Oka Mitsuo maintained that *Shufu no tomo* supported the conventional ideals of femininity as a means to preserve the status quo.[12] Fujitake Akira agreed, adding that women's magazines in general "made women compliantly conform to a set of moral standards that governed an entire country."[13] In the 1990s Saitō Michiko reiterated these claims, singling out *Shufu no tomo* as reenforcing a vision of the "ideal wife" whose identity was compatible with that of a "family state."[14] The premise of these critiques is that because the dominant representations of women in mass women's magazines had their basis in a patriarchal system, women readers must have been passive consumers who did not question their gender-differentiated roles. In the view of these scholars, mass women's magazines of the 1920s never crossed the boundaries of domestic concerns and showed no concern with rationalism and scientific inquiry. Rather, they continued to project a discourse similar to that found in women's magazines launched in the late nineteenth century.[15] Since they did not even attempt to question the legitimacy of a system that marginalized women, these magazines must have been of marginal importance for young women growing up in the 1920s.

Historian William Chafe, who has written widely on women's magazines in the United States during that period, also notes that "the role of mother and housewife represented the only path to feminine fulfillment."[16] According to historian Nancy Woloch, a few psychologists in the 1920s disputed the "glorification of domesticity," but they comprised a minority opinion in the United States.[17] Historical soci-

Advertisement for eye
drops, mass women's magazine,
late 1920s.

ologist Penny Tinkler's study of working girls' magazines from the
1920s through the 1950s in England documents that "marriage, and later
motherhood, were presented as the ambition and fulfillment of every
'normal' girl."[18]

The fact that mass women's magazines in Japan, like other expressions of mass culture, combined the old and the new cannot be denied.
Many articles did urge perseverance under the most adverse circumstances and instructed women on how to live virtuous lives. Almost
every issue of *Shufu no tomo* included articles such as "Rules a Housewife Must Know" (Shiraneba naranu shufu no kokoroe, March 1917),
"Suitable Sidework Even for Girls" (Joshi kodomo nimo dekiru yūri

Advertisement for
face cream, mass women's
magazine, late 1920s.

Advertisement for
eye drops, mass women's
magazine, mid-1920s.

na fukugyō, March 1917), "A Mother's Letter to Her Newly Married Daughter" (Shinkon no musume ni ataeta hahaoya no tegami, March 1917), and "Readers' Recommendations for Becoming a Model Wife" (Risōteki fujin no suisen happyō, January 1926). Nevertheless, it is more logical to assume that while in some ways mass women's magazines were instruments of the Meiji Civil Code, in other ways they undermined it.

Radio, which also took off in this period, exhibited a similar tendency toward the conservative. Radio stations may have encouraged Western classical music, but some of the most popular programs during the first five years of broadcasting featured old genres. An old-fashioned way of storytelling (kōdan), stories with a comic twist (rakugo), and stories of loyalty and human feelings recited with accompaniment on a traditional musical instrument (naniwabushi) occupied significant space in the airwaves.[19] Neither the new, nor the "modern," nor the Western drove out older forms of popular culture. Rather, the mass-direction the media had taken seemed to amplify tastes and attitudes, which ensured greater radio popularity and also boosted the sales of women's magazines.

Just as many people preferred older, more familiar forms of entertainment, some readers of women's magazines welcomed and appreciated articles that offered a doctrine they had been taught to respect from childhood. The construction of the "good wife and wise mother" philosophy exemplifies this point. When intellectual and educator Nakamura Masanao, who was influenced by the British educational system during his study trip to England in 1866, advocated this ideology as a yardstick for measuring the state of women's education, his intention was not for women to accept a status inferior to men's.[20] In effect, he was proposing a social role for women that he deemed progressive. The resurgence of Meiji conservatism in the 1880s, however, changed the valence of the term, and the "good wife and wise mother" ideology started to take on conservative trappings.[21] The editorials and articles carried in mass women's magazines corroborate the fact that many parents, and also the general public, supported education motivated by this philosophy, not solely because of its intrinsic value but also because it was familiar. Intellectuals' disdain for the magazines' policies reflected their annoyance with the complacency of women readers in holding on to what the intellectuals regarded as the status quo. Uchida echoed the thoughts of many intellectuals when he said:

> The contents of today's women's magazines betray the hopes of the *atarashii onna* because they show that most Japanese women still are not only on a different level than men, but it is like comparing the summit of a mountain to the bottom of the sea. When I see women on subways and trains who look like intellectuals [*sōtō na chishiki kaikyū no fujin rashii*] really enjoying reading women's magazines, which are an even lower level than [gossip magazines (*kōdan zasshi*)], it makes me so disappointed.[22]

A mass-directed medium alters its message, or content, according to profit motives. The *rakugo* artist was bound to experience difficulty performing in a setting designed for radio listeners. Similarly, as women's magazines went from small-scale endeavors with limited readership to mass-circulation operations, their character also underwent important changes. First, in order to garner the largest number of readers possible, the magazines were forced to publish articles that included a wide spectrum of views. The aggressive advertising campaign undertaken by *Kingu* is a well-documented success story of publisher Noma Seiji's tireless efforts to create a magazine that included something for everyone.[23] Competition for readers was severe. All women's magazines employed gimmicks that would help augment circulation figures. *Shufu no tomo* turned to special monthly themes like health tips for women (June 1919), birth control methods (January 1922), or Western clothes and the proper way to wear them (June 1923) to lure new readers. Another successful ploy adopted from 1918 onward included the periodic appending of supplements devoted solely to detailed coverage of topics such as leisure activities or the supervision of domestic help, ranging from ten to fifty pages in length.[24]

As the fight for readers intensified, a greater propensity for mixing the old with the new surfaced, minimizing individual differences between magazines. Tsugawa Masashi, the editor of *Fujokai*, maintained that "all the [women's] magazines have their own special features, but because of their subtleties, a cursory reading leads one to think there are no differences. The reason is that the editors of these magazines are basically aiming at the same reading public, the masses [*taishū*]; the pressure to achieve circulation goals is tremendous."[25] Standardiza-

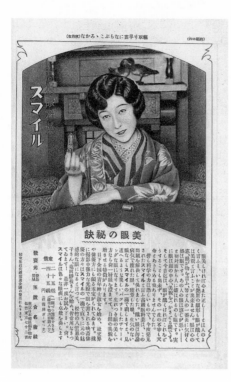

Advertisement for face powder and face cream: "If it comes from Paris . . ." Mass women's magazine, late 1920s.

tion, more than individuality, may have defined the temper of women's magazines at the time, but not all articles were uninspired or dull. Compared with the strongly enlightenment-oriented women's magazines of the early twentieth century, whose articles dealt largely with educational issues and ethical training, mass women's magazines of the 1920s went out of their way to carry a range of catchy topics. These magazines would have attracted very few young women readers if the information they disseminated dwelled only on timeworn subjects like morality. Much like Noma Seiji's declaration when he founded *Kingu* that there should be "something for everyone," the topics covered ranged from the conventional to the latest in foreign trends and popular customs. On the other hand, this practice led to the impression that magazines lacked editorial direction.

The modern girl attracted the attention she did precisely because of the sensational coverage she received, mainly in mass women's magazines. But while articles that focused on the modern girl whetted the imagination, they did little to revamp the average woman's everyday existence. It is unlikely that reading about the modern girl prompted young women in any number to imitate her. The "new" sophisticated family articles, practical articles, and confessional articles, on the other hand, informed the character of mass women's magazines in reinforcing and propelling women away from timeworn practices. The place occupied by basic but increasingly more complex domestic concerns like cooking, housework, and clothing, and the potential contradictions housewives faced in maintaining family relationships in a changing social and cultural environment, incited some readers to evaluate their everyday practices. By linking women and consumption on a personal level, mass women's magazines acted as a positive force encouraging women to become producers of the emerging urban culture.

Certainly the role women readers played in the construction of mass magazines was secondary to that of editors and publishers; and one must take care not to exaggerate their voices. Nevertheless, judging from the women who seized the chance to assert their will through reader participation, mass women's magazines were sites for a partial redefinition of femininity. Fundamental views of the home on which so many women's observations were grounded were also included in this process of redefinition. Although numerous articles counseled women on how they should function, such views did not prevent women from using magazines as forums for debating their positions. As key instruments in shaping mass culture, mass women's magazines offered women more than a release from the burdens of personal isolation. They also addressed women's responsibilities at home, at work, in society, and to themselves.

The Stage Is Set: Mass Women's Magazines in the 1920s

From the early twentieth century, the motivation behind women's magazines was no longer to promote and validate the interests of upper-class schoolgirls. The boundaries of the debate were widening. Women's publications were evolving into competitive profit-making ventures. The status of mass magazines reflected the wider development of mass culture and the general publishing boom, as well as the expansion of women's education.[26] None of these elements had matured sufficiently during the Meiji period for change to occur.

In 1898, only 1–2 percent of girls continued their education beyond the elementary-school level, and only 8,500 girls were enrolled

Cover of *Fujin sekai,*
September 1908.

in women's higher schools.[27] This extremely low figure was due both to the commonly accepted notion that higher education for women was unnecessary and also to economic conditions that blocked their way. Women's magazines operated under a similar set of economic restrictions. At a time when the middle class was still fairly small, female readership was composed primarily of women from upper-class households. In 1891, with the [Osaka] *Asahi shinbun* (morning edition) costing about 0.28 yen (equivalent to approximately 600 yen in today's currency), only a small segment of society constituted the readership.[28] Similarly, girls who subscribed to women's magazines were mostly Meiji upper-class young women who could afford to attend higher schools.

It has been said that although magazines "construct social class differences in terms of 'lifestyle' or consumption, [they] deny the existence of structured class."[29] Nevertheless, late-nineteenth-century women's magazines in Japan were heavy with fiction and refined articles and out of tune with young women who entered the labor force after graduation from elementary school. Nor could these publications have held the interest of urban figures like the modern girl, housewife, or professional working woman, whose objectives and ideals were displaying marked diversity from those of upper-class schoolgirls.

Among the large publishing houses of the Meiji period, Hakubunkan, established by Ōhashi Sahei in 1887, exhibited an interest in women from the outset. Nevertheless, its earliest women's magazine, *Nihon no jogakusei* (Japan's Women Students, 1887), was little more than a pamphlet and ceased publication after a few issues. Shortly thereafter, Hakubunkan embarked on a sophisticated marketing campaign to bolster sales. Astute marketing efforts, including dividing wouldbe readers on the basis of age, gender, education, and interests, distinguished Hakubunkan as a pioneer in the field and earned it the sobriquet "publishing don." Hakubunkan's impressive array of publications all claimed a high circulation, but *Jogaku sekai*, a magazine directed toward women's higher-school students that came out from 1900 to 1925, was among its top sellers.[30] This is one indication that in the late Meiji period, young, unmarried, financially secure women able to enroll in higher schools constituted the staying power behind women's magazines.[31] Other publications like *Fujo zasshi* (Woman's Magazine) and *Jogakusei* (Woman Student) took their cue from *Jogaku sekai*. They, too, pinned their hopes on higher-school (*jogakkō*) students and graduates as subscribers, although they did not gain the same prominence.[32]

Jogaku sekai appeared on the market when Hakubunkan was at the height of its success. As its name implied, and as the editor stated in his address to readers, the magazine aimed "to supplement those areas that are lacking in women's education today. By soliciting articles from authorities in the field of education, we will cover all facets of knowledge that a woman needs in order to become enlightened and knowledgeable in the necessary techniques required for understanding her household work. We hope to help form wise mothers and good wives."[33]

This statement, published in the magazine's second issue in January 1901, epitomizes the gender difference subscribed to in the Meiji period. Each issue of the two-hundred-page magazine boasted a colored frontispiece and assorted drawings of flower arrangements,

food, fashions, and the imposing figures of wives and families of prominent men. Although it contained a family section, practical articles of
the sort that filled the pages of later mass women's magazines were not
yet evident. The overwhelming concern was feminine cultural pursuits
like the tea ceremony and Japanese *tanka* poetry composition, with an
occasional article on Western cooking. *Jogaku sekai* catered to the hobbies of young "jogakkoites" with free time and a degree of economic
independence. Purchasing it was indeed an extravagant undertaking;
inasmuch as one copy sold for twenty sen, equivalent to approximately
four hundred yen in today's currency, *Jogaku sekai* was not suited to the
average young woman's pocketbook.[34] But then, neither was it suited
to the average woman's tastes.

Educators and intellectuals constituted the majority of *Jogaku sekai*'s
contributors. In the first issue, educator and intellectual Nishimura
Shigeki examined the state of women's education and Nagamawashi
Tomoe addressed the issue of ethical training for women's higher-
school students. Miwata Masako, founder of a private women's institution that became Miwata Women's Higher School in 1903, responded in
the March 1905 issue to changes in morality and their effects on young
women.[35] Anonymous higher-school teachers also contributed.

In keeping with the magazine's philosophy, the editors and contributors collaborated to create a journal for the continuing education
of women's higher-school graduates, who allegedly needed further
"moral" and "intellectual" guidance. *Jogaku sekai* acknowledged such
needs in articles like "Summer Thoughts—Manners and Morality"
(Shochū zakkan—dōtoku to reisetsu, September 1904) and "Ethics
and Women's Higher School Students" (Joshi no seishin kyōiku, April
1905). "A Noblewoman's Tastes" (Kifujin no konomi, January 1905),
"Letter Writing" (Tegami no kakikata, January 1905), and "English in
the Home" (Katei eigo, April 1905) were regular monthly features that
dwelled on the virtues of the Imperial Family. Most magazines for
young higher-school students in the late Meiji period set out not to alter
the status quo, but rather to enjoin young women to adopt the "traditional" lifestyle as it was then being reconstructed.

Thus, magazines like *Jogaku sekai* allotted space to conventional, un-
controversial subjects, but still saved space for fiction. Journalist and
critic Kimura Tsuyoshi maintained that the high priority given to fiction contributed to the magazine's downfall. "There were so many

articles that never answered the needs of women. More than anything else, there was too much fiction. If they had changed the cover and illustrations, it would have been similar to *Chūgakkō sekai* [Middle School World, Hakubunkan's publication for male junior high schoolers]."[36]

Jogaku sekai was eclipsed by rival publisher Jitsugyō no Nihonsha's *Fujin sekai* after the Russo-Japanese War.[37] Interestingly, *Fujin sekai*'s debut in 1906 caused little more than a ripple. Most people saw it as just another mainstream women's magazine. It, too, catered to schoolgirls and young unmarried women, devoted substantial space to fiction, and showed a deep regard for "traditional" culture and feminine grace.

Approximately one year after its founding, however, *Fujin sekai* began to veer in a different direction. In addition to articles on education, school life, plans for the summer holidays, and preparations for married life, the emphasis shifted to women's world after marriage. Conspicuous was the amount of space devoted to articles on home and family, which offered helpful tips to women. This section, as well as the space set aside for culture and entertainment, and even the short pieces that publicized the lifestyles of famous people, targeted married women. The female reading public had entered a transitional stage. The abrupt shift in *Fujin sekai*'s editorial policy reflected the expanding numbers and diversification of women readers.

This is not to say that family articles had no place in Meiji-period journalism before *Fujin sekai*. In 1898, when Hani Motoko was a fledgling reporter for the *Hōchi shinbun* (The Post), a sports and entertainment publication, her responsibilities included introducing "family articles" to women readers.[38] *Iratsume* (Young Women), a fifty-page women's magazine written in the colloquial style that sold for eight sen (0.08 yen), approximately 160 yen today, adopted an editorial stance comparable to that of the later *Fujin sekai* as early as 1887. Lack of marketing know-how coupled with a format that had little appeal contributed to its early demise.[39]

Fujin sekai, a magazine devoted entirely to women's tastes, easily positioned itself as the leading family magazine in the late Meiji years.[40] With popular writer and noted gourmet Murai Gensai as its editor, *Fujin sekai* reflected Murai's personal interests in popular literature, housekeeping, and food. Also notable was the amount of space devoted to entertainment. When one critic described the difference between *Jogaku sekai* and *Fujin sekai*, he commented that "much in *Jogaku sekai* would have been suitable reading for men, but not one page in *Fujin sekai* [would have] been."[41]

Fujin sekai's management policy, however, did not allow it to compete with magazines like *Fujokai* (1910), *Fujin kōron* (1916), *Shufu no tomo* (1917), and *Fujin kurabu* (1920). Nevertheless, some critics have labeled it "the most representative of the general magazines for the ordinary woman during Meiji" and "a prototype for the next generation of family magazines."[42] *Shufu no tomo* has usually been credited as the first magazine to set its sights on young married women as readers. In fact, *Fujin sekai* deserves that distinction. *Fujin sekai* incorporated practical family-oriented articles into its schedule of regular features with the young married woman specifically in mind. Its editorial policy became the model for Ishikawa Takemi, *Shufu no tomo*'s founder.

Ishikawa defied criticism when he settled on a title that singled out the housewife as the foundation on which to build the magazine's readership. Insisting that a woman's life began only after marriage, *Shufu no tomo* aimed to teach her the "mountain of things" she must learn.[43] The 1922 Tokyo City Office Survey reported that 1,184 of the 2,000 women interviewed were magazine readers. And 845 of that number, almost 80 percent, read women's magazines.[44] The large numbers of full-time housewives and professional working women who were readers during the 1920s spurred the growth of the new women's magazines. The information housewives gleaned from the readers' columns vitally affected the rise in circulation.[45]

The actual circulation figures are difficult to determine. Newspaper reporter Minemura Toshio complained about the unprofessional way circulation figures were publicized in a 1931 article for *Sōgō jānarizumu kōza* (Comprehensive Journalism Series):

> Why on earth do not only newspapers in our country, but also general women's magazines [*ippan no fujin zasshi*] adhere to a secretive policy regarding the disclosure of circulation figures? It is really a bad policy if we want to clean up advertising. In short, [the publishing companies] probably hold back on circulation figures because they think their advertising revenue will go down if they do not. Newspaper companies in America and other countries have been making circulation figures known for some time, but with the exception of *Shufu no tomo*, Japanese women's magazines today (unless they are pressed by the heads of advertising companies) refuse to make public their circulation.[46]

The magazine section of a bookstore features a wide selection, circa 1927 (Chikuma shobō).

The task of the researcher studying women's magazines of this period is indeed complicated by the fact that publishing companies were reluctant to release true circulation figures for their magazines. According to figures given out by the companies in 1931, *Shufu no tomo* reported a monthly circulation of 600,000 and a return rate of unsold magazines of 0.5–1 percent. *Fujin kurabu* reported a monthly circulation of 350,000 and a return rate of 25 percent; *Fujin kōron* 200,000 and a return rate of 15 percent; and *Fujin sekai* 120,000 with a 45 percent return rate.[47] Establishing the actual readership is difficult as well. By the mid-nineteenth century, women were positioned as consumers, but it was not until the 1920s that women and consumption defined each other through the dominance of women's magazines over the mass cultural landscape.

Women's Journalism Turns the Corner

In 1880, compulsory education, originally fixed at four years in 1871 by the Ministry of Education and then reduced to sixteen months during the decentralization of education in 1879, was extended without regard to gender first to three years, and then back to the original four years; in 1906 it was increased to six years. With the foundation laid for elementary-school education, families recognized, if reluctantly, that women, too, were entitled to some degree of schoolroom learning. The choices for further education narrowed considerably after the terms for compulsory education were set, but girls did have the option of entering a women's higher school, or *kōtō jogakkō*. Chronologically, women's higher schools were academically equal to boys' middle schools, or *chūgakkō*, which went from grades seven to eleven. Qualitatively, however, the differences between the two were vast.[48]

In 1887, 28 percent of all girls of elementary-school age were receiving an elementary education, and some 2,363 students were attending the 18 government-controlled higher schools then in operation. By 1912, 97.6 percent of the girls who were eligible were at least enrolled in elementary school. Moreover, 208 government-sponsored higher schools operated throughout the country with a total of 75,128 students.[49] Although the number of young women who received a secondary-school education was still small, by the early twentieth century, rising literacy among women and some economic latitude allowed greater numbers of women to purchase magazines.

Conscious of the connection between marketing and the potential occasioned by this new reading public, most women's magazines launched in the early twentieth century followed *Fujin sekai*'s example and sought the status of mass magazine. More than 40 percent of the two thousand professional women interviewed for the *Tokyo City Office Survey of 1922* received a monthly salary of 26–30 yen, the equivalent of approximately 60,000 yen today; the second most common salary was 31–35 yen, the equivalent of approximately 70,000 yen today.[50] The average monthly income for male government employees, based on figures compiled in 1921, was 96 yen, and for office workers, 98 yen, the equivalent of approximately 190,000 yen in today's currency.[51] Since the price of *Shufu no tomo* was 17 sen, or 0.17 yen (340 yen today), which amounted to approximately 0.5–1 percent of a professional woman's monthly salary, even women with low-paying jobs presumably could afford to purchase one magazine.[52] The magazines recognized this shift in women's economic position and courted women in their role as consumers. In fact, in January 1922, *Shufu no tomo*, buoyed by its spreading popularity, decided to become a bimonthly publication. This ambitious plan collapsed after only one month due to editorial complexities coupled with the economic strains involved in such a prodigious publishing endeavor.[53]

Acquiring mass readership meant meeting the demands and wishes of a new audience of women buyers and readers. This in itself posed an editorial challenge. One key to increasing readership lay in successfully wooing housewives. In the March 1927 issue of *Kaizō*, a journal that relied mainly on leftist intellectual contributors, Hirabayashi Hatsunosuke described the challenge.

> I do not think there is another foreign country that has achieved the success Japan has in marketing women's magazines. There are a number of reasons for this, but the main reason is because of the peculiar structure of Japan's family system. In Japan a housewife's work is clearly defined in its separateness from a man's work, and it is also extremely time-consuming. Consequently, the articles that make up the bulk of the magazine deal with a variety of topics like bringing up children, information related to illnesses, cooking, sewing, knitting, flower arranging and other artistic pursuits, and proper etiquette. In a country where a family system like Japan's prevails, these are the things that a housewife absolutely has to know.[54]

Hirabayashi linked the selling power of women's magazines to the structure of the family system, which had its basis in a code of law. Hirabayashi claimed, therefore, that the dominant domestic discourse carried in mass women's magazines was required reading for housewives and not a matter of choice.

Be that as it may, *Shufu no tomo*'s initial technique for winning the support of housewives lay in expanding and perfecting family articles. Unlike *Fujin sekai*, its predecessor, *Shufu no tomo* subdivided its so-called family articles into "practical" and "trendy" articles. *Fujin kōron*, determined to reject the family article approach for a more intellectually challenging agenda, was eventually forced to embrace *Shufu no tomo*'s policy as well. Soon, all the new mass women's magazines followed suit. Although family articles varied slightly from publication to publication depending on the editor's stance, their rationale was the same: to acquaint housewives with tips about home and family. For male editors, this was no doubt significant for the construction of a

Advertisement for a
Western-style hairpiece
for the modern woman,
in *Fujokai*, 1926.

woman's identity. Female journalist Inoue Matsuko wrote of the limitations this editorial policy imposed on women readers:

A shake-up in the cabinet, events concerning government policy, or
the rising and lowering of rice prices, were reported in the daily newspapers, and all of these things directly or indirectly affected the home.
But generally speaking, family articles [*katei kiji*] referred to articles
specifically related to a scientific [*kagakuteki*] approach in the home

A modern family welcomes the New Year, in *Fujokai,* January 1930.

and the various problems that confronted the housewife in a narrow sense. For example, ways to economize in the kitchen, making things by hand, entertainment, new trends, hairdressing, beauty tips, washing, cooking, compensation in times of sickness, preparing the family budget, and administering to the health needs of children.[55]

In other words, family articles lacked news value in that they did not apprise women of current events. Although the founding of *Shufu no tomo* coincided with World War I, one could easily have read the magazine unaware that a war was under way in Europe. According to one history of the journal, "the fact that only a smattering was written about the war was a conspicuous feature of the magazine."[56] With marriage still the main course open for middle-class women, the family articles served as the underpinning for the domestic discourse that prevailed in the magazine. Yet the presence of trendy articles that centered on beauty, clothing, and occupations suitable for women are an indication that the editor was responding to women entering the labor market as professional working women. The experiences that shaped women readers' lives were molded by factors that included gender and social class. Editor and publisher Ishikawa would probably have denied that his intent was to restrict the flow of public knowledge, or that his decision was linked to assumptions surrounding gender identity.

The Lifeline of Mass Women's Magazines: Practical Articles

Practical articles, or *jitsuyō kiji,* continued to cater to such domestic issues as cooking, cleaning, and sewing for the family. Hirota Masaki has noted that the home-related articles in *Fujin sekai* offered women, for the first time, a source of information different from the conventional one of a mother imparting information to a daughter.[57] *Shufu no tomo* took the level and quality of this information one step further. It would be more accurate to say that *Fujin sekai* set the stage, and *Shufu no tomo* performed the role. Information now meant indispensable advice on the latest, most up-to-date methods of homemaking. A sampling of the practical articles that appeared in the first issue of *Shufu no tomo* (March 1917) is illustrative. "Building a Convenient House on a Low Budget" (Anka de tateta benri na ie) taught the reader about the benefits of an eat-in kitchen and also offered the information that if entry to a home is limited to the front hall or kitchen, locking the house is simplified. "Five Secrets for Managing Money" (Okane o jōzu ni tsukau itsutsu no hiketsu) outlined how to avoid financial losses, offered cost- and time-saving measures for home repair (i.e., fix a leaking roof immediately before the hole gets bigger), and cautioned never to indulge in superfluous purchases. "New Family Lives on Thirty Yen a Month" (Tomokasegi de gesshū sanjūen no shin katei) clarified a young couple's budget strategies. Health-related articles like "Fool-proof Home Remedy for Gastrointestinal Disorders" (Kanarazu naoru ichōbyō no kateiryōhō) were a regular feature in all the mass women's magazines, but were especially frequent in *Shufu no Tomo.*[58]

When Nii commented that "there may well be large numbers of women who read women's magazines, but that doesn't necessarily mean that [the women who read them] have become any more intelligent," he left no doubt that he disapproved of the magazines' content, which smacked of the woman-only.[59] Nii labeled magazines like

Shufu no tomo, which made practical articles their raison d'être and implied that household work was women's work, ultraconservative. Socialist Yamakawa Kikue, who envisioned a genderless society, refused to see any woman as someone's daughter, wife, or mother and expressed disdain for a genre of mass magazines that caused women to "look inward" rather than "outward."[60] In Yamakawa's "Discussion on the Present State of Women's Magazines" (Gendai fujin zasshi ron) she remarked contemptuously: "The articles published in women's magazines emphasize only women's individual gains. Women are made to feel self-satisfied with their present status, which really is that of slaves in the bedroom and slaves to the family. [Women] become ostentatious and hedonistic."[61] Yamakawa was particularly critical of the content of the practical articles:

> As far as I am concerned, the topics taken up in women's magazines —namely, the practical articles [*jitsuyō kiji*] that are concerned with women in the home—are . . . without any practical value. And the articles on sex are nothing more than wordy descriptions about the coquettish behavior of prostitutes. . . . Among the practical articles, the doctors' statements on child rearing and caring for the sick are filled with generalities. No consideration whatsoever is given to specific problems. Sometimes advice from laypersons is solicited, but they give specious advice and, moreover, they never even explain how to treat an illness. It seems frighteningly crude and unkind that no warning is given about the dangers of these articles.[62]

Yamakawa strongly objected to limiting a housewife's role to that of nurse to her children, housemaid, or self-sacrificing giver of sexual pleasures. Nii agreed with Yamakawa on this point and concluded that "perhaps practical articles have the potential for being useful, but what is their basis scientifically and economically?"[63] Even if the modus operandi of most mass women's magazines was conservative in outlook and presumed a "traditional" role for women, by directing women's attention to other ways of thinking they unintentionally provided the opportunity for small upheavals in the home. While articles such as "An Economical, Attractive *Hakama* for Schoolgirls" could hardly have been inflammatory, articles like "Women Decide Their Fate" were sufficiently provocative to cause some women to alter aspects of their lives.

A state-initiated program urging rationalization (*gōrika*) became a propelling force underlying the process of altering everyday practices. And the impetus for this quest came to a large extent from the knowledge of a way of life that Japanese mass women's magazines helped depict.[64] Shortly after World War I, the government inaugurated the Daily Life Reform Movement (Seikatsu kaizen undō), one of the earliest organized attempts to achieve efficiency by cutting wasteful spending and simplifying everyday living.[65] Directives issued by the Ministry of Education urged people to proportion their time wisely; discard costly, irrational customs like exchanging year-end gifts; and even warned about the health dangers of eating white rice. Although the initiative for the reforms was state inspired, two "private" organizations that sprang up in Tokyo and Osaka in 1920 and 1921, respectively, assisted the authorities in promoting virtues such as prudence and thriftiness.[66] The wife of a jurist dedicated to the movement's precepts commented in *Fujin kōron:*

> Although it is late in coming, I am overjoyed that the need for this type of research finally has been recognized. All of us living in today's world—men and women alike, regardless of occupation—have to get together and find a way to make our lives rational [*gōriteki*] and economical as quickly as possible. We must strive to eliminate the tremendous waste around us, and the old-fashioned lifestyle that we are accustomed to. . . .
>
> Among the many things we should learn from the American family's lifestyle, most important, I think, is that the housewife's duty is to make her home a happy and beautiful place to live.[67]

The Daily Life Reform Movement was a campaign in which housewives were preached to but were not assumed to be the prime actors. The motivation to act came directly from the state rather than through indirect channels like mass women's magazines, which encouraged women to assume agency over their lives and to pursue their own goals. Nevertheless, the women's magazines jumped on the reform bandwagon—if not always successfully. An issue of *Shufu no tomo* that came out when the Daily Life Reform Movement was just taking off devoted two pages to extolling the benefits of the tomato in the hope of promoting a more nutritious and balanced diet.[68] Deep-fried tomatoes (tomato *tempura*) and tomato wheat noodles (tomato *udon*), however, never titillated the Japanese palate. Editorial urging inspired some women to try the untried, but the impetus for including creative practical articles also may be traced back to the Daily Life Reform Movement's push to cut costs and raise nutritional standards. For middle-class housewives, whose home was their workplace, practical articles in mass women's magazines helped make domestic labor like cooking a task that went beyond simply preparing food to be consumed. Even the increasingly elaborate recipes, though symbols of domesticity, imparted "special" knowledge to housewives, making them "experts" in their private spheres.

Do-it-yourself sewing patterns, which were a regular feature in mass women's magazines, are another example of the link between practical articles and the Daily Life Reform Movement's appeal for frugality and rational living. Economic conditions made handmade clothing a far more practical way to minimize household expenses than buying ready-made apparel.[69] The changes that the practical articles helped effect in women's everyday practices suggest that the ramifications of the Daily Life Reform Movement had proved greater than editors had anticipated.

While most intellectuals at the time commented on the parochiality of the practical articles, they did not seem to recognize the role that the articles were playing in the reconfiguration of domestic space and social relations. In middle-class housewives' lives, the home was starting to figure as the setting for a new concept, leisure. Mass women's magazines, the embodiment of the new mass culture, served both as guidebooks for modern lifestyles and as forms of home entertainment.[70]

Fashioning Trendy Articles

As was true in other countries, technological changes, industrial growth, spreading literacy, and expanded education all contributed to situate women as consumers of magazines on a new scale. Nor can the place of gender be ignored. We have seen how editors and contributors joined *Shufu no tomo* in making a concerted effort to determine women's "special" interests. To complement the practical articles that offered information on basic domestic tasks the magazines added a new genre of trendy articles, or *ryūkō kiji*, that prompted the direct importation of "foreign" things. The intent of the editors in publishing trendy articles was not to define a new social role for women, and so perhaps these articles also deserve the label "conservative." Still, like the practical articles, the trendy articles presented a perspective on the everyday that women may have desired but never considered actually attainable. Trendy articles acquainted readers with fads in fashions, hairstyles, accessories, and even the latest dance steps. "Makeup That Suits the Housewife" (Shufu rashiki okeshōhō, March 1917), "New Fashions to Wear for Cherry Blossom Viewing" (Shinryūkō no hanamigi, April 1918), and "How to Convert Unused Kimono into Western-Style Clothing for Women" (Fuyō no wafuku o fujin yōfuku ni shitatekata, February 1925) are representative of the trendy articles carried in *Shufu no tomo*. Although the titles differed depending on the magazines, similar trends prevailed in all.

Josei published articles like "A Study of Women's Clothing and Hairstyles Suitable for the New Age" (Shin jidai ni tekiō suru fujin no fukusō to riyō [rihatsu] no kenkyū, March 1923), which addressed questions of Japanese dress versus Western dress, how to make over clothes, and up-and-coming hairstyles. "Women's Styles in the New Age" (Atarashii jidai o tōru onna no sutairu, February 1925) discussed clothing for women of the future. "The Popularity of the Shawl" (Shōru no ryūkō, October 1927) described the shawl as a symbol of "today's modernism" (*modanizumu*). Detailed, step-by-step diagrams instructing women how they could do their hair to look more like a movie star or dance the tango and foxtrot like a professional enjoyed popularity.

As the quality of illustrations improved and new techniques in picture reproduction developed, the visual became an important element in facilitating the spread of trendy articles.[71] The first issue of *Shufu no tomo* in 1917 contained almost no photographs and only a smattering of trendy articles. Less than ten years later, the number of pictures and trendy articles had increased. Photography offered a medium for introducing modern lifestyles and allowed readers to go beyond word descriptions to see what was being offered. From an economic point of view, visual promotion was a convincing marketing ploy, stimulating a desire for new fashions—and other products in the process.[72] A particularly humorous photograph in an early issue of *Shufu no tomo* depicts a couple wearing "his and her" pajamas in a bold striped pattern. The woman is seated on an ornate velour sofa and the man stands stiffly behind her. Both are poker-faced, as if posing for a family portrait.[73] The extent to which this photograph contributed to pajama sales is not known. Nevertheless, the latest techniques in graphics and photography presented welcome additions to the line drawings of late Meiji women's magazines.[74]

The department store, yet another icon of "modernity," was one more force pulling women into the forefront of the modern.[75] By 1921, the doors of major Tokyo department stores like Matsuya, Takashimaya, Daimaru, and Isetan opened promptly at 10:00 A.M. There, one could see firsthand, and perhaps even purchase, what was being written about and illustrated in the magazines.[76] Just as mass women's magazines produced a new mass culture, department stores in the 1920s provided "a new concept of shopping" that formed "the heart of the cluster of leisure practices that constituted modern consumer culture." Department stores, too, were "assuming the power to define the modern in everyday life."[77]

Women Speak Out: Confessional Articles

Shufu no tomo's adeptness in charming women readers extended beyond the inclusion of family articles. Another resourceful formula for winning over readers was the solicitation of letters and other short pieces called "confessional articles," or *kokuhaku kiji*. Written by the readers themselves, a great many of these articles were published in each issue.[78] *Fujin kōron* adopted a similar editorial policy in its attempt to appeal to readers. Offering monthly themes like "Pride or Embarrassment" (Hokori ka haji) and "Educated Women and Marital Problems" (Kyōyō aru fujin to kekkon nan, June 1924), *Fujin kōron* formally requested contributions from readers pertaining to such subjects. In 1923, *Shufu no tomo* added an advice column to address quotidian concerns ranging from marital difficulties to worries consonant with the complicated web of Japanese-style human relations. The magazine's shift away from its earlier policy of having intellectuals and famous personalities write the confessional articles reflected a conscious effort to move closer to its readers. In so doing, it encouraged a new awareness in women. In time, most women's magazines adopted comparable editorial ploys to elicit active responses from readers. Even *Fujin sekai*, which pioneered the family article, capitalized on *Shufu no tomo*'s techniques. From 1924, it sponsored roundtable discussions with its own readers as the main participants.[79]

Women's magazines stood out among the plethora of commercial magazines printed in the 1920s for devoting space to readers' letters and confessional articles. The popularity of these letters hinged on the circumstances directing Japanese women's lives—especially women whose opportunities to mingle socially were limited. Men used the workplace and after-work activities to form liaisons with fellow workers and friends. But household management consisted solely of domestic tasks and childcare. Cultivating a life outside the home required time, a commodity that most women lacked. During the course of a roundtable discussion on the simplification of daily life held two months after the Great Earthquake, Shimanaka Yūsaku, editor of *Fujin kōron*, remarked that if women joined the labor force, ideally they would share the burden with men in an emergency. But it would not be a reciprocal arrangement. He also admitted that many men were not amenable to taking on the role of caretaker in the home.[80]

If domesticity implied the locus of a woman's space, the influence of women's magazines may have been even greater in rural areas than in the cities.[81] The following letter expresses one woman's view: "*Shufu no tomo* is my one and only friend. For someone like me tucked away in this mountain hamlet it is the only friend I have to teach me about all the new things going on in the world and to tell me interesting stories."[82] Women's magazines thus also filled a void in the lives of some country women and formed an integral part of their daily existence. By the early 1920s, then, the new mass women's magazines were drawing on a broad stratum of women readers, many with only the equivalent of an elementary-school education, who identified strongly with the confessional articles.

Literary and social critic Hirabayashi Hatsunosuke thought the success of these magazines was preordained. Since the structure of the educational system held women's aspirations in check, Hirabayashi felt justified in assuming that most women were unprepared intellectually to read anything more challenging than a magazine.[83] Be that as it may, up to this time, the majority of women, whether housewives or still unmarried, had not relied on print communication to express their hopes and disappointments, or as a significant source of information.

The *Yomiuri* had become the first national newspaper to include a section for women in 1914, but the one-page addition was discontinued the following year.[84] That a genre of reading that focused all its energies on average women should have elicited such an enthusiastic response seems obvious in hindsight. The state, however, thought differently. By 1913, the authorities had determined that the mass women's magazines posed a threat to "traditional morality." On April 20 of the same year, the Ministry of Education ruled that women's magazines opposed to the "good wife and wise mother" philosophy were not suitable reading. The February issue of *Seitō* and the May issue of *Jogaku sekai* were both banned from sales racks. Nevertheless, the repercussions of this decree were minimal.[85]

Hirabayashi understood women's fondness for confessional articles and aptly captured the temper of the times in an article printed in the September 1928 issue of *Shufu no tomo*: "Among all the people who are housewives or would-be housewives, I don't suppose there is anyone who hasn't experienced gloomy, tragic situations. Therefore, reading material that expresses such sentiments easily wins the sympathy of women. That is probably the reason that women's magazines welcome any kind of confessional article."[86] Hirabayashi expressed similar views on another occasion: "Because of the special character of Japan's family system, newlyweds are forced to live with their in-laws and other family members. Under such circumstances, the wife's position, when compared to women in other advanced countries, is incredibly low, and her life is filled with various tragedies. That is why all housewives and would-be housewives relate easily to reading material that describes depressing, heartrending moments that other women are experiencing."[87]

Confessional articles certainly helped to augment circulation figures. But they also helped transform the social function of women's magazines. From Meiji to early Taishō, a multitude of instructive articles concerned with morality and proper decorum set the tone (see chapter 4). The light reading, short stories, and practical articles had all offered women information, but they were one-sided, furnished by women educators, critics, and intellectuals. With the addition of letters and articles written by the women themselves, a forum for readers developed. The two-way flow of information between the readers and the magazines initiated a new balance with the media. The information they gathered from other readers' contributions formed a departure point from conventional behavioral patterns for women cut off from society and isolated from other women.

Readers identified with contributors who faced similar problems and voiced similar complaints. Emotionally, women realized that they were not alone in their uncertainty. Trivial though this identification may seem today, through it, women marginalized in the greater society came to recognize the benefits self-management offered. Even women's higher-school students created their own microsociety and formed relationships with their contemporaries within a school environment.[88] These young women already knew the power of magazines as a channel of communication. Since the late nineteenth century, several magazines had provided space for schoolgirls to write short letters about themselves using pen names.[89] A camaraderie developed among the young contributors that reflected the girls' everyday experiences and the aspirations that motivated them. Housewives were even happier to form attachments with other women through their contributions to women's magazines. The desire to escape from the conventions and inhibitions that constrained their actual female friendships can be interpreted as a response to family conditions that were often psychologically oppressive. Professor of Japanese literature Maeda Ai took note of the "personal style of communication" apparent in *Shufu no tomo* with the inclusion of readers' letters and confessional articles. Sounding slightly reminiscent of Hirabayashi, he remarked that "for housewives who had been shut up at home with no place of their own where they could communicate, personal accounts [*shuki*] provided a communication style they could relate to easily. It was closely akin to the style of communication promoted by the advice column."[90] By providing a forum for women to confront their anxieties and to learn about other women's problems, mass women's magazines registered a different set of attitudes toward love, marriage, divorce, and work that gave women the courage to contemplate change. The fact that women readers were contributing to the new wisdom offered in the magazine forums suggested that women themselves were going to chart their own course in domestic morality rather than have that course charted for them. Mass women's magazines became a kind of practical handbook that provided a window to the world outside the home.[91]

Love and Marriage: Editorial Bias?

Despite the gradual increase in the number of professional working women during the 1920s, middle-class women were still defined in relation to the family and were generally pressured to stay home after marriage. It was only natural that they gravitated toward family articles, advice columns, and readers' letters. Because of their close connection to women's everyday lives, family articles had a special appeal. Even the confessional articles that readers submitted themselves arose out of the various problems and emotional upheavals of daily life.

For most young women, the overriding concerns besides household tasks were finding a mate and adjusting to married life in the face of the challenges posed by the family. Gossip columns that dwelled on the romances and marital difficulties of famous people enjoyed great popularity. The use of sex and racy articles lured women readers and furnished them with rich sources for their fantasies. These stories also informed readers that there were already some women in society who refused to abide by the conventional standards governing marriage and married life.

In the early twentieth century, when mass women's magazines were still in their infancy, one of the first stories to receive sensational coverage concerned love and marriage. The event that set the stories in motion was Yoshikawa Kamako's attempted suicide in March 1917. Twenty-seven-year-old Kamako, the daughter of Count Yoshikawa Akimasa, was married to a prominent businessman who had been adopted into the Yoshikawa family. Along with her chauffeur, Kamako threw herself in front of a moving train. The chauffeur died instantly; Kamako survived, having violated two strict social laws—adultery and the propriety of her class. The twin violations made this a shocking incident. Not surprisingly, thunderous disapproval rang forth from various quarters. Kamako's neighbors branded her an outcast in a way that recalls Hester Prynn—attaching signs to the gates of the family estate that read "Neighborhood Disgrace" and "Shameless Hussy."[92]

The unusual circumstances surrounding the incident afforded perfect media material. The detailed coverage brought to light the facts that Kamako's husband habitually frequented geisha establishments and that Kamako's home life was anything but happy. A few male intellectuals rallied to Kamako's cause, one of them novelist Chikamatsu

Shūkō, who noted that "today's gentlemen of the nobility have absolutely no qualms about visiting the pleasure quarters and carrying on
with prostitutes. Kamako's disgrace pales in comparison." Christian
minister and educator Ebina Danjō added: "If one looks at the surface
of the case, the sole guilty party is the young wife. . . . [But] it was the
husband who invited this unhappy ending by his lack of love for his
wife and lack of integrity to protect his family."[93]

One may nevertheless ask why the Yoshikawa Kamako incident
aroused the sensation that it did. The answer involves the status accorded to upper-class women by the lower classes. Female novelist Enchi Fumiko astutely observed: "Until the debut of female actresses like
Kurishima Sumiko, upper-class women stood for objects of both adora-
tion and jealousy."[94] Enchi pointed out that before the age of the movie
queen, female celebrities were well-born daughters and wives like
Kamako. Their faces adorned the frontispieces of women's magazines.
Yoshikawa Kamako's transgressions had special significance precisely
because she epitomized the class celebrities of the time.[95]

Undeniably, women's magazines played on aspects of Japanese life
that emphasized social position. Two particularly respected women
whose pictures appeared time and again in women's magazines were
the esteemed poets Kujō Takeko and Yanagihara Byakuren.[96] Although
most of the reaction from the Yoshikawa incident had subsided by
June 1921, Yamakawa Kikue, who untiringly counseled women on the
importance of self-esteem, used this incident to draw an interesting
analogy between Yoshikawa, Kujō, and Yanagihara:

> Kamako may have been foolish and have had questionable morals, but
> I really do not think she was affected or hypocritical. She did not cal-
> culate things in terms of social position or appearances—she probably
> lacked the intelligence—she was merely governed by her instincts. I
> think she was honest, inoffensive, and far more human than many of
> her social peers such as Kujō Takeko and Itō [Yanagihara Byakuren's
> husband's family name] Byakuren, known for their arrogance, cow-
> ardice, ostentation, and grand airs.[97]

Yamakawa mentioned Kujō Takeko and Yanagihara Byakuren in her
article as examples of women who had been elevated to the status of
"star" during the period. Ironically enough, several months after the
publication of Yamakawa's article, Yanagihara Byakuren left her husband for Miyazaki Ryūsuke, a leading member of the Shinjinkai (New

Man Society, 1918–29), a political group organized by Tokyo University students in the Faculty of Law.[98] As the daughter of Count Yanagihara Sakimitsu, Japan's first ambassador to China and a cousin of Emperor Taishō, Byakuren's behavior was even more shocking than that of Yoshikawa Kamako. Kamako at least had attempted suicide. Byakuren "brazenly" lived with the man she loved. Moreover, she contributed an open letter to the October 22, 1921, *Tokyo Asahi* stating why she had acted as she did.[99] Byakuren's letter recounted a ten-year loveless marriage to a man twenty-seven years her senior, the nouveau-riche owner of a coal mine in Kyūshū. She described an emotionally barren life at the mercy of an incorrigible womanizer. A rebuttal printed in *Fujin sekai* by Yanagihara Byakuren's husband, Itō Denzaemon, aroused the further curiosity of readers.[100]

The Byakuren incident was not the only love-related scandal to cause an uproar in women's magazines in 1921. Just a few months earlier, the infamous poet Hara Asao's love affair with a married Tōhoku University professor had made the headlines.[101] Hara had been divorced several times, and the professor, Ishihara Atsushi, had a wife and three children. The fact that women received the brunt of the negative publicity in all of these incidents attests to the pervasiveness of the restraints placed on women for behavior not necessarily warranting condemnation as social aberration.[102] Certainly, gossip surrounding the "stars" was a factor in drawing attention to these incidents. The sensational coverage foretold the media's limitless potential to capitalize on women and sex. On the other hand, publicizing these affairs put female readers in contact with a class of women whose world differed from their own, but whose marital and romantic problems struck a familiar chord. Such women were amazed that these paragons of ideal Japanese womanhood had demonstrated the courage to break loose and exercise their own wills, and the knowledge made them all the more willing to share their own transgressions in the home, as shown by the vast number of letters and articles they submitted to the magazines.

Conclusion

In contrast to women's magazines of the preceding period, mass women's magazines of the 1920s no longer situated women within a sphere where their job was to educate and provide cultural refinement. Sensational stories brought glamour into women's lives while they satisfied the circulation demands of zealous editors and publishers. As the readership broadened, magazines were pressured into celebrating the needs of different types of women. Factory workers, farm women, elementary and higher-school students and graduates, and professional working women, who filled new urban positions and later became middle-class wives, all forged a place for themselves in their own "imagined communities." The strategic function played by the media in the articulation of the modern girl, the housewife, and the professional working woman was damned by some and praised by others. But it could not be denied. The language in which these women were represented in journalism clarified the changing nature of female identities—identities still in the process of negotiation.

In the late Meiji period, the new woman had been the subject of wide publicity; journalists were quick to report her "transgressions."[103] In the early twentieth century, mass women's magazines went further and addressed the love affairs and family problems of celebrities and other women. The impact of such stories on readers was far greater than anything published in the Meiji period had been. At the time of the Bluestockings, the public entertained an image of a group of eccentric young women doing peculiar things. The topics covered in later women's magazines, however, were no longer alien to readers, but reflected problems close to their hearts. Whereas the Bluestocking movement was generally regarded as the immoral, antisocial effort of a narrow group of literary young women, the small-scale resistance waged against the family in the subsequent era was not part of an organized movement inspired in connection with the state. This helps explain the degree of sympathy that romantic, passionate women who tried to be true to their hearts received from readers. The Bluestockings' escapades incurred social distrust. But the stories and events featured in the later magazines appealed to more common sentiments (like the commoner literature of the Edo period) and thus won the attention of many more women.

In the same way that family articles monopolized the pages of mass women's magazines when housewives joined the ranks of readers, most women's magazines pursued topics that women could relate to. This helps to explain why Yamakawa's politically charged views on women's liberation and the place women should assume in the labor movement failed to take hold on a broad level. Yamakawa expressed displeasure that *Shufu no tomo* enjoyed popularity "with factory girls and maids who are out-and-out members of the proletariat, and even with girls working in small businesses or on farms who are close to the proletariat."[104] She could not understand why young women who should have been attracted to socialist causes "wasted" their time reading "foolish bourgeois topics carried in mass women's magazines."[105] But while most intellectuals attacked the editors of mass women's magazines for creating this atmosphere, many women readers harbored a distrust of overly radical change. That is not to say that women opposed all change. The impact of family articles in altering conventional behavior attests to the magazines' ability to affect the everyday lives of women. Articles about the family lives and romantic liaisons of other women stirred women to an awareness of their own lives and loves. Even women from conservative middle-class families, previously too timid to express themselves at home, recognized possibilities for other lifestyles. The confessional articles written by a variety of women readers revealed that many women were beginning to exercise an independence of spirit. For some of these women, a desire to avail themselves of opportunities not necessarily in keeping with the desire of the state was in the making.

4

Work for Life, for Marriage, for Love

Women labor in many settings for many different kinds
of rewards.—Barbara Drygulski Wright[1]

The discourse surrounding the modern girl and the introduction of a
modern lifestyle that accompanied the emergence of the self-motivated
middle-class housewife and the professional working woman addressed disruptions that were occurring in established assumptions
about gender. Although harsh criticism of women's "deviant" behavior exacerbated the already adverse reactions to the prospect of change,
no one could deny that a new type of woman had emerged in the
guise of these three urbanites. Unless women themselves actively took
the transitional step, however, the shifts in the discourse surrounding
them would be of little significance in their lives. Journalism and mass
women's magazines played an important role in both chronicling and
shaping the transformation in progress. They also provided vital information about the emerging urban culture and described alternative
ways women could position themselves in public and private space.

The professional working woman, the subject of this chapter, occupied center stage in the clash of forces that "threatened" the boundaries of everyday practices. Struggles and contradictions marked the
increase in professional working women from the time of World War I.
The prospect of middle-class women participating actively in society,

however, was a growing reality.[2] As new jobs opened up for women in male-dominated spaces, the tensions between work, socialization, and home became conspicuous. A content analysis of mass women's magazines reveals numerous articles pertaining to self-cultivation, or *shūyō*, a concept that gained popular credence in the early twentieth century and was seen as a means of strengthening the resolve of some middle-class women to enter modern sectors of the labor force. Changing attitudes about love and marriage, also impelled in part by engagement with the possibilities of self-cultivation, went hand in hand with the motivation to become a professional working woman.[3]

Whereas the modern girl was an ephemeral concept, and the image of her constructed by intellectuals and the press reflected that, a more complex and multifaceted picture emerged of the professional working woman. First of all, the professional working woman was backed up by statistical reports: she therefore enjoyed a concrete quality that the modern girl lacked. Statistics from the Tokyo City Employment Bureau show that more than 370,000 women visited its nationwide offices in search of employment in 1923, figures that bear witness to the hard times triggered by the Great Earthquake in September of that year. Seven years later, that figure had risen above 870,000.[4] In 1924, the Tokyo City Employment Bureau for Women (Tokyo-shi fujin shoku-gyō shōkaijo), the first office set up exclusively for professional working women, opened in the Suidōbashi area of Tokyo. In 1926, the *Japan Labor Almanac* (*Nihon rōdō nenkan*) estimated that 865,078 professional working women held positions throughout Japan.

Figures obtained in a survey conducted by the Japan National Census Bureau and later referred to by socialist Yamakawa Kikue in her 1929 appeal for better working conditions for women at the lower stratum of society indicate that the number of women domestics and factory workers had already reached 534,348 by 1918. A 1930 report from the Japan National Census Bureau indicating that 697,116 women held manual labor jobs shows the class-based nature of women's work.[5] By 1934, the Tokyo City Employment Bureau was operating branch offices in thirty-nine Tokyo locations. Based on its data, 94,637 women, including those who sought positions as domestics and factory workers, visited the offices that year. Of that number, 27,244, or approximately 30 percent, boasted degrees from at least a women's higher school.[6]

One of the thirty-nine employment offices catered only to the needs

Professional working women clerking in a government office, early 1920s.
Reprinted with permission of Mainichi shinbun.

of the "intellectual class" (*chishiki kaikyū*), which was defined at the
time as men and women with the equivalent of a middle-school or
above education.[7] For women, this meant graduation from a four-year
women's higher school or normal school (also considered a higher
school though slightly inferior since the prewar educational track precluded girls from entering middle school after completing their elementary education). Among the 18,207 women who visited that particular office in 1934, 16,844 had graduated from women's higher school
or beyond. As many as 8,453 hoped to obtain positions as sales clerks,
and 4,537 were desirous of becoming office workers. The remaining
women looked for jobs as telephone operators, nurses, teachers, and
even bus girls. A small fraction sought work as domestics.[8] A significant number of women's higher-school graduates fixed their gazes on
the predominantly urban-centered positions opening up for women.

The salaries paid to women, being even lower than men's, made economic independence unlikely.[9] Nevertheless, entering the workplace
and earning their own money brought new expectations for women,
especially those who harbored even the slightest awareness of them-

selves as individuals apart from their families. This is confirmed by readers' letters and confessional articles in mass women's magazines. As a feeling of community developed among readers, women gradually broke the silence surrounding their personal lives. Some young women began questioning marriage as women's true destiny, voicing views that clashed with parental attitudes.[10] Others wrote letters asking for help in determining the necessary qualifications for obtaining gainful employment. Full-time housewives, who alluded to their frustration with caviling mothers-in-law and philandering husbands, inquired about the possibilities of engaging in side work.[11]

Unlike family articles and practical articles that offered the latest in household information but left out readers' reactions, confessional articles and letters from readers revealed a tone of intimacy and frankness.[12] The discussion of employment options—if only in terms of short-term jobs—attested to the value these women placed on the knowledge they obtained from reading mass women's magazines as a way of asserting their claims for agency. It is often remarked that mass women's magazines of the 1920s were distinguished by educational articles written by intellectuals, on the one hand, and by sensationalized gossip, on the other. But the letters penned by women readers and the editors' responses to them also show that a new set of social and cultural patterns that included the voices of women themselves was taking root. Women readers demonstrated a positive desire to avail themselves of new opportunities, and that is what encouraged their active participation as contributors.[13]

Although their main concerns may have centered on augmenting sales, editors could not ignore these voices. They recognized the power that reading held for women and deftly tried to take advantage of it by forging special relationships with their readers. *Fujokai* demonstrated its "good will" by setting up a committee of men and women writers to review readers' complaints and suggestions and to discuss innovative methods to improve the magazine. *Shufu no tomo* used a similar strategy, establishing the Society of Friends (Tomo no kai) to serve that purpose. The official fifty-year history of *Fujin kōron* stresses that from the outset the magazine encouraged middle-class women to realize their potential by welcoming and supporting their efforts in the labor force: "From the time of the magazine's inception [1916] employment for women was considered a serious enough matter to become a regular theme of the magazine. In keeping with the magazine's efforts to help direct the flow of women into the workplace, every issue dealt with some aspect of professional women. The topics were always presented to readers as social problems warranting attention."[14]

The lessons they derived from sophisticated family articles and practical articles in mass women's magazines helped create a challenging agenda for women as they moved into uncharted waters in the workplace and in their own homes. Impelled by changing social and economic conditions and the more personal desire for self-cultivation, the professional working woman had emerged as a new social figure, and she was prepared to make her way into previously male-dominated areas. The cultural power she achieved through the medium of mass women's magazines made her a symbol of modern life and a role model for autonomy. Even women without jobs identified with the challenges she faced and the opportunities she created for herself. The changes fashioned by professional working women resonated through the media.

Women: Objects of Sexual Curiosity

The negative views that equated the *moga* with a bar hostess or prostitute and led to her being labeled a delinquent (*furyō shōjo*) also made themselves felt in the discourse surrounding the professional working woman. The modern girl had drawn attention primarily because of her conspicuous hairstyle and mode of dress, not to mention her youth. It was difficult, however, to get a concrete picture of the *moga*'s psychological makeup and way of thinking. In spite of the diverse interpretations that surfaced in intellectual circles, the commentaries on the *moga* had an unmistakably abstract quality. The modern girl's "newness" was associated more with image than with identifiable social reality, making it difficult, for example, to ascertain her social class. The professional working woman, however, was unequivocally real as she commuted to and from work.[15] She became a familiar sight to city dwellers. The restlessness she embodied was discernible in other parts of the world in the 1920s as well.

The independent scholar Murakami Nobuhiko included domestics in his definition of the professional working woman. In contrast, the rendering used here follows the general usage of the period and confines the term's meaning to young women who had graduated from at least a four-year women's higher school.[16] These women were often referred to together with the white-collar workers, bureaucrats, and professionals who made up the "new middle class." (This concept did not gain recognition until after World War II, but the term *new middle class* was used by a few intellectuals during the period to differentiate the professional working woman, a post–World War I phenomenon, from the Meiji-period factory worker [*jokō*] and domestic [*jochū*].)[17] The term *professional working woman*, much like *modern girl*, caught on quickly. Although not every modern girl was a working woman, intellectuals and social critics such as Sakurai Heigorō and Chiba Kameo saw a direct correlation between the birth of the modern girl and the growing cadre of professional working women.[18] Some employment opportunities for the professional working woman, such as mannequin girl, also emerged because of the advent of the modern girl.

Many businessmen regarded the professional working woman as a sexual accoutrement and hired them to facilitate difficult business transactions and attract male customers. A number of women earned the appellation of a "such-and-such" girl (*gāru*) depending on their line of work. To the public, these jobs connoted sexually active women. It sounded titillating to call a female bus conductor a bus girl (*basu gāru*) and the clerk in a department store a salesgirl (*depāto gāru*) or shopgirl (*shoppu gāru*). Kitazawa Shūichi clarified the sexual nuance attached to the word *gāru* in an article he contributed to *Kaizō* in 1925: "Ten years ago women shop clerks were merely unusual. Nothing special stood out about them or was worth mentioning. But today's women salesclerks are very different from their predecessors. I refer to them as shopgirls [*shoppu gāru*] rather than using mundane terms like salesgirl or saleswoman. Foreign words seem much more 'high collar' [*haikara*, or modern] and really convey the modern [*modan*] air these women have."[19] If there was nothing "new" about women working outside the home, why did these young women cause so many eyebrows to rise? In their positions as shopgirls or office girls these young working women became figures of sexual fantasy encoded with consumerist value. For Kitazawa, the first to use the term *modern girl* in Japan to denote a new, unfettered, liberal kind of woman, the "modern" of the term represented the new sexual existence of middle-class women in the work-

Mannequin girl selling magazines, late 1920s. Compliments of Endo Noriaki.

place. Kitazawa believed that the shopgirl connoted a sexually attractive, though not necessarily sexually active, young woman who was on her way to becoming a pervasive social fact.

As the shopgirl became a feature of Tokyo shops and department stores, Kitazawa saw Tokyo exuding the same vibrant air as London and New York. Kitazawa predicted optimistically that the long hours professional working women spent in the workplace would change their thinking and behavior.[20] Kitazawa's observations and predictions regarding the transformation that young professional women would experience were perceptive, but he was overly positive in assessing the treatment the new breed of shopgirls or bus girls would encounter from their employers, the public, and even from intellectuals. When Kitazawa compared Tokyo with London and New York and called the shopgirl the perfect accompaniment to a metropolitan atmosphere, he was reiterating a view that saw women as accessories rather than as individuals in their own right.

In the course of the 1920s, the word *girl* (*gāru*) gained even more currency. But the nuance did not convey what women intellectuals like

Bus girl powdering her nose, 1932. Compliments of Endo Noriaki.

Hiratsuka Raichō had envisioned as the essence of the modern woman, namely, a socially and politically awakened woman. The magazine *Modan Nippon* (Modern Japan) devoted substantial space to the erotic and grotesque elements of the new consumer culture. The magazine's take on the various types of "girls" (*gāru*) and their distinguishing features added zest to its June 1930 issue. Among the girls included were the mannequin girl (*manekin gāru*), who earned her living as a department store fashion model; the one-yen taxi girl (*entaku gāru*), whose job was to look pretty and accompany the driver on his calls in the role of a billboard advertisement; the gasoline girl (*gasorin gāru*), whose primary task consisted of beckoning taxi drivers into gasoline stations; the mahjong girl (*mājan gāru*), who catered to customers frequenting the mahjong halls; and the usherette (*kinema gāru*), whose job was to seat people in a movie theater. These occupations had one point in common: all employed women as sex objects or commercial come-ons.[21] It is not surprising, therefore, that the magazine *Modan Nippon* should have included the geisha and prostitute in the same list of occupations under the rubric of street girl (*sutorīto gāru*). Murakami Nobuhiko, a teenager

Elevator girl in a
department store, mid-
1920s. Reprinted with
permission of Mainichi
shinbun.

Elevator girl in an
office building, 1932.
Compliments of Endo
Noriaki.

in the late 1920s, probably expressed the feelings of many of his contemporaries when he later confessed:

The female [bus] conductors, who were confined to a much smaller space than on a subway or train, always stood close to the male passengers, chatting with them and punching their tickets. With the exception of cafés and coffee shops [where hostesses were taken for granted], this was one of the only opportunities for [poor] young men to come into contact with young women. When they entered a darkened movie theater, a young woman took them by the arm and led them to their seats. They could not actually hold hands, but their fingers probably touched when they handed over their tickets. They probably stared boldly at the young women's faces and bodies and were really excited watching them move about at close range. Whenever necessary, they exchanged a few words.[22]

The "erotic and grotesque" aspects of the new urban culture, particularly eroticism, helped create some job opportunities for women. By the early 1920s, shopgirl was the in-vogue term for women sales clerks, but Kitazawa's predictions remained unfulfilled. Employers had succeeded in stirring up business by hiring women at lower wages and using the fact of their gender as a promotional technique to win over male customers. But sexuality, not efficiency, was the underlying reason why the shopgirl inspired attention.[23]

Women office clerks, another major group subsumed under the heading of professional working women, also achieved a certain glamour. These women attracted attention and lent flavor to the workplace mainly because they worked in offices populated by men. All day they sat side by side at desks with members of the opposite sex. Women factory workers, on the other hand, inhabited a community comprised almost exclusively of women. Factory workers lived in dormitories and worked in their own microcosms, and, with the exception of male overseers, rarely came into contact with men.[24] The world of professional working women was markedly different. From the moment they left home in the morning, they interacted with men. Such interactions posed a challenge to the accepted standards of femininity and masculinity.[25] The commute to work on a crowded subway or bus was a harrowing experience. The respondents interviewed for the *Tokyo City Office Survey of 1922* on working women complained of men's "vulgar behavior toward women on the trains."[26] The newness of this sexual environment is evident in the Ministry of Education's refusal to accord accreditation to Bunka gakuin, the first school to establish a co-educational program beyond the elementary level. Professional working women's assumption of sites in what had been male-dominated spheres conveyed ample proof of the effects of change in the broader scheme of consumption.

Many leading figures of the day believed that the social and economic changes occurring around women presaged a breakdown in sexual morality. Yamamuro Gunpei, an advocate for the abolition of public prostitution and a colonel in the Salvation Army, declared: "As young women leave home and start working and mixing with men, they are going to make mistakes when it comes to maintaining their chastity. . . . Or perhaps I should say, I think it will become a matter of course."[27] And a woman educator warned young professional women: "In the streetcar, be sure not to wear flashy clothing that men will find alluring or you will be the cause of your own ruined futures. Girls have to be aware of what they are letting themselves in for, and to be strong-willed."[28] Stories and speculative gossip circulated about the office girl and her behavior.[29] The Marunouchi Building, situated in front of Tokyo Station and associated with the trappings of the modern cityscape, formed the perfect setting for the following newspaper report:

> Located inside the Marunouchi Building are some three hundred large and small businesses employing 4,500 people. Herded together in this space are about 700 young women. If you add this [figure] to those working in other nearby buildings, more than 1,000 young women are employed in the Marunouchi area alone. Monthly salaries for women range from around thirty yen to a maximum of one hundred yen [as compared to a minimum of ninety yen for men]. Besides doing a lot of complaining, working women defiantly crack the whip when they take a break from their "heavy" work load, and are probably having sex orgies off somewhere in the corner of the office.[30]

Unquestionably, World War I and expanding Japanese capitalism provided the impetus to employ women as a new source of labor, but respect did not come along with most jobs. In the ogling eyes of their male counterparts in offices, working women found themselves seen in terms of their decorative rather than utilitarian value. The addition of

Streetcar girl, circa 1924. Compliments of Endo Noriaki.

women to the workplace livened up the atmosphere, providing an audience for men and an incentive for them to perform. Kitamura Kaneko, a pioneering woman journalist, disdainfully observed: "Women grow bored with their jobs because the men in the office are so sexually stimulated by just having them around that they try and show off their prowess by assuming responsibility even for those tasks that have been assigned to women."[31]

The notoriety accorded the professional working woman generated rumors of promiscuity about women journalists and editors who shared close ties with male intellectuals. Hatano Akiko, an editor for *Fujin kōron* who committed suicide in 1923 with her lover, the writer Arishima Takeo, reputedly used her feminine charms to extract manuscripts from famous writers like Akutagawa Ryūnosuke and Nagai Kafū. Murakami considered feminine guile an invaluable asset for a female editor. The leftist woman writer Sata Ineko insisted that Hatano did not win the trust of these authors because of any exceptional ability in her chosen profession, but rather because "she had confidence and

knew how to use her coquettishness as an editor."[32] According to Murakami: "It was a well-known fact that being a woman helped in obtaining articles and manuscripts easily." Murakami cited the case of
a woman reporter who stood on her head dressed in a kimono and
begged for a manuscript. Whether or not she was wearing underwear
is unknown.[33] Consequently, when Kitamura described the treatment
that this new breed of working women endured in the workplace, she
obviously wrote from experience: "Women taking their first jobs exhibit a tremendous amount of personal determination. But after working for a while, they begin to question their initial convictions and rely
on their looks to get by. Women are to blame for this behavior, but it
stems from their being a part of a capitalist system in which no attention
is paid to a woman's qualifications or to whether family circumstances
necessitate her working. For employers the sole criterion is a woman's
appearance."[34] Kitamura's analysis of the dilemmas facing the working
woman suggests the social dislocation that accompanied the articulation of gender differences in the workplace.

In 1924, 92,640 women were employed as office workers, sales clerks,
typists, and telephone operators.[35] Yet, women were still seen as ap-
pendages—to the head of the household, to their husbands and children, or, in this case, to the job. Rarely did they receive their proper due
for contributions made at work. The popular "Tokyo Marching Song"
echoed the pervasive sentiment toward professional working women.
Composer Saijō Yaso portrayed a young woman who had little to do
in the office other than think of her lover and write him love letters.
Seated by her office window in the Marunouchi Building, she remained
totally engrossed in her personal thoughts. As Japan's first million-
selling record, this song was well placed to reinforce this view.[36]

Much of the prejudice faced by professional working women in the
city had its roots in the conviction that women belonged at home. A
high official in the Home Ministry declared: "I know that the term 'good
wife and wise mother' has been around for a long time, but it has a profound meaning. . . . For a woman to seek employment as a means of
challenging a man's position is the greatest tragedy in the history of
women. The very idea that if a woman holds a job she will be liberated
and become independent smacks of hysteria."[37] At the time, this kind
of bias represented more than a psychological impediment for women;
it kept them from obtaining higher education and actively pursuing

job opportunities.[38] The preconception of the home as a woman's space worked to deposition women in the workplace. Similar issues continue to persist in the new era with different employment tracks for women and men. Indeed, women still must fight to rid themselves of the title "tea-pourer" (*ocha kumi*).[39]

Former prostitute Yamada Waka, famous for her advice column in women's magazines in the 1920s and for her column carried in the *Asahi shinbun* from 1931 to 1938, wrote that even women who chose outside employment would eventually end up in a domesticated setting.[40] Yamada's view of a carefully defined female sphere lent support to the legalized social system determined by the Civil Code. Such views disadvantaged professional working women and curtailed their chances for promotion. The crux of the problem concerned a woman's responsibility in the workplace. Not only was hers considered temporary employment, with immediate "retirement" upon marriage, it was also imbued with sexual overtones. Acceptance of the professional working woman was premised on a short-term social identity that would soon be replaced by the role of charming housewife.

Positioning the Professional Working Woman

Most intellectuals agreed that young women anxious to make their way in society as professional working women represented an unprecedented social development. Interestingly, the metaphor of "dolls' houses," which had captured the imagination of intellectuals and journalists in the early twentieth century, was also used to convey social change in the 1920s.[41] Journalist Sakurai Heigorō voiced a frequently shared opinion in 1927:

> To date, the traditional lifestyle for a woman meant being confined to the home and doing menial work. A woman devoted her life to serving her family—her husband, her parents-in-law, and her children—with no life of her own. To put it in the extreme, a woman lived a slave's existence. Economic changes brought women out of the home, and the intellectual climate filled women with a passion and motivation to liberate themselves from their conventional dolls' houses. Women moved onto the streets, and one of the first groups of pioneers was the professional working woman.[42]

The fascination of the press, intellectuals, and the public with the professional working woman did not stem from the novelty of women engaged in outside labor. That was not really new. In the Edo period, farming women and men had toiled in the fields as equals. In early Meiji, women factory workers were an indispensable segment of the labor force, a symbol of the social costs of modernization.[43] The professional working woman's arrival, however, paralleled the first stage in the growth of the so-called new middle class, to which they largely belonged and for whom upward advancement beckoned.[44]

Scholars frequently point out that the new middle class became a notable force after World War II. Nevertheless, an awareness and interest in the salaried class as a distinct social class developed much earlier. It accompanied the accelerated pace of industrialization around the time of World War I.[45] The "Ballad of the Happy-go-lucky" (*Nonki bushi*), a 1918 lyric composed by songwriter Soeta Azenbō, describes the emergence of the salaried class satirically:

> They dress up in Western clothes and they wear Western shoes.
> They're educated, too, but they don't have any money.
> They're poor all right, they're poor all right, but you sure can't
>   see it on their faces.
> Oh, to be happy-go-lucky.[46]

Outwardly, in their Western attire, the salaried class resembled the upper classes. From an economic perspective, however, they would not have qualified as affluent. Their annual incomes ranged between eight hundred and five thousand yen. For them, it was more a question of rising hopes. Education was the greatest asset of the salaried class because it distinguished them from the lower classes.[47] Just as education set the salaried man apart from the laborer, education separated the professional working woman from the woman factory worker.

The 1922 survey conducted by the Tokyo Bureau of Social Affairs classified professional working women into six categories: teacher, typist, office worker, sales clerk, nurse, and telephone operator.[48] Not all the professions listed required the same level of education. But based on the data from a survey conducted by the same office in 1931 and published the following year, more than 60 percent of office workers and typists, and as many as 40 percent of sales clerks, held diplomas from women's higher schools. In contrast, more than 90 percent of women factory workers and domestics ended their formal schooling at the elementary level.[49] Certainly, not all these professions were open only to graduates of women's higher schools. But higher education was influential in helping to break the pattern that located middle-class women's lives in a domesticated setting like the one envisioned by Yamada Waka.

According to a questionnaire prepared by the city's employment agency, which had been assigned the task of finding employees to fill positions for three major department stores, 1,797 of 5,779 women respondents had received a higher-school education or above. Of that number, more than 95 percent were under twenty-five years of age.[50] Although this amounted to just 31 percent of the survey's participants, these figures are astounding because the applicants were applying for positions in only three department stores. Moreover, statistics for 1923 and 1928 confirm that only about 10 percent of all elementary-school graduates proceeded to higher school.[51] Within a three-day period, applications from 3,744 men and 11,784 women flooded the office, further proof of the shopgirl's popularity. Working in a metropolis like Tokyo held great appeal for graduates of women's higher schools. One graduate wrote ecstatically about having quit her job as an elementary-school teacher in a rural community to assume a job in the city as a sales clerk.[52] The image of the professional working woman, compounded by the real need that motivated women's higher-school students to seek employment, helps clarify the attempt some women made to mold their own subjectivity.

Ōbayashi Munetsugu, the first scholar to conduct a sociological study of the café waitress, defined the professional working woman as an intellectual: "Originally the term professional working woman [*shoku-gyō fujin*] as used in our country provided a vague means of differentiating between women laborers and other women workers. The assumption was that women laborers [*rōdo fujin*] performed manual tasks as opposed to those women who performed intellectual work [*chinō no hataraki*]."[53] Honda Tōru agreed: "Their work, which requires some degree of intellectual ability [*chinō o yōsuru shigoto*], ties them [professional working women] to the intellectual classes."[54] Ōbayashi's definition resembles songwriter Soeda's description of the salaried class in that both stressed education as the criterion for determining who belonged to this group of professionals. Obviously, the term *woman intellectual* was defined far more broadly in the 1920s and early 1930s

than it is today.[55] The quality of a woman's education and the expectations held for her after graduation from higher school remained worlds
apart from that of men. Professional working women gladly performed
the job of sales clerk, while men aspired instead to become bankers or
company managers. Among the 177 young women hired by the city of
Tokyo as bus girls in 1924, 27 were higher-school graduates.[56] Because
these were new occupations, even middle-class women could perform
the same jobs as elementary-school or higher elementary-school graduates and escape the social stigma attached to being a woman factory
worker or farm laborer.[57] Robert Bellah stresses that with the emergence of the modern middle class in America, work became more than
a means of earning a living; it offered a path to self-advancement.[58] In
Japan, the motivation propelling women's higher-school students to
enter society and perform jobs shunned by males took on particular
meaning.

The Motivation to Work

Economic need, the formation of a woman's consciousness, and the
increasing number of jobs gave coherence to the unfolding of professional working women's experiences during the interwar period.[59]
Changes did not occur only because of social and familial demands;
shifts in women's consciousness made these transformations mutually
and reciprocally constitutive. Individual liberation, for example, does
not only occur because of a perceived inner need: it is also affected
by surrounding conditions, such as opportunities for wage labor. Was
it possible for women, who burned with the desire "to liberate themselves from their conventional dolls' houses," to take employment opportunities and use them to forge their own independence?

Economic Factors

One has only to check the passenger figures for buses and streetcars in
the 1920s or to examine photographs of the throngs of people crowd-
ing the streets during commuting hours and lunch breaks to recognize
that women were working outside the home in unprecedented numbers. The numerous surveys prepared by local government agencies

did more than clarify the numbers: they detailed the work women performed and the salaries they received, and they also provided insight
into the social background and class of the interviewees. Almost all
the surveys asked women why they sought employment.[60] Based on
the answers to the *Tokyo City Office Surveys of 1922 and 1931* (interviewees could choose only one answer), besides the predominant reason of
"supplementing family income," women worked to achieve "economic
independence," to "prepare for marriage," and for reasons related to
their personal "self-cultivation" (*shūyō*) (see table 2).[61] When we consider these surveys within the context of the world depression, it is clear
that Japan was no exception in the economic crisis that brought misery
to families the world over.

A clarification of the ambiguous nature of "economic independence"
may establish why almost 20 percent of those interviewed for the
1922 survey chose "economic necessity" as their motivating force.[62] By
definition, economic independence implies being self-supporting and
financially independent. On the surface, by affirming the word *independent*, some professional working women were expressing their awareness of the prospects that holding a job might provide. On the other
hand, work opportunities for women were still limited. Many young
women, particularly in rural areas, had little choice but to seek employment in the cities. By 1920, the economic and psychological toll from the
post–World War I depression was devastating Japan's agricultural sec-
tor. In the countryside, young women were automatically compelled to
become "independent." One employment agency claimed that all the
women who came to the city from the provinces in 1926 listed "economic independence" as the reason.[63]

Essentially, "economic independence" encompassed a double meaning. Not all respondents wanted to become completely independent
professional women. More relevant for many young women was reliev-
ing their families' financial burden by supporting themselves. A graduate of a mission-operated women's higher school in Osaka pointed out:
"My parents hoped that I would continue my education at a woman's
college [*senmon gakkō*], but our economic situation forced me to become
independent of the family. In my spare time, however, I plan to continue
studying music, my hobby."[64] "Economic independence" and "supplementing family income" both underscore the economic reasons behind
the largest percentage of women entering the workplace. This explains

TABLE 2 Motivation and Types of Work Available for Women
in 1922 and 1931

	Supplementing Family Income (%)	Economic Independence (%)	Self-Improvement (%)	Preparation for Marriage (%)	Other (%)
Teachers	23.5	20.5	25.0	0	31.0
Typists					
1922	26.9	42.3	3.8	3.8	23.2
1931	62.0	20.7	7.5	4.7	5.1
Office workers					
1922	52.1	20.5	5.8	3.4	18.2
1931	70.5	10.0	7.3	5.4	6.8
Sales clerks					
1922	56.0	13.1	7.1	1.2	22.6
1931	68.8	8.3	8.1	6.3	5.8
Factory workers	86.1	8.7	0.6	1.1	3.5
Domestics	79.5	17.3	0	0	3.2
Totals					
1922	52.3	17.8	7.3	2.3	9.4
1931	76.6	9.8	3.0	3.2	—

Source: Based on figures from the 1922 and 1931 *Tokyo City Office Survey.*
Note: Teachers were not included in the 1931 survey, and women factory workers and domestic workers were surveyed only in 1931. "Self-cultivation" and "social experience" were listed as separate categories in the 1931 survey, but since both reflect improving oneself or society, I have incorporated them into the category of "self-cultivation" (*shūyō*) in order to facilitate comparison with the 1922 survey.

why the *Tokyo City Office Survey of 1931* mentioned "self-cultivation" and "social experience" as the two factors instrumental in raising the awareness of the professional working woman, but made no reference to "economic independence."[65]

Given that "supplementing family income" and "economic independence" were the reasons offered by more than 80 percent of those interviewed, most intellectuals misinterpreted the "awakening" of professional women and their eagerness to become "independent" in much the same way as they misinterpreted the significance of the modern girl. Once again, intellectuals could not separate social realities from preconceived images. Hiratsuka Raichō's comments exemplify a common misconception. Raichō argued that the yearning for independence symbolized the new womanhood and influenced most of the women seeking employment. As a critic of radical gender equality, however, she cautioned women about the realities of attaining that goal in the workplace and instead urged them to reassess their priorities.[66] Oku Mumeo, publisher of *Fujin to rōdō* (Woman and Work), a magazine designed to inform professional women about the intricacies of the working world, voiced the opposite opinion and strongly disagreed with intellectuals who shared Hiratsuka's viewpoint. For Oku, the conflict did not hinge on women's self-awakening, but rather on their survival. Whether women wanted work experience or not, post–World War I economic conditions left them no alternative.[67]

Yet the proliferation of middle-class professional women cannot be explained solely by Hiratsuka's analysis or by Oku's interpretation of depressed economic conditions. Prior to World War I, a young woman's presence in the workplace was proof of her family's financial distress. Girls from middle-class families graduating from women's higher schools generally were not among the job seekers. In the Meiji period, negative pressures were strong enough to prevent young women from upper-level families from working outside their homes even if their families' fortunes had declined. For a woman, holding a job implied that her family had fallen into the ranks of the poor. The results of the *Tokyo City Office Survey* for 1922 and 1931, which classified working women according to their occupations, show this (see table 2).

The economic position of a woman's family and her level of education did much to determine the type of position she sought. Because "economic independence" conveyed a double meaning, it is impossible to say merely from the breakdown of professions whether the respondents had economic necessity, self-awakening, or both in mind when they made their choices. An extremely high percentage of factory workers and domestics worked to "supplement the family budget." However, economic motivation was not the decisive factor for a large number of office workers and clerks who had graduated from women's higher schools. This group considered work outside the home as useful "preparation for marriage" and a way to achieve "self-cultivation," luxuries factory workers and domestics rarely had the chance to consider.[68] Besides the misery wrought by the world depression, economic upheaval brought a challenge for some middle-class women in Japan to adapt to new possibilities. Clearly, educated young women occupied a unique position in the ranks of professional working women.

Self-Cultivation as Preparation for Marriage

In addition to economic necessity, self-cultivation, or *shūyō*, was another compelling reason why young women from middle-class families entered the workforce at this time. The term *self-cultivation* encompassed a variety of different meanings, evoking connotations of "character building," "moral training," and "spiritual and cultural growth." Middle-class women's concern with self-cultivation can be traced back to Taishō culture, which emphasized individual freedom and the importance of intellectual cultivation for its own sake.[69] Intellectuals such as Abe Jirō, Kurata Hyakuzō, and Kagawa Toyohiko saw individualism as nurturing personal salvation. In their search to give meaning to the self, some intellectuals immersed themselves in philosophical and religious meditation and subjected themselves to constant self-examination.[70] Self-cultivation was a key word expressing their attempts at spiritual and cultural cultivation.[71]

Professional working women also became caught up in the general self-cultivation boom. The popularized form of self-cultivation had an empowering effect on women in the home and in the workplace. Many professional women looked to reading as a way to achieve self-cultivation. One section in the *Tokyo City Office Survey of 1922* listed the most popular books among professional women for that year. Approximately 20 percent of the respondents cited Kurata Hyakuzō's best-selling essay, "Shukke to sono deshi" (The Priest and His Disciples), which made the thirteenth-century Buddhist priest Shinran a popular figure. Also included was the autobiographical novel *Shisen o koete* (Crossing the Line between Life and Death) by Kagawa Toyohiko, which dealt with Kagawa's personal involvement in Christianity, a philosophy widely embraced by intellectuals since the mid-Meiji era.[72] The fact that religious novels, plays, and books on religion and the humanities constituted more than 45 percent of their favorite books is an indication that self-cultivation shaped the reading choices of these professional women.[73]

The 1922 survey included a question asking professional working women how they readied themselves for marriage. Here again, self-cultivation played an important role. Thirty of the forty-nine respondents called self-cultivation the light that guided them in preparing for their future life. Miyake Yasuko, who counseled numerous young women on personal problems, admitted that some women regarded work as a chance to become more independent (something that Miyake herself wished to interpret as a rise in self-awareness). Others, however, spoke of work as a release from the boredom of daily life. "Actually, the overwhelming number of aspirants only want a suitable job until they marry."[74]

A female office worker for whom self-cultivation symbolized conventional etiquette training commented: "For me, self-cultivation entails attending a nightly sewing class and taking lessons in tea ceremony and flower arrangement on the weekends." A typist who was no less enthusiastic about self-cultivation entertained a different opinion. Rather than dwelling on the virtues of self-cultivation as preparation for marriage, she addressed its advantages from the standpoint of personal growth: "I am working to improve myself. I want to become a whole person." Self-cultivation for these women was obviously something quite different from the religious and philosophical conceptions of the intellectuals. These young women did not attach esoteric meaning to self-cultivation, but reconstructed it to fit their own development. In the words of a sales clerk: "It is hard working outside as a professional working woman, but I am doing it to get an idea of what life is really like after marriage."[75] Thus, holding a job represented another form of self-cultivation, which assumed a place in the life plans of middle-class young women. The longing for self-cultivation, which centered on the values of self-improvement, was directly related to the growing number of women's higher-school graduates.

The need to defray wedding costs could have been a reason why women from middle-class homes worked in "preparation for marriage," but more likely the majority who selected this response considered social experience a prerequisite for married life. The following statement on the changing requirements for brides by Kawai Michiko, a director of the Tokyo YWCA, supports this explanation:

Formerly, as long as a woman could perform such basic tasks in the home as sewing, cooking, washing and cleaning, she had sufficient qualifications to become the woman of the house. The only thing that a girl of marriageable age needed was good manners. But for a woman to run a home in today's busy society, she must be cultivated in more than just the basics. She really needs the experience that comes from being directly involved in society to acquire the sort of practical knowledge she cannot learn at a women's higher school. I see absolutely nothing wrong in women doing some kind of work outside the home, for the same reasons they used to study proper etiquette before getting married, to develop social skills and acquire common sense.[76]

Recognition of the importance of "social experience" for housewives demonstrates a shift in the perception of some male and female intellectuals about the educated woman's role in the home. Kawai's thinking reflected the belief that self-cultivation implied a rite of passage for married life. Prior to the 1920s, graduates of women's higher schools either married immediately on leaving school or else spent the interval before marriage helping out at home and studying the three prerequisites for prospective brides: tea ceremony, flower arrangement, and sewing. If having a job offered social experience, then, as one woman remarked, "even when women get married, that kind of concrete knowledge will be far more valuable than acquiring a few chests for a dowry and having a meaningless school diploma."[77] Outside employment became one more item on the list of "musts" that guided young middle-class woman into the practicalities of married life. Even liberal social critic Chiba Kameo adhered to this opinion: "Holding down a job — or at least having economic independence — will assure that when a woman marries and enters the home she will have the same rights and status as a man. It is only by going out and working that a woman will be able to change and improve her subservient position in the family."[78]

Some critics voiced fears that work led women away from marriage and the home. Educator Hatoyama Haruko, an outspoken advocate of conventional gender relationships, warned: "It is a total mistake for women to reject marriage just because they can work and earn money to support themselves and do not want their lifestyles to be restricted after marriage."[79] Chiba and Hatoyama, in contrast, identified self-cultivation as a preliminary step for improving personal relations in the home. That alone made working worthwhile. Hatoyama located self-cultivation in terms of "physical, mental, and financial self-improvement."[80] She equated "financial self-improvement" with economic independence. Outside employment would teach women to budget money, an essential skill in fulfilling their duties as helpmates to their husbands. A women's higher-school student who wrote to *Shufu no tomo* in 1922 was certain that a job would prepare her for a successful marriage: "As I see it, marriage is really the cornerstone of a person's life. I think that for two people to trust and help each other and grow together is their most valuable work. But for many people petty things like the fear of growing older or being influenced by the neighbors' gossip cause them to rush into marriage and then to fail. That is why after I graduate from women's higher school, I will live with my parents and take a few years to master skills and get a job that will prepare me for marriage. I want to wait until I can find the right person to marry."[81] This young woman associated being a professional working woman with "mastering skills" like dressmaking, cooking, and embroidery, which would ultimately help her find a suitable mate.

By the 1920s, then, at least some middle-class professional women regarded work as self-cultivation. Some scholars have argued that self-cultivation gave working women a heightened sense of themselves.[82] We should not, however, exaggerate the extent of that awareness. From the vantage point of the media, and particularly mass women's magazines, the liberating aspects of the self-cultivation discourse were less important than its role in enhancing a woman's time-honored role as wife and mother. Magazines were not counseling their readers to make radical changes in their lives. And most young women entering the workforce never considered the possibility of sacrificing marriage for a career. This does not mean, however, that women were not in the process of redefining themselves.

Reading was not the only means to achieve self-cultivation, but many women believed that subscribing to newspapers and magazines offered a concrete way to fulfill their goals. One teacher commented that she hoped to become a complete person by "reading widely and going to lectures."[83] In the words of a telephone operator: "Reading magazines is my way of improving myself spiritually."[84] More than 70 percent of those interviewed subscribed to women's magazines; the majority of professional women favored magazines like *Fujin kōron* and *Fujokai*, which addressed themes related to enlightenment and self-cultivation.[85]

The mass women's magazines placed a high value on introspection and cultivating the mind, but they stayed within the realm of the practical. As one intellectual lamented: "Today's scholars are inclined to be overly idealistic and self-righteous." Unquestionably, many intellectuals preached a kind of self-cultivation far removed from the actual lives of professional women.[86] Mass women's magazines avoided abstraction and pomposity and featured more popular aspects of self-cultivation. Indeed, the popularization of self-cultivation captured the imaginations of women readers, who in turn felt a bond with the magazine. Excerpts from readers' letters published in *Shufu no tomo* are telling: "How can I ever express how I have benefited from all the instructive articles published in each issue?"[87] "Please help guide someone like me who is lacking in personal cultivation [*shūyō*]."[88] One reader celebrated the role of women's magazines in the attainment of self-cultivation using the words "teacher, friend, cane to lean on, and pillar for support."[89]

Articles that invoked self-cultivation were far more useful for professional working women than the family articles and practical articles that introduced a new kind of expertise for housewives. Particularly beneficial to aspiring professional working women were discussions about work opportunities and hints on how to succeed on the job. Personal accounts, many written by the readers, provided such information. "Professional Women's Salaries and the Experience Required for These Jobs" (Kakushu shokugyō fujin no shūnyū to shoku o eru made no keiken) detailed a female attendant's work experiences on an ocean liner traveling to Australia, Europe, and America. Although her monthly salary was only sixty yen, the job put her in constant contact with the passengers, and, coupled with tips, her take-home pay averaged two hundred yen a month. A woman who had studied photography and opened her own studio in 1910 claimed that by hard work and perseverance, after less than fifteen years she averaged approximately five hundred yen a month.[90] In "Employment for the New Woman—Woman Driver" (Atarashii fujin no shokugyō—jidōsha no onna untenshu), a women's higher-school graduate recounted how her greatest desire had been to obtain her driver's license, an unusual feat for anyone, but especially for a woman. Hired as a taxi driver, she took home three hundred yen a month.[91] In the column "Diary of a Professional Woman's Life" (Shokugyō fujin no seikatsu nikki—aru hi no nikki), women whose professions included doctor, journalist, music teacher, and tourist guide for foreigners shared their daily experiences and described the people they encountered enthusiastically enough to fill any young woman with ambition.[92]

In "The Road Young Women Higher-School Graduates Should Follow to Find Employment" (Jogaku de no wakai fujin no shokugyō wa nanika), a female reporter warned young women that "easy work carries no responsibility. You receive a paycheck for performing a job that anyone without any knowledge can do. Work that has value entails commitment and training. Women who pay attention to these two requirements will be the first to succeed in the working world and command high salaries."[93] The office manager of a telephone company told readers that a professional working woman's success depended on perseverance, even if the work was considered boring by some people's standards.[94]

The popularization of self-cultivation did not necessarily circumvent the desire to get ahead in the workplace (risshin shusse); total dedication to one's work was the prerequisite for success.[95] Considering this statement, it is probably correct to assume that success stories written about professional working women and articles that apprised women of job openings comprised the core of women's reading material about possibilities in the wider world.[96] Moreover, after reading these articles, even young women still enrolled in women's higher schools understood that self-cultivation was a viable path to future employment. The daughter of a well-to-do colonel in Niigata explained that just thinking about entering the working world put her mind at ease and filled her with excitement. Her father, however, was adamantly opposed to her becoming a professional working woman after graduation from women's higher school because of the gossip it would invite.[97]

By spreading news about jobs, women's magazines precipitated an increase in middle-class women seeking employment. Murakami noted that the exodus of young women from rural areas accounted for the bulk of that increase.[98] Many of the young women who left the country to take jobs in urban areas as domestics or factory workers did so immediately after finishing elementary school. Not to be disregarded, however, is the role women's magazines played in informing graduates of rural women's higher schools about urban employment. Rural women often spoke of being unable to endure the constraints of life in the country, the strenuous work, and the power exercised by domineering mothers-in-law.[99] It is highly unlikely that they considered farm work to be self-cultivation.

Reading how common it was for women to work in the city, some graduates of women's higher schools took comfort in knowing that holding a job was not shameful. Articles that suggested work as a form of self-cultivation helped assuage the fears of those anxious to procure employment in the cities. *Ie no hikari* (Light of the Home), a magazine directed toward farming communities, expressed alarm about the exodus of young women, especially women's higher-school graduates, from the countryside to the city. "If you live in the country and think about women in the city," the article's author warned readers, "you probably imagine them wearing beautiful clothes and going out and having a good time. But the women who actually can afford the comforts of city life and have freedom to enjoy themselves are about one in a thousand. Most city women work harder than country girls do, fighting to make a living in the unbearable heat."[100] This article struck a chord among young men and their parents in several villages, but it did little to stem the tide of young rural women streaming to the cities, which continued unabated.[101] In fact, the *Tokyo Asahi* reported that an agency opened in Tokyo Station to assist young women arriving from the country: "As might be expected, of the 819 cases that were handled, the most common problem concerned finding suitable employment: 280 women raised that issue. Among the coveted jobs, department store sales clerk and office worker ranked highest on the list. In most instances, young women said reading about these things in women's magazines brought them to Tokyo."[102]

The self-cultivation boom stimulated by women's mass magazines and books influenced many higher-school graduates to seek employment. With self-cultivation as an incentive, even those who worked because of economic need could overcome the humiliation that paid employment held for young women from middle-class families. The realization that other women were entering society for reasons like "preparation for marriage" lessened the psychological stigma attached to outside employment. Although only a small fraction of the women interviewed for the *Tokyo City Office Survey* of 1922 and 1931 listed "preparation for marriage" and "self-cultivation" as their reasons for working, the media focused on these opinions. More significant, such articles gave moral support to the increasing number of middle-class women forced to seek employment to "supplement family income" because of "economic necessity."

Qualifying for a New Type of Marriage:
Self-Cultivation and Changing Expectations

Having described the connection between work and self-cultivation, it is pertinent to examine the marital status of these young working women and how self-cultivation affected their approach to matters of the heart. To equate the increase in professional women in the 1920s with a nationwide reassessment of gender roles would be an overstatement. True, some young women no longer unequivocally subscribed to the view that a woman's place was in the home. Nevertheless, questioning conventional gender roles did not mean wanting to change completely how they lived. Total independence was not the propelling factor for professional working women. Young women continued to link the future possibility of marriage with self-cultivation. Rather than denouncing the patriarchal family, they envisioned a transformation directed at fulfilling their own expectations for a successful marriage. "Self-cultivation," as described in women's magazines, provided a sense of emotional support that led to changing conceptions of themselves.

The changing social position of women affirmed the possibility of alternative perceptions of love and marriage. The *Tokyo City Office Survey of 1922* reported that 83.6 percent of the professional women interviewed were single; in the 1931 survey, the percentage remained almost identical at 83.4 percent. According to the 1922 survey, 71.4 percent of the respondents were young women under twenty-four years of age; in 1931, 80.5 percent were younger than twenty-five years of age.[103] No doubt, the percentage rose slightly in the later survey because women factory workers and domestics (*jochū*) were included for the first time. Nevertheless, the figures show that professional working women were overwhelmingly young and single.[104]

Reasons given for the paucity of married women among professional working women included poor working conditions, the atmosphere in the workplace, and employers who frowned on them. The *Tokyo City Office Survey of 1931*, however, contradicted this rationale and placed the blame on women. The survey reported that 22.6 percent of employers expressed dissatisfaction with the short time young women spent in the company's service and admonished women for assuming that marriage gave them license to sever company ties.[105] Whether businesses shunned married women or young women regarded termination after marriage as the natural course is a source of debate. Nevertheless, both sides seem to have looked on the home as the proper place for a married woman. Performing household tasks ultimately symbolized a woman's "divine mission" (*tenshoku*). Any deviation from that course would likely have aroused strong opposition from husbands and mothers-in-law.[106]

Yet it was not only social norms and the atmosphere in the workplace that governed such decisions. Young women themselves believed that gender-differentiated labor was appropriate.[107] Most single young women stopped working after marriage and handed over all economic responsibility to their husbands. The assumption that a woman's happiness was contingent on her marriage remained unchanged. Neither the hope for economic and spiritual independence nor women's fears about authoritarian mothers-in-law and family burdens was sufficient to deter them from marriage.

The head of the Bureau of Social Affairs, established within the Home Ministry in 1920 to deal with the "woman problem" (*fujin mondai*), urged women to exercise prudence in choosing a partner:

> Perhaps the biggest problem [a woman] faces in her lifetime is selecting a husband. A man's fate is completely governed by his own efforts. With a woman, however, no matter how prominent her family may be, no matter how much money she may have saved or how smart she may be, if she chooses the wrong husband, there is no greater unhappiness that she will have to endure for the rest of her life. In spite of this, the careless way of deciding on a partner in Japan shows a lack of any great concern for this most important event in a woman's life. That is the reason why so many tragedies arise.[108]

Women needed no lecture in morals from a civil servant to understand the seriousness of selecting a marriage partner. Being married was regarded as natural, but choosing one's own husband was not. Moreover, a parent's decision generally hinged on economic factors and the enhancement of the family's fortune.[109] Tago Kazutami notes that "for parents the only criteria were a man's school record, his assets, and his position in society. If the parent was especially materialistic, these conditions took on all the more significance. There are numerous examples of marriages being forced for these reasons."[110] If a young woman had exercised her own judgment in selecting a partner, she would likely have clashed with her parents. This is not to say that the desire to marry the person of one's choice did not exist. One of the first expressions of the intellectual Bluestockings' "awakening" was the endorsement of free love or marriage based on romantic love. Itō Noe broke her engagement to a man from her hometown to marry the artist Tsuji Jun. Nishizaki Hanayo wrote about her love affair with the poet Ikuta Shungetsu and later described their married life together in a series of articles published in Seitō. Although the Swedish feminist Ellen Key influenced both women, it was not unusual for young intellectual women with a sense of themselves to voice concerns about free love and marrying for love.[111]

Middle-class women and the educated few who had graduated from women's higher schools required special circumstances to resist accepted marriage practices. The social experience that the professional working woman gained from entering society and working for a salary often provided the confidence and moral support to oppose controlling parents. A salary, no matter how small, guaranteed a degree of economic independence. But these factors pertained only to the professional working woman. A third, and the most important, factor supporting women's freedom to choose their husbands was the self-cultivation boom embraced by professional working women and other young middle-class women. Self-cultivation instilled hope for a marriage that offered the chance of self-fulfillment. Marriage became more than an economic agreement that bound two households (ie). A marriage that promoted spiritual union between two individuals could not deny women their sexuality.[112] In fact, male intellectuals were the first to link shūyō and marriage by insisting that marriage joined a couple spiritually and physically.[113] In the July 1919 issue of Fujin kōron, a jurist called attention to the meaning of marriage: "Marriage in the true sense of the word means that a man and a woman must love each other and become one mentally and physically. They have to help each other, continue to be diligent in their practice of self-cultivation and contribute to the development of world civilization. Traditional marriages in our country were completely opposed to these objectives. Frankly speaking, the reason a woman married had nothing to do with the man, but with the family [ie]."[114]

Whenever the sacredness of love and married life involved the articulation of self-cultivation, a love marriage was always the ideal. The reasons were clear. A marriage that normalized parents' feelings rather than the couple's had little chance of becoming a spiritual union. The social position and personal worth of the prospective groom, factors that governed a parent's decision, were antithetical to self-cultivation. Hence, they were considered vulgar. Kurata Hyakuzō's essay "Ai to ninshiki no shuppatsu" (The Origins of Love and Understanding), which views love as an essential part of life, exemplifies the explicit connection between love and self-cultivation among Taishō intellectuals.[115] Kuriyagawa Hakuson's essay "Kindai no ren'ai kan" (Modern Views of Love), published in 1920 and widely read by young women, links the ideal of marriage to the underlying ethos implicit in self-cultivation: "Only love has the total power to join two individuals mentally and physically and influence the formation of their character."[116] The popular phrase "unity of body and soul" (rei niku icchi), which referred to the ideal image of love and marriage at the time, had its roots in self-cultivation thought.

Chiba Kameo explained this concept of marriage: "If a young woman wants to make a good life for herself today, she has to be patient and do her utmost to find the best possible partner she can in the world. That is the person she will give her heart and body to. Because of the need to devote oneself totally to one another, virginity is a woman's treasure. The same thing holds true for a married woman. A husband and wife realize that in this whole wide world they are the only two who matter and they must be willing to give everything to each other."[117]

Self-cultivation encouraged an egalitarian view of marriage that stipulated "only two people in the world mattered," a premise that negated the primacy of the ie. A reader's letter published in Fujin kōron in 1928 shows the extent to which intellectual views on self-cultivation and its relationship to love and marriage shaped young women's thoughts: "What gave me pleasure was what one would probably describe as his simple purity and the fact that he expressed himself more in spiritual than in physical terms. He said that it was a sin for a husband and wife to live without love and that being virtuous meant giving everything, mind and body, to the one and only partner we have. You can imagine the tremendous feeling of trust I felt for him when he said that."[118] The high value that the husband attached to the spiritual side of their relationship attracted this young wife. In her letter she used a term used at the time to convey a pure, spiritual love in which both parties were of one mind and body (*yurushiau*).[119] However, unlike intellectuals who used the word abstractly to express love, these young women demanded concrete proof of a deep spiritual bond that would join them with their partners. The young woman who wrote the letter insisted that her husband be chaste; any man who had visited the pleasure quarters even once lacked the qualifications to be her husband.[120] Such expectations conveyed a longing for a more equal relationship. Visiting a geisha or engaging a prostitute was not considered immoral at this time. But for a woman to make a man's virginity a requirement for marriage attests to the new expectations women voiced in their search for a "true partnership." Some women questioned the assumption that sexual promiscuity was a man's natural right, both before and after marriage: "Even after they get married most men in Japan have no sense of virtue and think they have a right to visit the pleasure quarters. I can't excuse that kind of behavior after marriage as being a 'necessary' social practice (?) [original punctuation] If my husband feels that that is something he has to do because it is expected of men in our society, I am always going to be anxious and dissatisfied with our life. I think that we will both be unhappy. Unless I am convinced that our life is not going to be like this, I cannot foresee any other way but to separate."[121]

The problem went beyond virtue. Increasingly more women disavowed their husbands' arbitrary authority and attempted to stand on an equal footing with them. A relationship without an exchange of ideas was considered flawed. The following reader's letter exemplifies this point: "I am one of four sisters and the only one who is still single. All the men who have proposed to me, however, were concerned with our family name, finances, and my father's position. Unless someone wants to marry me for myself, and if I cannot find somebody who is manly and not going to treat his wife like a slave and be a tyrant, then I have decided never to wed. I, too, want to put my parents' minds at ease. Even so, I cannot entrust my marriage to them. I feel very anxious about ever finding a man who meets my needs."[122] This young woman grew up in a wealthy merchant family proud of its social standing. Generally, such families tended to observe established practices. Even living in such an atmosphere, however, this young woman was intent on maintaining her sense of self after marriage. Because she insisted that marriage should be satisfying, she sought a partner who shared her ideals even though that required challenging her parents' absolute authority. A letter from the daughter of a prosperous Akita farmer records one young woman's dogged resistance to marriage. After much pleading, the writer had been allowed to attend a women's higher school in Tokyo. Shortly before her graduation, however, her parents summoned her back to her native village. "Now that you have received an excellent education at a school in Tokyo," her father said, "don't you think you ought to show a little devotion to your parents? Isn't it about time you stopped being so selfish and doing only what you want? How about putting your parents' minds at ease?" This, of course, was the father's way of pressuring his daughter into marrying the son of a prominent member of the same village. The daughter indignantly replied: "Father, I refuse to become the bride of someone I have never met. There is no way I am going to have a marriage without love and understanding. You are acting like a tyrant. No father has this absolute kind of power." In the end, the young woman disregarded her father and married a man of her own choice. At the end of her letter she addressed a few lines to her father, who wanted to benefit economically from her marriage and "never thought of his own daughter's happiness": "Father, I have always been strong-willed and not a very dutiful daughter, but have I really done anything to make you so unhappy?"[123]

The perennial emotional collisions with parents over the right to love and marry the person of one's choice are given a modern (*modan*) twist in this letter. Young women's determination not to compromise their feelings and willingness to oppose their parents' will owed something to the self-cultivation boom and the value it placed on individual thinking. Even parents who intellectually recognized the progressiveness of a marriage that considered the couple's emotions were reluctant to consent to such a marriage for their own daughters. The daughter who fell in love with a man who met with her mother's approval is a good case in point. Although the mother was "definitely not opposed" to this match, she believed that "an unevenly balanced marriage owing to differences in family status is doomed to failure."[124] A professor insisted that deciding on a marriage partner required a parent's wisdom. Correlating wisdom with age, he expressed doubt that a young woman could make a judicious choice. A doctor asked by *Shufu no tomo* to comment on new trends among young women noted: "As prerequisites for a marriage partner, women are less concerned with the person's looks, the extent of his fortune, and the standing of his family. I am glad to see them emphasizing education and personal cultivation [*shūyō*]." He went on to say, however, that young women "are self-centered, do not listen to their parents, are lacking in purpose, change their minds at whim, and, moreover, are frivolous and extravagant."[125]

As young women spoke out in favor of the freedom to marry for love and daringly put their hopes into practice, conflicts with parents and others of the older generations intensified. Articles carried in women's magazines and printed in advice columns vividly recounted both sides of the story. Just as women's magazines fostered self-cultivation among readers, they also fanned an attraction for love marriages. Articles like "A Discussion for Those Who Would Marry the Person of Their Choice" (Jiyū kekkon o nozomu hitobito no tame no sōdan, *Shufu no tomo*, January 1925) and "Over One Hundred Ways to Win in Love" (Ren'ai hisshō no hiketsu hyakkajō, *Shufu no tomo*, July 1928) served this need. Asked whether a woman should marry the man she loved or the person selected by her parents, the director of the Christian Temperance Union advised young women to obey their parents:

> In Western countries there is a saying that "love is blind." In Japan we say "love blinds us to all imperfections." [The literal translation is "To the lover's fond eye a pockmark looks like a dimple."] This is an expression that came into being because the emotional state of being in love makes people lose their ability to reason, and they often fail to make impartial judgments. Lacking in worldly experience . . . one might say you lack the ability to judge wisely. . . . When the time finally comes and you want to be a dutiful daughter, your parents will already be gone. How much will you grieve then?[126]

This argument made an impression on some young women. One woman whose love marriage failed because of her husband's infidelity said: "In the eyes of a rash and impudent young girl, my mother seemed ignorant, blind, and unworldly . . . but now I know that being submissive was her way of finding happiness. When I think back on how

I rushed into marriage as if it were a dream and proclaimed love for love's sake without having laid down any roots myself, I am absolutely mortified."[127] This young woman rued her own decision and came to accept the criticism that members of the older generation leveled against young people like herself. She succumbed to the prevailing opinion that seniority was tantamount to good judgment. Nevertheless, in spite of the counterattack launched by the older generations against love marriages and young women's stories of contrition, when readers read letters like the following, they realized the significance of self-cultivation as a means to validate their ideals:

> We were married before I even had time to remember my husband's name. My only feeling was that he was disgusting, short, fat and old. Without a chance to say whether I liked him or disliked him, I had become his wife. Of course, I knew the word *no*, but I thought that my parents would never agree with me. At the time it seemed absolutely impossible to marry the person I truly love and since I was young this is how things turned out. I have been married six months now and I think only of him. I don't know if I can endure living with someone who is of the same generation as my parents just for the sake of money. When I think I might have to go on this way and that all I have are my beautiful dreams, I feel so wretched and ashamed of myself for what has happened. If I am unhappy, my husband will be unhappy. . . . Our marriage could break up someday.[128]

Self-cultivation won the sympathy of similarly inclined young women because of examples like this that described married life as a form of repression. Although women had always encountered problems and dissatisfaction with conventional marriages, self-cultivation offered a new context within which to express their opinions and desires.

Conclusion

Self-cultivation went from being an abstract idea embraced by a small group of intellectuals to a popular concept because of the growth of mass journalism. The popular-based mass magazine *Kingu,* together with other mass women's magazines, held a prominent position in the lives of a widening array of readers, of whom middle-class women comprised a significant segment. The rise in the number of women subscribers was particularly noticeable with the spread of higher education. Publishers of women's magazines introduced a popularized variation of self-cultivation to their readers.[129] Although economic reasons topped the list of reasons for the majority of professional working women seeking employment, the self-cultivation boom drew a number of women's higher-school graduates to the workplace. Self-cultivation offered personal fulfillment. And while intellectual discourses sparked the initial interest in self-cultivation, professional working women interpreted self-cultivation in their own fashion and molded it to fit the patterns of their lives.

Working outside the home to gain social experience and a holding view of marriage that emphasized the spiritual bond between husbands and wives were considered by many young women as kinds of self-cultivation. Discussions pertaining to both issues filled the pages of women's magazines. Readers' letters, confessional articles, and personal testimonies printed in the advice columns acknowledged the specific problems that women battled. Women's magazines, in spite of their own vested interests, provided a forum where women could communicate hitherto unspoken wishes, sorrows, and disappointments. And self-cultivation satisfied the need for a conceptual framework to justify entry into the workplace and marry the person of one's choice.

Not all articles encouraged women in Japan to explore the world of the professional working woman, find employment, and contemplate marrying for love; and not all readers championed these notions. Mass women's magazines took care not to endorse love marriages outright. Critical accounts written by prominent members of the community and parents, together with examples that detailed failed love-marriages, were also featured.

The responses to the Tokyo office surveys of 1922 and 1931 confirm that the expectations some young women harbored about the compatibility of work and self-cultivation showed a misguided naïveté. Statements like "When I first began to work, I was surprised to learn how different the real world was from the visions I entertained at school" are not unusual in any age or any country. Yet, the degree of discrimination women faced in the workplace should have made it clear that media-inspired fantasies were out of touch with reality. Young women's bitter complaint that even "in the train on the way to the job, men exhibit inappropriate behavior" reveals the blatant sexual curiosity with which men greeted professional working women. Indeed, sex-related issues and a general mistrust of women's ability to contribute constructively in the business world elicited pronouncements like, "people look with contempt on us professional working women." Other young women voiced similar objections: "The first time I heard the uncomplimentary comments made by the officials at the government office [*yakusho*], I was reduced to tears." Or, "I want the male employees to stop using all kinds of abusive language like idiot [*baka*] about us."[130] Harassment directed against professional working women dashed the romanticized ambitions of many young women to achieve self-development through working.

The most commonly voiced protests by professional working women, however, involved the physical exhaustion that accompanied long hours on the job. Fatigue prevented them from participating regularly in other forms of self-cultivation. Plans to take music lessons, read, or enjoy the conventional cultural pursuits of flower arrangement, tea ceremony, and calligraphy after work had to be curtailed. "At the end of a ten-hour day, all I want to do is go home as quickly as possible." "No sooner do I finish work and return home than I am ready to sleep." "The only recourse I have to recover from fatigue is sleep. Consequently, I am unable to help at home or accomplish anything to enhance my personal improvement [*shūyō*]." Such observations capture the frustration professional working women encountered.

Many women disliked the changes the workplace was making in them. "After I return home, I have no strength to do anything other than make small talk with the family. I feel a sense of disappointment and no longer have the desire to meet nice men." "I have lost the gentle heart that is a woman's by nature and my behavior lacks humility." "The longer I work, the tougher I become. I am losing the delicacy and softness of a woman, and there is no warmth left in me. To use extreme language, I am like a stone." "I have reached the point where it is easy for me to use rough language and be unkind to those around me."[131] Conflicts arose over women's personal expectations and the prevailing social representations of femininity. Confessional articles written by unemployed middle-class women were not necessarily examples of what professional working women were thinking, but such opinions influenced readers, and vice versa. If outside employment was to occupy a central site in women's lifestyles, attitudinal changes experienced on the job should have been welcomed as positive proof that women were anxious to perform challenging tasks. But even bosses measured women's capabilities by their subordination, and used it as a ploy for maintaining unequal wages. Reality indicated that women's future was still linked to marriage. As marriage defined the goals of education and work, it assumed an even larger position for women. With femininity a sign of virtue, the professional working woman's struggle within the masculine space of the workplace continued.

5

Hard Days Ahead

WOMEN ON THE MOVE

Among the changes that were occurring in Japanese society in the 1920s, those that affected the everyday lives of women, particularly of urban middle-class women, were perhaps the most irrefutable.[1] The transition these women underwent, though not unproblematic, was more than a superficial and temporary process. Yet, studies of modern Japan have largely ignored it. The virtual dismissal of their experiences may be attributed to the fluidity of their "new" middle-class identity, which was advanced by industrial capitalism and the growth of consumerism, the development of the media, and the expansion of higher education.

Yosano Akiko was one of the few intellectuals of her time who pinned her hopes on middle-class women. But the social commitment that she envisioned as a natural by-product of their "favored" status was nowhere in sight:

Within the ranks of the middle class [*chūryū kaikyū*], I know there are women whose eyes have been opened to new ways of thinking. There are even more educated women with high standards, good morals, and knowledge of society among these women than there were among the former "new women." If they take the initiative and pool their energies as a group, they could be several times more influential than the so-called "new women" and any movement they might have orchestrated. Instead they choose home and family. They lack the courage to become socially active. Because they do not have to worry about the bare necessities of life, they have time to participate in demonstrations. But out of deference to their husbands and relatives, they retreat into their own worlds. Their main concern is their families. If you ask whether or not they are able to realize their ideals, as far as I am concerned, they just compromise and continue to maintain the same old customs. Like other ordinary housewives, once in a while they might follow a fad, but usually they spend their days absentmindedly reflecting on nothing in particular.[2]

The middle-class women Yosano envisioned as harbingers of social change, like Yamakawa's factory workers, lacked the capacity to reform society. The economic stability these women enjoyed, though fragile in many cases, no doubt contributed to their conservatism and support for a lifestyle hostile to their personal needs. In Japan and in other parts of the world as well, a consciously designed, maternally centered socialization implanted in young women an array of traits including gentle consciences, frugality, temperance, and self-control. The bonds that linked these women, though not necessarily at the same point in time, were not only such values, but also the mundane details of their everyday lives.

The concept of public and private spheres has disguised many of the variations, complexities, and contradictions that were a part of the actual experiences of middle-class women. In Japan, for example, the "good wife and wise mother" philosophy of education empowered women to train young boys for occupational roles in the public sphere while they themselves were expected to remain within the carefully drawn social boundaries delineated by the private sphere of the home. Of course, not all middle-class women in Japan were satisfied with their lives. The confessional articles in mass women's magazines show that finding a suitable marriage partner, the strain of entering a home where a couple's wants were subordinated to those of the family, and the frustrations of having received an education that left one unprepared to deal with a domineering mother-in-law were among the most pressing problems young middle-class women faced. Some young women voiced their desire to enter the workforce, a decision that would take them outside the main unit of domesticity, if only temporarily.

Why were these emotional strains not sufficient to stimulate these women to organize and articulate their discontent as a group? While the reasons that prevent mobilization by disenfranchised populations are many, the concerns about the morality and ethics that dominated the patterns of middle-class women's lives in Japan during this period deserve special attention here. Subservience to men was considered one of women's greatest virtues, and maintaining the sanctity of the home contributed to sustaining this climate. The exaltation of patience and self-abnegation cloaked in the rhetoric of Confucian values continued to appear alongside new ideas permeating the lifestyle of middle-class women to a far greater extent than that of lower-class women.

The changes that were affecting women in general in Japan during the 1920s and that were implied by the consumer culture were not in themselves sufficient to alter middle-class women's lives. Economically, culturally, and even institutionally, the illusion of stability made it difficult for women to embrace the new or different. As I pointed out in chapter 4, a higher-school (*kōtō jogakkō*) education did not provide a direct route to economic independence. It was no easy task for the middle-class woman to defy a family who clung to the conventional expedients of the home. The growth of journalism, and especially mass women's magazines, which worked to create a new women's reading public, was but the first step on the road to change. Nevertheless, its significance cannot be overlooked, both from the standpoint of the reservations many middle-class women harbored vis-à-vis reform and also the actual conditions in society that prevented them from availing themselves of further opportunities for change.

The fact that numerically the middle class was becoming the dominant section of Japan's population meant that news of even the faintest sign of change that became manifest in society would spread to women throughout the country.[3] For the most part, the conspicuous changes involved urban women, most strikingly in Tokyo. Indeed, the most coveted places of employment for young women, department stores, were strictly an urban phenomenon.[4] Women in rural areas were more often bystanders. The rapid growth of journalism and the visual excitement offered by movies brought consumerism to more provincial areas of the country. But the knowledge that other young women were moving into society as professional working women or the yearning to become a professional working woman oneself was not always enough to trigger the actual move to the city.

The changes portended by the figures of the modern girl, the new type of housewife, and the professional working woman in the areas of public and private life were limited in scope. Of primary concern to most women was emotional fulfillment. The chance to exercise one's will in choosing a marriage partner and becoming an enlightened housewife, or the satisfaction a growing number of women's higher-school graduates gained from briefly joining the labor force as professional working women became vehicles for self-improvement. Holding a job was a way to learn about the real world, but it also, and more importantly, offered the chance to make women better people who were better situated for a happy married life. However, the reality was that the larger discourse of self-cultivation for the sake of marriage kept most women tethered to the home.

The modern girl, the housewife, and the professional working woman had neither the desire nor the intention to clash with the system in the 1920s. They shunned radical change. Had there been an organized woman's movement, they probably would not have joined it. The small-scale resistance these women conducted in the Taishō and early Shōwa periods focused on areas of life considered more private and individual. This is perhaps one of the main reasons why their challenges and changing attitudes and desires have remained largely undocumented. The very personal nature of these urban women's struggles, however, does not diminish the importance of the fledgling steps taken by women to map out new possibilities for self-fulfillment, or the role consumerism played as an agent of change.

During the 1920s, when consumerism flourished, intellectuals created their own idealized image of the modern girl in the guise of a politically and socially aware woman unencumbered by conventional norms, although they realized that middle-class women were interested only in private concerns and rarely became involved in broader social issues. In the words of socialist Yamakawa Kikue:

> Young women today put a high value on love marriages. But they are interested only in personal issues and have no social perspective, never demanding economic independence or trying to become independent beings in their own right. If they attempt to change the traditional relationship that exists between husbands, wives, and families by merely adding the element of romantic love to it and not reforming the economic structure of society, then the changes that occur will be cosmetic change. It is like changing one's hairstyle from hair pulled

back in a bun [*shimada*] to a short cut that barely covers the ears [*mimi kakushi*].[5]

Yamakawa's criticism of women for choosing love and personal fulfillment over social and political concerns was not unlike the criticisms other intellectuals directed against the modern girl when they labeled her "hedonistic" (*kyōrakuteki*) and "impulsive" (*setsunateki*).

As Time Goes On: Reflections

If the concept of society (*shakai*) is extended to include the state (*kokka*), a parallel may well be drawn between the thought prevalent in the 1920s and that of the 1930s. The emphasis in the 1930s rested on loyalty to the state and was symbolized by such slogans as "dispense with frivolities" (*kyōraku haishi,* 1937) and "sacrifice one's personal interest for the good of the state" (*messhi hōkō,* 1939). These slogans reflected the criticisms intellectuals voiced about women in the 1920s for their lack of social perspective.[6] Writing in 1959, Hashikawa Bunzō pointed out that even the Marxists were not concerned with the development of a strong ego that would enable individuals to distance themselves from and offer resistance to Japan's family system, which supported the notion of a family-state under fascism.[7] From the Marxists on the left to the militarists on the right, all placed a higher value on social change than on the individual.

From the late 1930s onward, women seeking employment in the cities were commonplace. In contrast to 1927, when the Tokyo City Employment Bureau opened an office to provide counseling for "intellectuals" (Tokyo-shi chishiki kaikyū shōkaijo) and a total of 275 women voiced the hope of becoming professional working women, as many as 4,579 women registered for assistance in 1931. Three years later that figure had jumped to 18,207.[8] As war fever within Japan heightened in the wake of the Marco Polo Bridge incident (July 1937) and the outbreak of full-scale hostilities, the number of young women taking jobs outside the home increased.[9]

Comments made at a roundtable discussion sponsored by *Shufu no tomo* in 1938 on the responsibility of professional working women during the "national crisis" reflect the sentiments of single middle-class women from relatively economically secure families. "Having a job has become something of a fad." "During this time of national emergency when everyone around you is so wrought up, it just doesn't feel right to stay at home." "We have to understand that this is the age we are living in." "In any event, working is important before getting married."[10] A female social critic observed: "Making money is not our sole aim. In wartime, helping the country by our efforts in the workplace is essential. If the war continues indefinitely, even [married] women will have to get out and work."[11] By the late 1930s, middle-class women's link to established conventional Confucian ethics no doubt made them more receptive to the government's fascist rhetoric.

War fever fanned by organized networks like the National Women's Defense Association (Kokubō fujinkai, 1932) as well as government-orchestrated campaigns, however, were not the only reason for the increase in working women in the late 1930s. The prolonged economic recession was affecting the lives of more and more young women. In contrast to earlier times, fewer than 10 percent of those aspiring to become professional working women still spoke of work as a form of social training in preparation for marriage. Women readily admitted: "Economic hardships are forcing us to join the work front [*shokugyō sensen*]."[12]

By 1939, practicality, not glamour, dictated women's job choices.[13] Although department stores continued to need female sales clerks, the image of the department store sales clerk (*depātō gāru*) that had epitomized the dreams of the professional working woman in the 1920s and early 1930s had now lost its luster. No longer satisfied with long hours and low wages with few benefits, as they formerly had been, these women now preferred office work. In contrast to the eagerness with which professional working women voluntarily entered the workforce with the flourishing of consumerism in the 1920s, economic conditions, and to a lesser extent war fever, drove most young women from their homes into the workplace in the late 1930s.

Just as the personal incentive to become professional working women changed in the late 1930s, so too did the discussions that centered on the question of sexuality in the workplace. From the outset, the move of women into the working arena formerly dominated by men had raised eyebrows and sparked heated debates. While the "chastity problem" (*teisō mondai*) remained a contentious issue, the growing number of working women now meant that the prospect of romance and love in the office was no longer a mere possibility but a distinct reality.

A very few companies attempted to recruit young women by depicting their firms as places to fulfill the hope for a love marriage. Sumitomo Trust and Banking Company (Sumitomo shintaku), with offices nationwide, alleged: "Join our bank with the intention of finding your future mate." And Japan Life Insurance Company (Nihon seimei), a leading insurance firm, asserted: "Our company encourages staff marriages."[14] Most companies that enlisted women employees, however, declared unequivocally that love in the workplace was taboo. According to the results of a questionnaire sent to the personnel managers of seventeen large companies and published in the March 1938 issue of *Fujin kōron*, only one company denied having interfered in employee love affairs. The other sixteen firms categorically banned romantic liaisons: if discovered, both parties faced dismissal.[15] Coupled with the fear that expressions of sexuality would induce a breakdown in company morals was an underlying concern that such behavior violated social norms.

Although young women in the early twentieth century seriously contemplated love marriages, this did not signify approval from the state. An ethics textbook prepared for female high school students and widely used from the time of its first printing in 1921 through the war years instructed women that "the custom in our country is to discuss marriage with our parents and to comply with their wishes," and that "going out and fraternizing freely is not appropriate behavior for young women from good families."[16] In light of this generally accepted idea, employers considered it their responsibility to assume the role of surrogate parent and "protect" their female employees from the dangers posed by romantic involvement. Companies that did not risked losing both parental trust and social credibility.

Even parents whose daughters joined the ranks of professional working women in the 1930s as a form of social preparation (*shūyō*) for marriage did not consider a marriage that had its roots in the workplace a "proper" marriage. The personnel manager of the Meiji Confectionery Company (Meiji seika) explained his company's policy in the aforecited questionnaire: "The reason we exercise such strict control over female employees is to ensure their future happiness. . . . As a result, our company has a reputation for hiring young women whom anyone would be pleased to recommend as prospective marriage partners."[17] The "modern" ideal of marriage that women in the 1920s and 1930s turned to for legitimization of their call for a new identity and life-style was a short-lived dream. Love marriages were still a rare com-modity in the late 1930s. The quantitative increase in professional work-ing women did not afford women greater independence in choosing their marriage partners; the strict control exercised by employers en-sured the exact opposite, and it was a position that parents endorsed.

By the late 1930s, it was no longer the intellectuals who demonstrated sharp insight or attempted to dominate the new culture; it was the state under the leadership of the military. Conspicuous aspects of urban cul-ture—dance, dress, movies, and popular songs—all came under state control.[18] Restrictions hampered consumerism and stymied the flow of Western culture. As could be expected, the media came under strict surveillance from the government censors.[19] In the new political and economic climate, consumerism was no longer a viable lifestyle for women. The move toward ultranationalism had begun.

In 1940, in compliance with the state's policy to increase the popu-lation, marriage became women's duty carried out for the good of the country (kekkon suru koto ga naniyori no gohōkō). This policy led to a tem-porary decline in the trend toward love marriages as official doctrine left no room for individualism in marriage.[20] "We can't think anymore about marriage being for our personal happiness," Shufu no tomo told its readers. "A good marriage is one that will help strengthen the state."[21]

The changes in lifestyle that had accompanied the growth of con-sumerism in the 1920s provided the impetus for the emergence of fig-ures like the modern girl, the housewife, and the professional working woman. In the postwar years, the motivation for the changes surround-ing marriage and divorce, for example, were closely bound up with the Occupation reforms. Japan's defeat in World War II brought an end to the family system that had legally restricted women from the time of the promulgation of the Meiji Civil Code. Women's historian Itō Yasuko pointed out that while "on point of principle, women supported the abolition of the family system [ie seido], their main reason was that they saw it as an impediment to the realization of love marriages, their sole concern."[22]

Further possibilities for resistance opened up during the Occupation. On orders from General Douglas MacArthur, supreme commander for the Allied Powers, reforms concerned with raising the status of women received top priority—a decision that jolted Japanese society.[23] In accordance with the new Constitution of 1946, the revised Civil Code of 1947, and other government regulations, women gained voting privileges, had the right to become property owners, and enjoyed equal access to the family inheritance.[24] Former minister of foreign affairs Shigemitsu Aoi, who was present on the uss Missouri at the time of Japan's surrender, spent five years in Tokyo's Sugamo Prison for war crimes. Although he had never expressed an interest in women's issues during his term of office, he called the Occupation reforms "eye-opening for the Japanese people" and cited those reforms that concerned women as the most radical.[25]

It is thus interesting that in surveys taken in the years following the war, women's suffrage was invariably cited in response to the question "What was most significant about the reforms for women?" In a 1950 survey that targeted farm women, 49 percent mentioned voting rights, 2.2 percent referred to the abolition of the family system, and a mere 0.8 percent listed freedom to marry the person of one's choice when asked "In what way did the new laws change women the most?" In a 1955 survey, 22.3 percent said the right to vote and 11.4 percent gave freedom to marry the person of one's choice when asked "What contributed most to the change in the position of women after the war?"[26] Indeed, in the April 1946 election, thirty-nine women won seats in the lower house of the Diet; but the number of women dwindled to fifteen in 1947 and twelve in 1949 and 1952, and then dropped to nine in 1953.[27] Thus, despite the fact that suffrage topped the list of significant changes for women in attitudinal surveys, the records show that the most conspicuous change for women resulting from the postwar reforms may have been the increase in love marriages.[28]

When one left the realm of politics and moved into the everyday world where problems relating to marriage and family emerged, however, the confusion wrought by Article 24 was apparent. The article stated that "marriage shall be based on the mutual consent of both sexes and shall be maintained through mutual cooperation with the equal rights of husband and wife as a basis." Although Japan has a long history of campaigning for women's political rights, and feminist activities date back to the Meiji period, political activists often ignored love and marriage, considering these private and personal matters. The con-

TABLE 3   Marriage Configurations in Postwar Japan

	1942–1947 (%)	1947–1952 (%)	1952–1957 (%)	1957–1962 (%)	1962–1967 (%)
Love marriages	15.8	28.5	34.7	38.2	46.3
Arranged marriages	65.2	57.0	55.0	52.3	47.8
Other	19.0	14.5	10.3	9.5	5.9

Source: Based on figures for the 1978 survey on birthrate from the Institute of Population, Ministry of Welfare, and quoted in Itō Yasuko, *Nihon josei seikatsu shi,* pp. 27–28.

stitutional changes did not necessarily make it easy to realize a love marriage.

The figures in table 3 indicate that it took approximately twenty years for the annual rate of love marriages to reach that of arranged marriages (*miai*). Inasmuch as the reforms were not the result of a spontaneous movement, how women would react to and deal with their new status was a matter for concern. The new status did not remove women from the social and familial webs that entangled their lives. In 1955, almost ten years after the promulgation of the revised Civil Code, more than half the participants in a series of roundtable discussions dealing with love and marriage spoke of love marriages as their ideal. But some young women doubted that it was actually possible to live lives different from those of their mothers.[29] One participant who shared this opinion said: "I can't imagine that passion can assure me a happily married life."[30] For several women involved in these discussions, love and marriage remained two different realms. Frightened by the risks of a love marriage, one young woman remarked: "We Japanese have no tradition of love. We have never been taught what love is all about. Won't we fail?"[31] Despite the ideal of love marriages held by many young women, love was not necessarily conceived of as part of their everyday existence, and therefore was not a prerequisite for marriage.

That is not to say, however, that there was no optimism regarding the possibility of achieving a love marriage among the participants in the 1955 discussions, which included salesgirls, office clerks, young women employed in the field of banking, and beauticians. A feisty young woman from Osaka remarked: "These days women believe they should be finding their own husbands. Married life is long. Even if a part of us feels that we should give in to our parents' demands, in the long run we are bound to feel discontent. I know we will regret our decisions."[32] Another young woman agreed wholeheartedly and said: "I don't want to be forced into marriage."[33] And yet another participant added: "In the old days *omiai* [arranged marriage] was the only way to marry. The parties involved did not decide for themselves and as a result they entered into marriage reluctantly. But we are the ones who are getting married, and personally, I hope to be able to find my partner at work."[34] All of these comments reflect the importance of marriage for young women and a desire to exercise their own wills.

Nevertheless, it was not easy even for working women to meet a suitable mate. When the war broke out, most of the eligible young men were drafted. Young women of marrying age at that time were considered too old when peace came and were forced to bear the name *sanjū musume* (thirty years old and still a miss). Although many held jobs and expressed satisfaction with their work, one woman who participated in a roundtable discussion on the topic sponsored by *Shufu no tomo* in 1950 spoke for the group when she said: "I love my office and I adore my work. In fact, I like it so much that even if I marry, I would want to continue working. But true happiness for a woman comes only from marriage. That is where the joy of living is found."[35] In fact, women did not know how to go about meeting men after the war. "How someone in my position can find an opportunity to meet men is beyond my comprehension," one woman remarked.[36] Although the postwar reforms provided for coeducational schooling, the custom of dating did not exist and no single word existed to refer to the practice of men and women socializing. Author Mishima Yukiko defined the problem: "Wouldn't you agree that Japanese people have no social graces when they get together? They have no idea how to act with the opposite sex. Even when they walk together, they look comical. Before marriage, a woman doesn't know what it is to have a male friend, let alone think of love and marriage developing naturally out of such a friendship."[37]

Just as the changes affecting women in the 1920s were characterized by the promise of rationalization of everyday life and changing attitudes toward love and marriage, both symbols of modernity, so, too, was the transformation taking place for women after World War II.

The promise of a rationalized home and a solid middle-class identity often referred to in the 1920s finally fell within the grasp of the post–World War II housewife. Sociologist Ishikawa Hiroyoshi's analysis of Japanese society in the early 1950s evokes Hirabayashi Hatsunosuke's vision for women in the 1920s:

> The electrification of the home was what first influenced the housewife's way of thinking. Because time-consuming tasks such as cooking, washing, and cleaning were shortened as a result of electrification, the housewife began to enjoy "leisure time" [yoka] or at least a degree of latitude in her life. . . . As a member of the new "leisure class" [yoka kaikyū], the housewife used this "leisure time" to move into society and enter the labor force. If nothing else, she was able to get out of the narrow confines of the home and broaden her horizons. After the war, the reform of the civil code brought an end to the family system, and that no doubt was related to women having more free time.[38]

Some doubted that things had really changed. Itō Yasuko's postwar criticism of Japanese women as being backward closely resembles the prewar position of feminist Yamakawa Kikue: "The problem is that Japanese women command a low position in society, have no vision of the world around them, are unable to make rational decisions, are not moved to action by politics, and mentally they remain confined to the home."[39] Despite these intellectuals' frustrations over women's purported backwardness and lack of political and economic awareness, the alacrity with which the postwar reforms were *accepted* in Japan show that the changes in women that started in the 1920s with the modern girl, the self-motivated middle-class housewife, and the professional working woman, and were symbolized by the ideals of work, love, and the marriage of one's choice, were not destined to remain in hibernation.

Notes

Prologue: Women and the Reality of the Everyday

1 Stuart Hall, "The Meaning of New Times," in *Stuart Hall: Critical Dialogues in Cultural Studies*, ed. David Morley and Kuan-Hsing Chen (London: Routledge, 1996), p. 226.
2 Ozu demonstrates that the stereotype of a single type of traditional woman can no longer apply. A similar reference to multidimensional women can be found in Tanizaki Junichirō's *Sasameyuki* (The Makioka Sisters, 1943–47), a novel set in the 1930s about the compelling dispositions of four sisters. Yukiko, the "traditional" sister, shows a passion for French movies, while Taiko, portrayed as a rebel, takes up the profession of Japanese doll making.
3 *Ozu Yasujirō sakuhinshū*, vol. 4 (Tokyo: Rippū shobō, 1984), pp. 109–10. For a discussion of the similarities between Ozu's *Tokyo Story* and Leo McCarey's *Make Way for Tomorrow*, see Arthur Nolletti Jr., "Ozu's *Tokyo Story* and the 'Recasting' of McCarey's *Make Way for Tomorrow*," in *Ozu's Tokyo Story*, ed. David Desser (Cambridge: Cambridge University Press, 1997), pp. 25–34.
4 *Tokyo Story* is reminiscent of Lidia Curti's argument that "fact and fiction are different but both crucial aspects of the same reality." Lidia Curti, "What Is Real and What Is Not: Female Fabulations in Cultural Analysis," in *Cultural Studies*, ed. Lawrence Grossberg, Cary Nelson, and Paul Treichler (New York: Routledge, 1992), p. 142.
5 Ishigaki Ayako's *Onna wa jiyū de aru* (Tokyo: Bungei shunjū, 1955) was one of many guides advising women about life in a democratic society.
6 Inoue Kiyoshi, *Nihon joseishi* (Tokyo: San'ichi shobō, 1948).
7 Tanaka Sumiko, *Josei kaihō no shisō to kōdō—senzen-hen* (Tokyo: Jiji tsūshin, 1975); Ide Fumiko, *Hiratsuka Raichō—kindai to shinpi* (Tokyo: Shinchōsha, 1987); Horiba Kiyoko, *Seitō no jidai—Hiratsuka Raichō to atarashii onnatachi* (Tokyo: Iwanami shoten, 1988).
8 Maruyama Masao, *Nihon no shisō* (Tokyo: Iwanami shoten, 1961); Maru-

yama Masao, *Gendai Nihon no seiji to kōdō* (Tokyo: Miraisha, 1964); Ōtsuka Hisao, *Shūkyō kaikaku to kindai shakai* (Tokyo: Misuzu shobō, 1948).

9 Murakami Nobuhiko, "Joseishi kenkyū no kadai to tenbō," *Shisō*, no. 549 (March 1970): 94.

10 Further analysis of this debate appears in *Shiryō joseishi ronsō*, no. 3, ed. Kosho Yukiko (Tokyo: Domesu shuppan, 1987), p. 76; for Irokawa's and Kanō's views, see Irokawa Daikichi (*Fujin kōron*, 1975) and Kanō Masanao (*Ajia josei koryūshi kenkyū*, October 1975), in ibid., p. 288. For an insightful argument on people's history (*minshūshi*), see Yasumaru Yoshio, "*Hōhō*" *toshite no shisōshi* (Tokyo: Azekura shobō, 1996).

11 A good example is *Nihon joseishi—gendai*, vol. 5, ed. Joseishi sōgō kenkyū-kai (Tokyo: Daigaku shuppankai, 1982).

12 Mitsuda Kiyoko, "Kindaiteki, boseikan no juyō to henka—'kyōiku sura hahaoya' kara 'ryōsai kenbo'e," in *Bosei o tō—rekishiteki hensen*, vol. 2, ed. Wakita Haruko (Kyoto: Jinbun shoin, 1985), pp. 100–129; Koyama Shizuko, *Ryōsai kenbo to iu kihan* (Tokyo: Keisō shobō, 1991); Kiyonaga Takashi, *Ryōsai kenbo no tanjō* (Tokyo: Chikuma shobō, 1995); Kathleen Uno, "The Origins of 'Good Wife, Wise Mother' in Modern Japan," in *Japanische Frauengeschichte(n)*, ed. Erich Pauer and Regine Mathias (Marburg: Forderverein Marburger Japan-Reihe, 1955); Ulrike Wöhr, "Early Feminist Ideas on Motherhood in Japan—Challenging the Official Ideal of 'Good Wife, Wise Mother,'" *Hiroshima Journal of International Studies* 2 (1996): 6–36.

13 *Nihon josei seikatsushi—kindai*, vol. 4, ed. Wakita Haruko (Kyoto: Jinbun shoin, 1990), preface. Other studies that show the progress being made in women's studies include Yamada Masahiro, *Kindai kazoku no yukue—Kazoku to aijō no paradokusu* (Tokyo: Shinyōsha, 1994); *Jendā no Nihonshi*, vols. 1 and 2, ed. Wakita Haruko and S. B. Hanley (Tokyo: Tokyo daigaku shuppan, 1995); *Onna to otoko no jikū—Nihon joseishi saikō*, ed. Okuda Atsuko (Tokyo: Fujiwara shoten), esp. vols. 5 (1995) and 6 (1996); Shinozuka Eiko, *Josei to kazoku—Kindai no jitsuzō, nijū seiki no Nihon*, vol. 8 (Tokyo: Yomiuri shinbunsha, 1995); Muta Kazue, *Senryaku toshite no kazoku* (Tokyo: Shinyōsha, 1996); Ōkoshi Aiko, *Kindai Nihon no jendā* (Tokyo: San'ichi shobō, 1997); Koyama Shizuko, *Katei no seisei to josei no kokuminka* (Tokyo: Keisō shobō, 1999); Kaneko Sachiko, *Kindai Nihon joseiron no keifu* (Tokyo: Fuji shuppan, 1999); Fukawa Kiyoshi, *Kindai Nihon—Josei rinri shisō no nagara* (Tokyo: Ōtsuki shoten, 2000); Nishikawa Yūko, *Kindai kokka to kazoku moderu* (Tokyo: Yoshikawa kōbunkan, 2000); *Onna no bunka, Kindai Nihon bunkaron*, vol. 8, ed. Aoki Tamotsu, Kawamoto Saburō, Tsutsui Kiyotada, Mikuriya Takashi, and Tamanori Tetsuo (Tokyo: Iwanami shoten, 2000).

14 Refer to Harry Harootunian, *History's Disquiet: Modernity, Cultural Practice, and the Question of Everyday Life* (New York: Columbia University

Press, 2000); and Harootunian, *Overcome by Modernity: History, Culture, and Community in Interwar Japan* (Princeton: Princeton University Press, 2000). These are landmark studies that put the everyday in the broad perspective that it deserves. See Harry Harootunian, "Introduction: A Sense of an Ending and the Problem of Taishō," in *Japan in Crisis: Essays on Taishō Democracy,* ed. Bernard S. Silberman and H. D. Harootunian (Princeton: Princeton University Press, 1974), pp. 3–28; Sheldon Garon, *Molding Japanese Minds: The State in Everyday Life* (Princeton: Princeton University Press, 1997).

15 Judith Butler, *Gender Trouble: Feminism and the Subversion of Identity* (New York: Routledge, 1990), p. 4.

16 See Carol Gluck, Introduction to *Shōwa: The Japan of Hirohito,* ed. Carol Gluck and Stephen R. Graubard (New York: W. W. Norton, 1992), p. 6.

17 Of interest here are Andreas Huyssen, *After the Great Divide: Modernism, Mass Culture, Postmodernism* (Bloomington: Indiana University Press, 1986); and Raymond Williams, *The Politics of Modernism: Against the New Conformists,* ed. and intro. Tony Pinkney (London: Verso, 1993). Also see *Modernism—1890–1930,* ed. Malcolm Brady and James McFarlane (London: Penguin Books, 1976); Matei Calinescu, *The Five Faces of Modernity: Modernism, Avant-Garde, Decadence, Kitsch, Postmodernism* (Durham: Duke University Press, 1987). For Daniel Bell's analysis, see "The Double Bind of Modernity," in *The Cultural Contradictions of Capitalism* (New York: Basic Books, 1978), pp. 46–54. Harootunian's *History's Disquiet* and *Overcome by Modernity* are the most helpful sources from my perspective.

18 Astradur Eysteinsson provides a solid discussion of modernism art and literature in *The Concept of Modernism* (Ithaca: Cornell University Press, 1990).

19 On the ideological and cultural underpinnings of modernism, refer to Harootunian, *Overcome by Modernity,* pp. xx–xxvi.

20 Natalie Zemon Davis, in *The Return of Martin Guerre* (Cambridge: Harvard University Press, 1983), also addressed the question of choice when she asked: "Did individual villagers ever try to fashion their lives in unusual and unexpected ways?" (p. 1).

21 *Nihon modanizumu no kenkyū—shisō, seikatsu, bunka,* ed. Minami Hiroshi (Tokyo: Burēn shuppan, 1982); *Shōwa bunka—1925–1945,* ed. Minami Hiroshi (Tokyo: Keisō shobō, 1987); *Kindai shomin seikatsushi,* vols. 1–10, ed. Minami Hiroshi et al. (Tokyo: San'ichi shobō, 1984–88). A helpful collection of literary materials is *Shiryō shihon bunka no modanizumu—bungaku jidai no shosō,* ed. Sekii Mitsuo (Tokyo: Yumani shobō, 1997). Japanese scholars like Mitsuda, Koyama, and Sechiyama Kaku (*Higashi Azia no kafuchōsei —jendā no hikaku shakaigaku* [Tokyo: Keisō shobō, 1996]), and Western scholars such as Uno and Wöhr, in an attempt to clarify by whom and in what way *ryōsai kenbo* emerged, have broached new questions for histori-

ans. Did most women accept this new ideological construct because it was in keeping with already ingrained Confucian thought, or was there resistance on the part of women to submitting to an ideology that contravened other ingrained values? Relying on a social historical approach for understanding such questions, *Recreating Japanese Women, 1600–1945,* ed. Gail Lee Bernstein (Berkeley: University of California Press, 1991), is the first history of Japanese women in English to go beyond feminist concerns and deal with nonelite women in the early modern and modern periods. Recent research—again, I refer to Harootunian's *History's Disquiet* and *Overcoming Modernity*—fill an important void in our knowledge of modernism and the everyday.

22 Nancy Cott, "The Modern Woman of the 1920s, American Style," in *A History of Women,* vol. 5: *Toward a Cultural Identity in the Twentieth Century,* ed. Françoise Thébaud (Cambridge: Belknap Press of Harvard University Press, 1994), p. 77.

23 Among the three modern women dealt with in this study, chronologically the housewife appears first in modern literature. However, the midnineteenth- and early-twentieth-century woman who bore the appellation *"shufu"* resembled the 1920s housewife in name only. Thus, it is more appropriate to begin this study with an analysis of the modern girl.

Chapter One
The Emergence of Agency: Women and Consumerism

1 *The Sex of Things: Gender and Consumption in Historical Perspective,* ed. Victoria de Grazia with Ellen Furlough (Berkeley: University of California Press, 1996), p. 1.

2 On Hiratsuka Raichō and meditation, see Sasaki Hideaki, *"Atarashii onna" no tōrai: Hiratsuka Raichō to Sōseki* (Nagoya: Nagoya daigaku shuppankai, 1994), pp. 120–27.

3 *Yomiuri shinbun,* "Atarashii onna," May 5, 1902–June 13, 1902.

4 There are many excellent studies on the new woman. See, for example, Ruth Brandon, *The New Women and the Old Men: Love, Sex and the Woman Question* (New York: W. W. Norton, 1990), pp. 3, 11, 22, 29; Vivien Gardner, Introduction to *The New Woman and Her Sisters: Feminism and Theater 1850–1914,* ed. Vivien Gardner and Susan Rutherford (Ann Arbor: University of Michigan Press, 1992), pp. 1–6. See Elaine Showalter, "New Women," in her *Sexual Anarchy: Gender and Culture at the Fin de Siècle* (New York: Viking Penguin, 1990).

5 "Atarashi onna tokushū," *Chūō kōron,* February 1913. Also see Hiratsuka Raichō, *Genshi josei wa taiyō de atta, Hiratsuka Raichō jiden,* vol. 2 (Tokyo: Ōtsuki shoten, 1971), pp. 422–24. For a discussion of Matsui Sumako and

the new woman, see Ayako Kano, *Acting Like a Woman in Modern Japan: Theater, Gender, and Nationalism* (New York: Palgrave, 2000), pp. 123–82.

For further insight on the new woman in Japan, see Yamada Keiko, "Atarashii onna," in *Onna no imēji, Kōza joseigaku*, vol. 1, ed. Joseigaku kenkyūkai (Tokyo: Keisō shobō, 1984), pp. 210–34; Arai Tomio, "Bosei ishiki no mezame—'Seitō' no hitobito," in *Bosei o tō—rekishiteki henyō*, pp. 130–57; *"Seitō" o yomu*, ed. Shin feminizumu hihyō no kai (Tokyo: Gakugei shorin, 1987); Muta Kazue, " 'Ryōsai kenbo' shisō no ura omote," in *Onna no bunka*, vol. 8, ed. Aoki, Kawamoto, et al., pp. 24–45; Ulrike Wöhr, "Mō hitotsu no *Seito*-onnatachi no rentai o mezashista zasshi *Shinjin fujin*," in *Nihon joseishi saikō-kindai*, vol. 5, ed. Okuda Akiko (Tokyo: Fujiware-shoten, 1995), pp. 312–34.

6 Henrik Ibsen's *A Doll's House* (1879) was first translated into Japanese by Shimamura Hōgetsu. See Henrik Ibsen, *A Doll's House* (unabridged republication of anonymous, undated English translation, New York: Dover, 1992).

7 Dorothy Day maintains that in the United States, the new woman's "coming had been announced, heralded, and denounced since 1900. By 1920 her numbers included veteran reformers, victorious suffragists, powerful athletes, pioneering scientists, Marxists, bohemians, and aviators." But she, too, "was joined by an even more troubling version in the 1920s—the flapper." Dorothy Day, *Setting a New Course: American Women in the 1920s* (Boston: G. K. Hall, 1987), pp. 29, 31.

Atina Grossmann calls the German "new woman" a political tool of the state in the 1920s. See Atina Grossmann, "The New Woman and the Rationalization of Sexuality in Weimar Germany," in *Powers of Desire: The Politics of Sexuality*, ed. Ann Snitow, Christine Stansell, and Sharon Thompson (New York: Monthly Review Press, 1983), p. 154.

8 Some wives actually took their grievances against their husbands to court, and in some cases, though few, the higher courts overturned verdicts in favor of women. One case involved a divorcée's suit against her former husband for having contracted syphilis while still married to her. Here the Supreme Court overturned the original verdict. See Tomotsugu Jutarō, *Mezurashii saiban jitsuwa* (Tokyo: Hōrei bunka kyōkai, 1932), pp. 126–29. However, the more common view can be found in a December 1935 supplement (*furoku*). See "Important Tips for New Brides and New Grooms" (Hanayome hanamuko hitsuyō chō), appended to the magazine *Fujin kurabu*. Young women, many of whom contracted sexual diseases from their husbands, were urged to forget past transgressions and remember that the basis for "true love" is forgiveness. "Sex Education for Young Women before Marriage" (Yomeiri mae no musume ni taisuru seikyōiku no shikata), pp. 178–86.

9 Barbara Sato takes up this issue in " 'Sōgōkasareta' zasshi ni okeru jendā—

no hyōshō—*Taiyō* 'Kateiran' o megutte," in *Nihon kenkyū*, no. 17 (Tokyo: Kadokawa shoten, 1997), pp. 276–79. Also see Barbara Sato, "Sōkan 'kinji no fujin mondai' to katei no rinen," in *Zasshi 'Taiyō' to kokumin bunka no keisei*, ed. Sadami Suzuki (Kyoto: Shibunkaku shuppan, 2001), pp. 554–67. For more on the family, see Muta, *Senryaku toshite no kazoku—Kindai kokumin kokka keisei to josei*, esp. section 2, "Kindai Nihon no kazoku saikō," pp. 51–77; Ueno Chizuko, *Kindai kazoku no seiritsu to shūen* (Tokyo: Iwanami shoten, 1994), esp. pp. 69–124; 'Kazoku' no shakaigaku, *Iwanami kōza gendai shakaigaku*, vol. 19, ed. Ueno Chizuko et al. (Tokyo: Iwanami shoten, 1996), esp. the selections by Ueno Chizuko, Ochiai Emiko, Muta Kazue, Nishikawa Yūko, and Sechiyama Kaku.

10 Sakai Toshihiko, *Katei zasshi*, reprint, vols. 1–5 (Tokyo: Ryūkeishosha, 1982). One of the most representative discussions of the home at the time appears in the family column (1895–1903) of *Taiyō*, the most widely read general magazine in the late Meiji period.

11 For a discussion of morality and frugality advocated by the Meiji state, see the 1908 edict, Boshin sōsho. Carol Gluck, *Japan's Modern Myths: Ideology in the Late Meiji Period* (Princeton: Princeton University Press, 1985), pp. 92, 176–77, 273. Also see Ōkoshi, *Kindai Nihon no jendā—Gendai Nihon no shisōteki kadai o tō*, esp. pp. 77–124.

12 See Paul Glennie, "Consumption within Historical Studies," in *Acknowledging Consumption*, ed. Daniel Miller (London: Routledge, 1995), p. 185. Andreas Huyssen questions "the notion which gained ground during the 19th century that mass culture is somehow associated with women, while real, authentic culture remains the prerogative of men." Huyssen, *After the Great Divide*, p. 47.

13 Richard Ohmann, *Selling Culture: Magazines, Markets, and Class at the Turn of the Century* (London: Verso, 1996), p. 172.

14 Ibid., p. 170.

15 Kitada Akihiro, *Kōkoku no tanjo* (Tokyo: Iwanami shoten, 2000), pp. 144–46.

16 See Hiratsuka Raichō, "Nora san ni" (*Seitō*, January 1912), in *Hiratsuka Raichō chosakushū*, vol. 1, pp. 79–85; Ikuta Chōkō and Honma Hisao, *Shakai mondai jyūnikō* (Tokyo: Shinchōsha, 1919), pp. 314–20; Suzuki Bunshirō, *Fujin mondai no hanashi: Asahi jōshiki kōza*, vol. 9 (Tokyo: Asahi shinbunsha, 1929), pp. 98–105; Kiyosawa Rei, "Gendai no shokugyō fujin no sho mondai," in *Fujin kōron daigaku: fujin shokugyōhen* (Tokyo: Chūō kōronsha, 1931), pp. 55–57. Also see Yamada Yoshie, Torii Toshiko, Yoshizawa Chieko, and Nakai Yoshiko, " 'Seitō' ni kakawatta hitobito," in *Taishōki no josei zasshi*, ed. Kindai josei bunkashi kenkyūkai (Tokyo: Ōzorasha, 1996), pp. 149–222.

Yamakawa recalls this incident in her later article "Fujin wa kawaru," written for *Nihon kokumin* (1932), using examples of the new woman to focus attention on the power of the media. Reprinted in *Yamakawa Kikue shū*, vol. 6, pp. 32–33.

17 Tokutomi Sohō, "Seinen no fuki," in *Dairoku nichiyō kōdan* (Tokyo: Minyū-sha, 1905).

18 See *Jogaku zasshi* (reprint, Tokyo: Rinsen shoten, 1984); Fujita Yoshimi, *Meiji jogakkō no sekai* (Tokyo: Seieisha, 1984), pp. 50–78; Harada Kyōko, "Iwamoto Yoshiharu no fujin kaihō shisō to sono hen'yō," in *Josei kaihō no shisō to kōdō*, pp. 65–68; Inoue Kiyoshi, *Shinpan Nihon joseishi*, p. 229.

19 Fukuzawa Yukichi, *On Japanese Women: Selected Works*, trans. and ed. Eiichi Kiyoka (Tokyo: University of Tokyo Press, 1988), pp. 7, 12, 15, 17, 21, 24. Also see Nakamura Toshiko, "Bunmei ni okeru josei to kazoku," in *Fukuzawa Yukichi: Bunmei to shakai kōzō* (Tokyo: Sōbunsha, 2000), pp. 124–72.

20 See Shimoda Utako, *Nihon no josei* (Tokyo: Jitsugyō no Nihonsha, 1912), pp. 569–76; *Tsudajuku rokujūnenshi* (Tokyo: Tsudajuku daigaku shuppan, 1960), pp. 35, 61; Naruse Jinzō, "Kyōiku shoken" (1911), in *Naruse Jinzō chosakushū*, vol. 2 (Tokyo: Nihon joshi daigaku, 1956), pp. 102–6.

On the role of Christian missionaries in the development of modern educational facilities for women, see Hiratsuka Matsunori, *Joshi kyōikushi—jinbutsu chūshin ni* (Tokyo: Teikoku chihō gyosei gakkai, 1965), esp. pp. 7–53; also see Chino Yōichi, *Kindai Nihon fujin kyōikushi—taiseinai fujin dantai no keisei katei o chūshin ni* (Tokyo: Domesu shuppan, 1979), pp. 56–70. In English, see Ann M. Harrington, "Women and Higher Education in the Japanese Empire (1869–1945)," *Journal of Asian History,* no. 21 (February 1987): 170.

21 On the late Meiji reform societies, see Kaneko, *Kindai Nihon joseiron no keifu*, pp. 66–86. In English, see Sharon L. Sievers, *Flowers in Salt* (Stanford: Stanford University Press, 1983), pp. 89–103. Most women active in welfare organizations came from well-to-do upper-class households.

22 For a look at Yosano Akiko through her poetry, see Steve Rabson, "Yosano Akiko on War: To Give One's Life or Not—a Question of Which War," *Journal of the Association of Teachers of Japanese* 25, no. 1 (1991): 45–74. Also see Kōchi Nobuko, *Yosano Akiko—Shōwaki o chūshin ni* (Tokyo: Domesu shuppan, 1993), pp. 12–19. The complete *Teihon Yosano Akiko zenshū,* 20 vols. (Tokyo: Kōdansha, 1980), and the *Hiratsuka Raichō chosakushū,* 10 vols. (Tokyo: Ōtsuki shoten, 1983), are indispensable sources.

23 Good examples are Sakai Toshihiko, "Shakai to katei" (*Yorozu chōhō,* April 29, 1903), and Sakai Toshihiko, "Warera no kateishugi" (*Katei zasshi,* January 1906), both in *Sakai Toshihiko josei ronshū*, pp. 178–82 and 227–30. Also see Yamakawa, "Jiyū shakai ni okeru tsuma to haha" (*Fujin kōron,* October 1920), in *Yamakawa Kikue shū*, vol. 2, pp. 88–96.

24 Yamakawa, "Jiyū shakai ni okeru tsuma to haha," *Yamakawa Kikue shū,* vol. 2, p. 185.

25 Yamakawa, "Fujin undō ni arawaretaru shinkeikō," *Yamakawa Kikue shū*, vol. 1, p. 203. Also "Rōdō kaikyū no shimai e," *Onna no tachiba kara* (1919), in *Yamakawa Kikue shū*, vol. 1, pp. 247–53; "Chūryu fujin to rōdō mondai" (*Warera*, January 1919), in *Yamakawa Kikue shū*, vol. 2, pp. 88–96.

26 Karl Marx, *Capital: A Theory of Political Economy* (reprint, New York: Vintage Books, 1977), pp. 163–77.

27 Fukuda Hideko, "Fujin mondai no kaiketsu," *Seitō*, February 1913, supplement, pp. 1–7. August Bebel's *Die Frau und der Sozialismus* (1883) was translated from the German into Japanese in its complete form in 1922 as *Bēberu fujinron* and published by Arusu publishing company in 1923. The book contains a short introduction written by Yamakawa Kikue. For a critique of Bebel's treatise on women, see Furukawa Sachiko, "Bēberu no fujin kaihōron," in *Nyūmon josei kaihōron*, ed. Ichibangase Yasuko (Tokyo: Aki shobō, 1975), pp. 62–94.

For a general discussion in English of Meiji women socialists, see Sievers, *Flowers in Salt*, pp. 115–38. The most extensive study in English on women and socialism is Vera Mackie, *Creating Socialist Women in Japan: Gender Labour and Activism, 1900–1937* (Cambridge: Cambridge University Press, 1997). For a Foucauldian reading on the subject of socialist women, see Helen Bowen Raddeker, *Treacherous Women of Imperial Japan: Patriarchal Fictions, Patricidal Fantasies* (London: Routledge, 1997).

28 Fukuda Hideko, "Fujin mondai no kaiketsu," *Seitō*, February 1913, supplement, pp. 1–7.

29 See Kanda Michiko, "Fujinron no hensen—josei no chii kōjō o motomete," in *Gendai no esupuri—fujinron*, no. 56, ed. Matsubara Jirō and Kanda Michiko, March 1972, pp. 19–20.

30 Hirabayashi, "Fujin undō no mokuhyō" (*Tane maku hito*, August 1922), in *Hirabayashi zenshū*, vol. 1, pp. 153–54, 156.

31 "Musan fujin no undō e" (*Fujin kōron*, June 1922), in ibid., p. 157.

32 Yamakawa, "Meiji bunka to fujin" (*Kaihō*, October 1921), in *Yamakawa Kikue shū*, vol. 3, p. 35. Also see "Fujin o uragiru fujinron" (*Shin Nihon*, August 1918) and "Yosano Akiko ni atau" (*Shin shakai*, September 1916), both in *Yamakawa Kikue shū*, vol. 1, pp. 156–75 and 76–87.

33 Ruth Whitaker, "The First World War I Memoirs of Miss R. Whitaker" (unpublished, c. 1970, Department of Documents, Imperial War Museum), quoted in Sharon Ouditt, *Fighting Forces, Writing Women: Identity and Ideology in the First World War* (London: Routledge, 1994), p. 28.

34 Using Britain as an example, feminists in the 1920s involved themselves in a similar movement that pressed the state to provide mothers with remuneration commensurate with their jobs as mothers.

35 For an account of the debate (1915–18) in English, see Laurel Rasplica Rodd, "Yosano Akiko and the Taishō Debate over the 'New Woman,'" in

Recreating Japanese History, pp. 189–98; also Diane Bethel, "Visions of a Humane Society: Feminist Thought in Taishō Japan," *Feminist International,* no. 2 (1980): 158–60; and Mackie, "The Motherhood Protection Debate," in *Creating Socialist Women in Japan,* pp. 86–93.

36 The assumption that innate gender differences dictated separate spheres within home and society, or that women's economic subordination presupposed an eternal dependency that would persist unless women left home and engaged in outside employment with men as their equals, are issues Mary Wollstonecraft, John Locke, and others pondered in the eighteenth and nineteenth centuries. See Mary Wollstonecraft, "Of the Pernicious Effects Which Arise from the Unnatural Distinctions Established in Society," in *A Vindication of the Rights of Woman* (1792), ed. Carol H. Poyson (New York: W. W. Norton, 1988), pp. 140–50.

37 Yosano Akiko, "Joshi no tettei shita dokuritsu" (*Fujin kōron,* March 1918), and Yosano Akiko, "Hiratsuka Raichō-san to watakushi no ronsō" (*Taiyō,* January 1918), both reprinted in *Shiryō bosei hogo ronsō,* ed. Kōchi Nobuko (Tokyo: Domesu shuppan, 1984), pp. 85–86 and 96–104.

38 For Hiratsuka's translation of Ellen Key's *Love and Marriage* (1911), see *Seitō,* February and March issues, 1913. For other views on Key by Raichō, see "Ellen Key, ren'ai ni tsuite" (*Seitō,* March 1913) and "Ellen Key-shi" (*Shin Nihon,* September 1914), both reprinted in *Hiratsuka Raichō chosakushū,* vol. 1, pp. 177–81 and 398–406. Of further interest is Murata Makoto, *Nihon ren'ai shi* (Tokyo: Shūeikaku, 1925), pp. 302–5. Key's quote on the role of a mother can be found in Ellen Key, *The Century of the Child* (New York, 1909). Also see Ellen Key, "Bosei to kenri," in *Ren'ai to kekkon* (Love and Marriage), trans. Harada Minoru (Tokyo: Shūeikaku, 1913), pp. 201–39. Other discussions include Hedwig Dohm's analysis of Key, quoted in Biddy Martin, *Woman and Modernity: The (Life)styles of Lou Andreas-Salome* (Ithaca: Cornell University Press, 1991), pp. 167–69, 171–72. Nancy F. Cott takes up the question in *The Grounding of Modern Feminism* (New Haven: Yale University Press, 1987), pp. 46–48.

39 Raichō, "Bosei hogo no shuchō wa irai shugi ka" (*Fujin kōron,* May 1918), reprinted in Kōchi, *Shiryō bosei hogo ronsō,* pp. 86–91. For a critique of the debate, see Tsukamoto Shūko, "Yosano Akiko, Hiratsuka Raichō, Yamakawa Kikue no bosei hogo ronsō," in *Nyūmon josei kaihōron,* ed. Ichibangase Yasuko, pp. 223–55.

40 Yamakawa, "Bosei hogo to keizaiteki dokuritsu—Yosano, Hiratsuka ni shi no ronsō," *Fujin kōron,* September 1918; Kōchi, *Shiryō bosei hogo ronsō,* pp. 132–46. Also see Mackie, *Creating Socialist Women in Japan,* pp. 84–93.

41 Kōchi, *Shiryō bosei hogo ronsō,* p. 289.

42 Yamakawa, "Fujin wa kawaru," in *Yamakawa Kikue shū,* vol. 6, pp. 33–36.

43 After the passage of the Kōtō jogakkō rei (Women's Higher School Act) in February 1899, women's higher schools were officially known as *kōtō jogakkō* although they continued to be referred to as *jogakkō*.

44 *Meiji Taishō kokusei sōran* (Tokyo: Tōyō keizai shinpōsha, 1927), p. 678; also Murakami Nobuhiko, *Nihon no fujin mondai* (Tokyo: Iwanami shinsho, 1978), p. 27.

45 Ōhama Tetsuya and Kumakura Isao, *Kindai Nihon no seikatsu to shakai* (Tokyo: Hōsō daigaku kyōiku shinkōkai, 1989), pp. 72–73.

46 Hiroshima joshi kōtō shihan gakkō, established in 1908, was added to the list after its founding. See *Tsuda juku rokujūnenshi* (Tokyo: Tsuda juku daigaku shuppan, 1960), pp. 35, 61. On the founding of Joshi eigaku juku, see Wakamori Tarō, *Nihon no joseishi—atarashisa o motomete*, vol. 4 (Tokyo: Shūeisha, 1966), pp. 55–62. For a useful discussion of women's higher-school students, see Honda Masuko, *Jogakusei no keifu* (Tokyo: Seidōsha, 1990).

47 Shinotsuka, "Josei to kyōiku," *Josei to kazoku—Kindaika no jitsuzō*, pp. 70–136. Also see Harrington, "Women and Higher Education," pp. 174–75.

48 For Itō Noe's criticism of Shimoda Utako's stance on women's education, see Itō Noe, "Shimoda Utako joshi e," *Seitō,* October 1914, pp. 64–72. Also see Shimoda Utako, *Kōsetu sōsho,* vol. 5 (Tokyo: Jissen jogakkō shuppanbu, 1933), esp. "Ikuji to katei kyōiku," pp. 371–429.

49 Hamada Shirō, *Hyakkaten issekiwa* (Tokyo: Nihon denpō tsūshinsha, 1927), p. 224.

50 Ibid., p. 242; also see *Mitsukoshi sanbyakunen no shōhō: sono hatten no mono-gatari,* ed. Sanyū shinbunsha (Tokyo: Hyōgensha, 1972).

51 Eric Hobsbawm, *The Age of Empire: 1875–1914* (New York: Vintage Books, 1987), p. 335.

52 Kuwabara Takeo, "Taishō gojūnen," in *Kuwabara Takeo shū,* vol. 6 (Tokyo: Iwanami shoten, 1980), p. 300.

53 See Miriam Silverberg, "Constructing a New Cultural History of Prewar Japan," in *Japan in the World,* special edition of *boundary 2,* 18, no. 3 (1991): 65–68; *Taishō bunka,* pp. 150–67, 350–61; also see *Goraku no senzenshi,* ed. Ishikawa Hiroyoshi et al. (Tokyo: Tokyo shoseki, 1981), pp. 96–109.

54 Wakamori Tarō, *Taishū bunka no jidai—zusetsu, Nihon rekishi,* vol. 8 (Tokyo: Chūō kōronsha, 1961).

55 Figures cited by Itō Sō, "Zōdai suru shin chūsan kaikyū," in *Taishō bunka,* ed. Minami, p. 240. In addition to Itō's research, I have relied on Ōkō-chi Kazuo, *Nihonteki chūsan kaikyū* (Tokyo: Bungei shunjū shinsha, 1960). Factors such as age and job status should be taken into account when determining a middle-class family's expenses. That said, however, the Department of Statistics in the Tokyo central government "fixed" the living expenses for a middle-class family at 100–200 yen per month. *Tokyo-shi: Tōkeikoku, 1926–1927,* in *Kindai shomin seikatsushi,* vol. 7, ed. Minami Hiroshi

et al., pp. 274–76. Sonoda Hidehiro's research on "culture" and the middle class has been valuable in helping me form my own views on a complicated subject. See, for example, Sonoda Hidehiro, "Kindai Nihon no bunka to chūryū kaikyū," in Toshi bunka, Kindai Nihon bunkaron, vol. 2, ed. Aoki, Kawamoto, et al., pp. 100–16.

56 Gonda Yasunosuke, "Modan seikatsu to hentai shikōsei" (Kaizō, June 1929), reprinted in Gendai no esupuri—Nihon modanizumu, no. 188, pp. 67–72.

57 Rudolf Kayser, "Amerikanismus," Vossiche Zeitung, no. 458, September 27, 1925; reprint, "Americanism," in The Weimar Republic Sourcebook, ed. Anton Kaes, Martin Jay, and Edward Dimendberg (Berkeley: University of California Press, 1994), pp. 395–97. For an expansion of this view, see Yoshimi Shunya, "Amerikanaizeishon to bunka no seiji," in Gendai shakai no shakaigaku, Gendai shakaigaku, vol. 1, ed. Mita Munesuke, Inoue Shun, Ueno Chizuko, Ōsawa Masachi, and Yoshimi Shunya (Tokyo: Iwanami shoten, 1997), pp. 157–231.

58 Hirabayashi, "Amerikanizumu no chikara," in Hirabayashi zenshū, vol. 3, pp. 650–51. See Harootunian, Overcome by Modernity, pp. 22–30 and 57–65.

59 Frederick Lewis Allen, Only Yesterday: An Informal History of the 1920's (New York: Harper and Row, 1931), p. 78.

60 Ibid., p. 79.

61 Ibid., pp. 74, 73.

62 Marx could not have come up with the theory of capitalist production without a clear awareness of consumerism. As Marx argues, production does not exist when there is no need, and the process of consuming is what produces that need. Karl Marx, Grundrisse: Foundations of the Critique of Political Economy (1857–58) (Harmondsworth: Penguin, 1973), pp. 90–92.

63 Hirabayashi, "Geijutsuha, puroretariaha oyobi kindaiha" (Shinchō, May 1930), in Hirabayashi zenshū, vol. 2, p. 239.

64 Hirabayashi, "Bungaku ni okeru shinkeishiki no yobo—gendai no seikatsu wa ikani kawaritsutsu aruka (2)" (Shinchō, February 1929), in Hirabayashi zenshū, vol. 1, p. 331.

65 Kimura Shōhachi, Zuihitsu josei sandai (Tokyo: Kawade shobō, 1956), p. 86.

66 Minami Hiroshi, "Masu bunka no seiritsu," in Taishō bunka, ed. Minami Hiroshi (Tokyo: Keisō shobō, 1965), pp. 265–68; also see Taishō daishinsai dai kasai (Tokyo: Dainihon yūbenkai—Kōdansha, 1923); S. Doke, "The Reconstruction of Tokyo," in The Japan Year Book: Earthquake Edition 1924–25, no. 18 (Tokyo: Eibun Nihon nenkansha, 1924), pp. 87–109.

67 Hirabayashi, "Amerikanizumu no chikara" (Tokyo Asahi shinbun, May 8, 1929), and "Modanizumu mo shakaiteki no konkyo" (Shinchō, March 1930), both in Hirabayashi zenshū, vol. 3, pp. 650–51 and 836–37.

68 Nakajima Kenzō, Shōwa jidai (Tokyo: Iwanami shoten, 1957), pp. 12–28.

69 Fujimori Terunobu, Kenchiku tantei no bōken (Tokyo: Chikuma shobō, 1986), pp. 38–74.

70 Writer Unno Hiroshi, concerned with the impact that the growth of urban centers like Tokyo had on Japanese literature, commented: "As far as I am concerned, the 1920s was the period in which city life as we know it today, took off. Everything from the automobile to women's fashion and makeup became popular at that time." Unno Hiroshi, *Modan toshi Tokyo—Nihon no senkyūhyaku nijū nendai* (Tokyo: Sanyōsha, 1983), p. 10.

71 Natsume Sōseki, "Gendai Nihon no kaika," speech delivered in Wakayama, Japan, August 1911, reprinted in Natsume Sōseki, *Watashi no kojinshugi* (Tokyo: Kōdansha, 1988). Also see Yamazaki Masakazu, *Fukigen no jidai* (Tokyo: Kōdansha, 1986), pp. 47–48; Matsuo Takayoshi, "A Note on the Political Thought of Natsume Sōseki in His Later Years," in *Japan in Crisis: Essays on Taishō Democracy*, ed. Silberman and Harootunian, pp. 73–75 and 443.

72 Yamazaki, *Fukigen no jidai*, p. 62.

73 In contrast to Japanese intellectuals in the 1920s, Walter Adamson points out that in Italy, "modernists generally were from a generation of frustrated intellectuals desirous of keeping their own threatened social role intact while building a new culture of modernity." Walter L. Adamson, "Modernism and Fascism: The Politics of Culture in Italy," *American Historical Review* 95, no. 2 (1990): 390.

74 Hirabayashi, "Beikoku no kikan toshite no eiga" (*Kaizō*, February 1929), in *Hirabayashi zenshū*, vol. 2, pp. 411–15; Nii, "Eigato josei no kindaigata," reprinted in *Gendai no esupri—Nihon modanizumu*, no. 188, pp. 191–99; Harootunian, *Overcome by Modernity*, pp. 21–22, 59–60.

75 William Leach, *Land of Desire: Merchants, Power, and the Rise of a New American Culture* (New York: Vintage Books, 1993); Erika Diane Rappaport, *Shopping for Pleasure: Women in the Making of London's West End* (Princeton: Princeton University Press, 2000); Rosalind H. Williams, *Dream World: Mass Consumption in Late Nineteenth-Century France* (Berkeley: University of California Press, 1992); see photographs from p. 244, including insert no. 18. Also see Daniel Boorstin, *The Americans: The Democratic Experience* (New York: Vintage Books, 1974).

76 *Toshi taishū bunka no seiritsu*, ed. Hirai Tadashi et al. (Tokyo: Yūhikaku, 1983), pp. 136–37; Hirai Tadashi, *Berlin—1923–1945* (Tokyo: Serika shobō, 1981), p. 186. Also pertinent to the discussion are Harootunian, *Overcome by Modernity*, pp. 47–65; Jeffrey E. Hanes, "Masu karuchyā/sabu karuchāzu/popyura karuchā," in *Toshi no kūkan toshi no shintai, 21 seiki no toshi shakaigaku*, vol. 4, ed. Yoshimi Shun'ya (Tokyo: Keisō shobō, 1996), pp. 91–136; and *Toshi bunka, Kindai Nihon bunkaron*, vol. 5.

77 Minami Hiroshi, *Shakai shinrishi—Shōwa jidai o megutte* (Tokyo: Seishin shobō, 1960), p. 67.

78 Saijō Yaso, *Uta no jijoden* (Tokyo: Sikatsu hyakka kankōkai, 1956), pp. 61–

69. Edward Seidensticker, *Tokyo Rising: The City since the Great Earthquake* (New York: Knopf, 1990), p. 70. Seidensticker renders the first stanza of the "Tokyo Marching Song" as follows (p. 70):

> The Ginza willows bring thoughts of the past.
> Who will know the aging, fickle woman?
> Dancing to jazz, liqueur into the small hours.
> And in the dawn a flood of tears for the dancer.

79 Daniel Boorstin refers to department stores in the United States such as R. H. Macys, John Wanamakers, and Marshall Fields, all of which were operating in the late nineteenth century, as "consumers' palaces." He remarks: "If the department store was not an American invention, it flourished here as nowhere else." Boorstin, *The Americans: The Democratic Experience*, pp. 101, 104–7. For a discussion of department store building in Japan, see Izeki Jūjirō, *Wanamēkā hōten* (Tokyo: Jitsugyō no Nihon sha, 1926); and Katō Saburō, *Māsharu Fīrudo to sekai ichi no daishōten* (Tokyo: Kaizōsha, 1929). Also see Jinno Yuki, *Shumi no tanjō: hyakkaten ga tsukutta teisuto* (Tokyo: Keisō shobō, 1994); and *Nihon no hyakkaten no bunka: Nihon no shōhi kakumei*, ed. Yamamoto Taketoshi and Nishizawa Tamotsu (Tokyo: Sekai shisōsha, 1999). In English, see Louise Young, "Marketing the Modern: Department Stores, Consumer Culture, and the New Middle Class in Interwar Japan," in *International Labor and Working-Class History*, no. 55 (New York: International Labor and Working Class History, 1999), pp. 52–70.

80 Raymond Williams, *Communications* (London: Penguin Books, 1962), pp. 14–24; *The History of Popular Culture*, ed. Norman Cantor and Michael Wetham (New York: Macmillan, 1968).

81 Who can forget Bernard Rosenberg's comment regarding the "erroneous assumptions" about mass culture? "Capitalism is responsible for mass culture. America is responsible for mass culture. Democracy is responsible for mass culture." Rosenberg hypothesizes that "modern technology is the necessary and sufficient cause of mass culture. Neither national character nor the economic arrangement nor the political system has any final bearing on this question. All that really matters is the most recent industrial revolution." Bernard Rosenberg, "Mass Culture in America," in *Mass Culture: The Popular Arts in America*, ed. Bernard Rosenberg and David Manning White (New York: Free Press, 1957), pp. 11–12.

82 See *Shinpan dai Tokyo an'nai*, ed. Kon Wajirō (Tokyo: Chūō kōronsha, 1929), p. 64; also Ōtsuka Akira and Okada Kōnosuke, "Bunka sangyō no seiritsu," in *Taishō bunka*, p. 135.

83 See *Shinbun gaku o manabu hito no tame ni*, ed. Wada Yōichi (Tokyo: Sekai shisōsha, 1980), p. 40.

84 R. P. Dore, *Education in Tokugawa Japan* (Berkeley: University of Califor-

nia Press, 1965), pp. 254, 291–95. For more on this subject, see Richard Rubinger, "Who Can't Read and Write? Illiteracy in Meiji Japan," *Monumenta Nipponica* 55, no. 2 (2000): 163–99.

85 Maeda Ai, "Taishō kōki tsūzoku shōsetsu no tenkai—fujin zasshi no dokusha-sō," in *Maeda Ai chosakushū*, vol. 2 (Tokyo: Chikuma shobō, 1989), p. 156; also see Wada, *Shinbun gaku o manabu hito no tame ni*, pp. 38–39.

86 Hirata Yumi, *Josei hyōgen no Meiji-shi* (Tokyo: Iwanami shoten, 1999).

87 Honma Nagayo and Kamei Shunsuke, *Amerika no taishū bunka* (Tokyo: Kenkyūsha, 1975), pp. 8–12.

88 Kurahara, speech delivered February 22, 1930, in *Kurahara Korehito hyōronshū*, pp. 50–52. Author and literary critic Hayashi Fusao's criticism of "mass" culture written in 1929 is almost identical with that of Kurahara. See "Kakuteru no koseibun" (*Chūo kōron*, October 1929), in *Gendai no espuri—Nihon modanizumu*, no. 188, pp. 39–43. Tetsuo Najita and H. D. Harootunian point out, however, that Hayashi and his group called for the "restoration of 'timeless' cultural values in order to combat utilitarianism, bureaucratism, functional specialization, and mass production, and consumerism," which shows a change in Hayashi's way of thinking. See Tetsuo Najita and H. D. Harootunian, "The Debate on Modernity," in *Cambridge History of Japan*, vol. 6: *The Twentieth Century*, ed. Peter Duus (Cambridge: Cambridge University Press, 1988), pp. 766–67. (Hayashi publicly renounced Marxism in 1933.)

89 Murobuse Takanobu (Kōshin) frequently changed his stance on issues. Murobuse generally used the words "*shin chūto kaikyū*" or the English "white-collared" to describe the "new" middle class. See Murobuse Takanobu, *Chūkan kaikyū no shakaigaku* (Tokyo: Nihon hyōronsha, 1932), pp. 44–47. Also see Koyama, *Katei no seisei to josei no kokuminka*, especially "Katei seikatsu ni kansuru kokka no kanshin," pp. 67–76.

90 Ōya, *Ōya Sōichi zenshū*, vol. 2, p. 5.

91 Sawamua Torajirō, "Amerikanizumu," *Bungei shunjū*, March 28, 1928, p. 10.

92 Sociologist Takahashi Akira points out that "Japanese intellectuals consider Shōwa popular culture to be an alternative to Taishō culturalism. [The earthquake] showed the power of nature as opposed to the powerlessness of man. It made people turn away from the culturalistic, personalistic, and moralistic Taishō culture. Coupled with a temporary dislocation that occurred in the traditional order, [the earthquake] led people toward out-and-out hedonism aimed at the release of inner stress rather than emphasizing a moral culture, which put a strain on the ego." Takahashi Akira, "Toshika to kikai bunmei," in *Kindai Nihon shisōshi kōza*, vol. 6 (Tokyo: Chikuma shobō, 1960), p. 186.

93 Max Horkheimer and Theodor W. Adorno, *Dialectic of Enlightenment* (1944) (New York: Continuum, 1993). For Horkheimer and Adorno, "mass"

leisure created the illusion of providing variety and choice. The only possible way to go against consumerism was through "negation." According to Andrea Huyssen, Adorno "never saw modernism as any other than a reaction formation to mass culture and commodification." See Huyssen, *After the Great Divide*, p. 57.

94 Walter Benjamin, "The Work of Art in the Age of Mechanical Reproduction," in *Illuminations: Essays and Reflections*, ed. and intro. Hannah Arendt (New York: Shocken Books, 1969), p. 234.

95 Takasu Yoshijirō, "Taishō, Shōwa no kokumin shisō," in *Nihon seishin kōza*, vol. 8 (Tokyo: Shinchōsha, 1934), pp. 116, 121.

96 Lawrence Grossberg, Ellen Wartella, and D. Charles Whitney, *Media Making: Mass Media in a Popular Culture* (Thousand Oaks, Calif.: Sage Publications, 1998), pp. 268, 399.

97 Allen, *Only Yesterday*, pp. 82, 85.

98 Hirabayashi, "Fujin undō no mokuhyō" (*Tane maku hito*, August 1922), in *Hirabayashi zenshū*, vol. 1, pp. 161–62. Women like revolutionary Alexandra Kollontai in the Soviet Union from the early twentieth century and feminist and socialist Lily Braun in Vienna in the late 1890s called for collective family services.

99 Hirabayashi, "Bunka no joseika" (*Josei*, April 1926), in *Hirabayashi zenshū*, vol. 3, pp. 778–80.

100 Hirabayashi, "Modanizumu no shakaiteki no konkyo" (*Shinchō*, March 1930), in *Hirabayashi zenshū*, vol. 3, pp. 840–46.

101 Lewis Mumford's fear of mechanization as expressed in *Technics and Human Development: The Myth of the Machine*, vol. 1 (New York: Harcourt, Brace and World, 1967), sounds similar to that voiced by the majority of Hirabayashi's contemporaries:

> The absolute validity of the machine has become a conditioned validity: even Spengler, who has urged the men of his generation to become engineers and men of fact, regards that career as a sort of honorable suicide and looks forward to the period when the monuments of the machine civilization will be tangled masses of rusting iron and empty concrete shells. The decay of this absolute faith [in the machine] has resulted from a variety of causes. One of them is the fact that the instruments of destruction ingeniously contrived in the machine shop and the chemist's laboratory, have become in the hands of raw and dehumanized personalities a standing threat to the existence of organized society itself.

102 Hirabayashi, "Fujin undō no mokuhyō" (*Tane maku hito*, August 1922), in *Hirabayashi zenshū*, vol. 1, p. 154.

103 Ibid., p. 153.

104 Hirabayashi, "Gendai no seikatsu wa ikani kawaritsutsu aruka (1, 2)," in *Hirabayashi zenshū*, vol. 1, pp. 333–38.

105 See Hamill on the concept of women's education as formulated by Hani Motoko and Nishimura Isaku. "Josei—modanizumu to kenri ishiki," in *Shōwa bunka—1925–1945*, pp. 201–4; also see Laurel Rasplica Rodd, "Yosano Akiko and the Bunka gakuin: Educating Free Individuals," *Journal of the Association of Teachers of Japanese* 21, no. 1 (1991): 75–89; Hani Motoko, "Katei kyōiku yori gakkō kyōiku o miru, 1926," in *Hani Motoko chosakushū*, vol. 1 (Tokyo: Fujin no tomosha, 1928), pp. 227–357; Saitō Michiko, *Hani Motoko—shōgai to shisō* (Tokyo: Domesu shuppan, 1988), pp. 129–34.

106 Nishimura Isaku, "Bunka gakuin no setsuritsu," in *Ware ni eki ari* (Tokyo: Kigensha, 1960), and "Bunka gakuin setsuritsu shuisho," in *Ai to hangyaku —Bunka gakuin no gojūnen, Bunka gakuin shi hensanshitsu* (Tokyo: Bunka gakuin shuppanbu, 1971). Both are reprinted in *Nihon fujin mondai shiryō shūsei*, vol. 4, pp. 545 and 557.

107 Ibid., pp. 562, 568.

108 Hani Motoko, one of Japan's first women newspaper reporters, together with her husband founded the women's magazine *Katei no tomo* (Home Companion) in 1903. Renamed *Fujin no tomo* (Woman's Friend) in 1908, it is still published today.

109 Hamill, *Shōwa bunka—1925–1945*, pp. 203–4; also Hani Motoko, "Jiyū gakuen no kyōiku" (*Kyōiku sanjū nen*, 1932), and "Jiyū gakuen no sōritsu" (*Fujin no tomo*, February 1921), both reprinted in *Nihon fujin mondai shiryō shūsei*, vol. 4, pp. 557 and 545.

110 Matsushita Keiichi's article, "Taishū kokka no seiritsu to sono mondai-sei," *Shisō*, no. 389 (November 1956): 31–52, is one of the earliest analyses on Japanese mass society by a Japanese scholar. This article later became a substantive part of the book Matsushita Keiichi, *Gendai seiji no jōken* (Tokyo: Chūō kōronsha, 1959). Matsushita's arguments formed the basis for Inaba Michiō's, Satō Tomō's, and Sasaki Ayao's analyses of mass culture found in *Kōza shakaigaku*, vol. 7, ed. Fukutake Tadashi (Tokyo: Tokyo daigaku shuppankai, 1957), esp. pp. 165–80.

After World War I, the word *mass*, or *taishū*, was used synonymously with *minshū* to mean "the people." It was not until after the Great Earthquake that *taishū* conveyed the meaning of "mass" as in mass society or mass production. Uncertainty over the "proper" way to define *mass* led to a variety of intellectual narratives in the 1950s and 1960s. Discourses on mass society (by Matsushita, Tsurumi Shunsuke, Minami Hiroshi, Tada Michitarō, and Katō Hidetoshi) and on the influence of the media on the general public also elicited responses from Western sociologists.

111 Kanō Mikiyo, *Jiga no kanata e—kindai o koeru feminizumu* (Tokyo: Shakai hyōronsha, 1990), p. 7.

112 Ibid.

113 Jean Baudrillard, "The Masses: The Implosion of the Social in the Media," trans. Marie MacLean, *New Literary History* 16, no. 3 (1985): 577–89, reprinted in *Jean Baudrillard: Selected Writings*, p. 202.

Chapter Two
The Modern Girl as a Representation of Consumer Culture

1 Stewart Ewen and Elizabeth Ewen, *Channels of Desire: Mass Images and the Shaping of American Consciousness* (Minneapolis: University of Minnesota Press, 1999), p. 171.

2 Although the fictional character Naomi is from a lower-working-class family, her relationship with Jōji and the lifestyle she becomes accustomed to allow her to assume some accoutrements of a bourgeois middle-class existence. See Anthony H. Chambers's English translation of Junichirō Tanizaki, *Naomi (Chijin no ai)* (New York: North Point Press, 1999). The novel first came out in English as *A Fool's Love* (New York: Alfred A. Knopf, 1985).

3 See Hamill [Sato], "Nihonteki modanizumu no shisō—josei to modanizumu," in *Nihon modanizumu no kenkyū*, pp. 109–13; "Modan gāru no jidaiteki imi," in *Gendai no esupuri—Nihon modanizumu*, no. 188, pp. 84–85; "Josei—modanizumu to kenri ishiki," in *Shōwa bunka—1925–1945*, pp. 198–231; "Modan gāru no tōjō to chisikijin," *Rekishi hyōron* 3 (March 1991): 18–26; Barbara Hamill Sato, "The Moga Sensation: Perceptions of the Modan Gāru in Japanese Intellectual Circles during the 1920s," *Gender and History* 5, no. 3 (1993): 361–81. The latter article is the basis for chapter 2. Also see Harry Harootunian, "Overcome by Modernity: Fantasizing Everyday Life and the Discourse of the Social in Interwar Japan," in *parallax*, issue 2, Theory/Practice (Leeds, U.K.: Wild Pansy Press/University of Leeds, February 1996), pp. 80–81. Also see Takeuchi Yō, *Taishū modanizumu no yume no ato* (Tokyo: Shinyōsha, 2001). For an ambitious interpretation of the modern girl, particularly as she was portrayed in fiction, see Miriam Silverberg, "The Modern Girl as Militant," in *Recreating Japanese Women*, pp. 239–66. For a journalistic portrayal of five women of the period who represent Phyllis Birnbaum's modern girls, see Phyllis Birnbaum, *Modern Girls, Shining Stars, the Skies of Tokyo: Five Japanese Women* (New York: Columbia University Press, 1999). For a persuasive positioning of the modern girl, see Suzuki Sadami, *Modan toshi no hyōgen: jiko, gensō, josei* (Kyoto: Hakuchisha, 1992). A convenient anthology on the modern girl in fiction is *Modan gāru no yūwaku, Modan toshi bungaku*, vol. 2, ed. Suzuki Sadami (Tokyo: Heibonsha, 1989). For more on the modern girl, see Horiuchi Fumiko, *Modan gāru*

no koi—Horiuchi Keizō to watashi (Tokyo: Sōshisha, 1987); Katori Shunsuke, *Modan gāru—Takehisa Chieko to iu joyū ga ita* (Tokyo: Chikuma shobō, 1996); Saitō Minako, *Modan gāru ron—Onna no ko ni wa shusse no michi ga futatsu aru* (Tokyo: Magajin hausu, 2000).

4 Kon Wajirō, "Tokyo Ginzagai fūzoku kiroku" (*Fujin kōron,* July 1925), in Kon Wajirō, *Kōgenkau* (1927), *Kon Wajirō shū,* vol. 1 (Tokyo: Domesu shuppan, 1971), pp. 107–24. A nationwide survey of twenty-six thousand women conducted by *Fujin no tomo* in 1937 found that 13 percent of those surveyed in Tokyo wore Western dress versus 12 percent in Osaka, 12 percent in Kobe, and 7 percent in Sendai. In the Marunouchi area of Tokyo, approximately 39 percent of the professional working women (*shokugyō fujin*) wore Western dress.

5 For an account of the Ginza during the period that "modernism" flourished, see Matsuzaki Tenmin, *Ginza* (1927; reprint, Tokyo: Shinsensha, 1986); Kon Wajirō, *Shinpan dai Tokyo an'nai* (Tokyo: Chūō kōronsha, 1929), esp. "Sakariba Ginza," pp. 105–11; Andō Kōsei, *Ginza saiken* (1931; reprint, Tokyo: Chūō kōronsha, 1977). The magazine *Modan Nippon* regularly carried articles on leisure and the consumer lifestyle that came to epitomize the city. "My Schedule on the Ginza" (Watashi no Ginza sukejūru) (January 1934) is but one example.

6 On fashion trends in Taishō and early Shōwa, see Yanagi Yōko, "Taishō Shōwa shoki no fasshon," in *Nihon modanizumu no kenkyū,* pp. 187–206; also Yanagi Yōko, *Fasshonka shakaishi—haikara kara modan made* (Tokyo: Gyōsei, 1987), pp. 236–44. Articles like "Studies on Women's Fashions and Hairstyles Suitable for the New Age" (Shinjidai ni tekiō suru fujin no fukusō to rihatsu to no kenkyū), *Josei,* December 1923, pp. 228–55, appeared in many popular women's magazines of the period.

7 *Meiji Taishō Shōwa sesōshi,* Katō Hidetoshi et al. (Tokyo: Shakai shisōsha, 1967), p. 60.

8 "Kamigata-zu," in *Nihon fūzokushi jiten* (Tokyo: Kōbundō, 1979), pp. 738–39.

9 See Nishizawa Sō, *Zatsugaku—Kayō Shōwa shi* (Tokyo: Mainichi shinbunsha, 1980), p. 33.

10 Ryū Kaori, *Danpatsu* (Tokyo: Asahi shinbunsha, 1990), pp. 184–88; Takahashi Yasuo, *Danpatsu suru onnatachi—modan gāru no fūkei* (Tokyo: Kyōiku shuppan, 1999).

11 "Yuigami to keshō no jissendan" (Discussions on the "Bun" and Makeup), *Shufu no tomo,* April 1925, pp. 308–10. A magazine published in the United States, *American Hairdresser* (May 1922), predicted that the bob, which had been gaining in popularity in the United States since 1918, would probably run its course by the summer. By 1924, however, the bob was a regular feature of this magazine. See Allen, *Only Yesterday,* p. 87. On popular Western

hairstyles in Japan, see "Yōgamino yuikata to biyō no hiketsu" (1928), in *Kindai shomin seikatsu shi—fukushoku, biyō, girei,* ed. Minami Hiroshi et al., vol. 5, 1986, pp. 271–94. One of the most useful accounts on changing hairstyles is "Sokuhatsu ni shutsugen" and "Short Hair no jidai," both in Murakami Nobuhiko, *Onna no fūzoku shi* (Tokyo: Daviddo sha, 1957), pp. 102–20.

12 Mochizuki Yuriko, "Shindanpatsu monogatari" (*Josei,* March 1928), in *Dokyumento Shōwa sesōshi senzen hen* (Tokyo: Heibonsha, 1975), pp. 122–23. Mochizuki was not alone in her desire to follow new trends and simplify everyday life. The magazine *Shin katei zasshi* (New Home), which targeted women's higher-school graduates, printed a special issue on the short cut (*danpatsu*) in December 1920. Articles included "How I Felt After I Cut My Hair" (Kitta ato no kimochi), p. 35; "Doubts about the Short Cut for School Girls" (Jogakusei no danpatsu wa kangaemono), pp. 36–42; "A Health Specialist's Views on the Short Cut" (Kenkō gakushi yori mitaru fujin no danpatsu), pp. 40–42; and "Kansai Women Speak Out about the Short Cut" (Danpatsu ni tsuite Kansai fujin no iken), p. 43.

13 Ishimaru Kiyoko, "Modan gāru zakkan—modan gāru to atarashii onna," *Fujin kōron,* January 1927, p. 64.

14 Nishikawa Fumiko, "Modan gāru zakkan—nijussai zengo no ryūkō," *Fujin kōron,* January 1927, p. 63.

15 Okada Hachiyo, "Modan gāru no zakkan—modan gāru to wa," *Fujin kōron,* January 1927, p. 65.

16 Suzuki Bunshirō, *Fujin mondai no hanashi: Asahi joshiki kōza,* vol. 9 (Tokyo: Asahi shinbunsha, 1929), p. 192.

17 Yosano, "Joshi no danpatsu" (*Yokohama bōeki shinpō,* January 1926), in *Teihon Yosano Akiko zenshū,* vol. 19, pp. 282–83.

18 Ibid., pp. 292, 294.

19 See Kitazawa Chōgo, "Modan gāru no hyōgen—Nihon no imōto ni okuru tegami," *Josei kaizō,* April 1923. Special thanks to Suzuki Sadami for introducing me to this article, the earliest reference in Japanese to the *modan gāru.* See Suzuki, *Modan toshi no hyōgen: jiko, gensō, josei,* p. 60.

20 Kitazawa Shūichi, the author of this article, and Kitazawa Chōgo ("Modan gāru no hyōgen—Nihon no imōto ni okuru tegami") are no doubt the same person. See Ueda Yasuo on this point, in "Fujin zasshi ni miru modanizumu," *Gendai no esupuri, Nihon no modanizumu,* no. 188, p. 112. Although the phonetic spelling of *modan gāru* caught on immediately, Chinese characters continued to be used occasionally. In one combination, the Chinese characters for *modan* humorously read "to cut off one's hair."

21 Ōya Sōichi, in a 1925 newspaper article entitled "Josei sentānjin hihyō," for the *Osaka Asahi,* credits Nii Itaru with having introduced the word *modan gāru* to Japanese readers. The phrase is still attributed by many to Nii, as it is in the *Gendai ryūkōgo jiten* (Tokyo: Tokyodō shuppan, 1974), p. 253. How-

ever, at a roundtable discussion, "Zadankai—kindaiteki josei no hihan," sponsored by the women's magazine *Fujin no kuni* in May 1926, Nii said that Kitazawa was the first to use the word in Japan. Also see Ueda, "Fujin zasshi ni miru modanizumu," *Gendai no esupuri, Nihon no modanizumu,* no. 188, p. 112.

22 Kitazawa, "Modan gāru," *Josei,* August 1924, p. 230.

23 Ibid., pp. 226–27.

24 Nii Itaru, *Kindaishin no kaibō* (Tokyo: Ijōsha, 1925), pp. 153–58.

25 Ibid., pp. 159–60. For more on the *modan gāru,* see Ōkubo Hokushu, *Modan gāru hiwa* (Tokyo: Nishōdō, 1927); Tsumuraya Hiroshi, *Kafe bunka no shogenshō* (Tokyo: Shakai gaitōsha, 1928), esp. "Modan gāru no imizuke," and "Modan gāru to gaijin no motsure," pp. 18–33.

Writer Sasaki Kuni, well known for humorously depicting Japanese family life in his novels, equates the *modern girl* with nouveau riche young women like the daughter of a landowner whose circumstances fortuitously changed with the rise of land prices. According to Sasaki, the appellation *gāru* depended on family finances. Sasaki Kuni, *Sekensō ningensō* (Tokyo: Meiji insatsu, 1927), pp. 124–25.

26 "Zadankai," *Fujin no kuni,* pp. 6, 8–9. On "high-collar" tastes, see "Tōsei haikara shugyō" (1903), in *Kindai shomin seikatsushi—fukushoku, biyō, girei,* ed. Minami et al., vol. 5, pp. 368–76. The high collar literally referred to a man's starched stand-up collar, a style that was introduced to Japan from England in the early Meiji years.

27 Ibid., p. 8.

28 "Jōryū shinsai zengo kondankai" (*Fujin kōron,* November 1923), reprinted in *Nihon fujin mondai shiryō shūsei-seikatsu,* vol. 7, pp. 221–38.

29 Kitamura Kaneko, "Josei taitō jidai—shokugyō josei," *Hyōhi wa ugoku* (Tokyo: Heibonsha, 1930), pp. 123–24. In Atina Grossmann's article "Girlkultur or Thoroughly Rationalized Female: A New Woman in Weimar Germany?" Grossmann makes the point that an important motivation behind the sex reform movement in post–World War I Germany was to "redomesticate a putative New Woman—independent and sexy—back to an identity that would accommodate marriage and family as well as wage labor and active sexuality." See *Women in Culture and Politics: A Century of Change,* ed. Judith Friedlander, Blanche Wiesen Cook, Alice Kessler-Harris, and Carroll Smith-Rosenberg (Bloomington: Indiana University Press, 1986), p. 63.

30 Ōya Sōichi, "Hyaku pāsento moga" (*Chūō kōron,* August 1929), in *Ōya Sōichi zenshū,* vol. 2 (Tokyo: Eichōsha, 1982), pp. 12–13.

31 See "Popular Entertainment: A Critical Discussion [roundtable] on Movies" (Minshū geijutsu to kangaete no katsudō shashin hihankai), in *Josei,* February 1925, pp. 124–44. Also see Minami Hiroshi, "Gendai no

fūzoku (1) Senzen no fūzoku," in *Nihon fūzoku shi* (Tokyo: Yūzankaku, 1959), reprinted in Minami Hiroshi, *Nihonjin no shinri to seikatsu* (Tokyo: Keisō shobō, 1980), pp. 167–77. For more on movies, see Kawamoto Saburō, "Shoshimin eiga no 'tanoshii wagaya,'" in *Taishū bunka to masu meideiya, Kindai Nihon bunkaron*, vol. 7, ed. Aoki, Kawamoto, et al., 1999, pp. 2–17.

32   *Tokyo Nichi Nichi shinbun*, May 4, 1927; *Yomiuri shinbun*, May 7, 1927. Also see Ōkubo, *Modan gāru hiwa*, pp. 1–11.

33   Kataoka Teppei, "Modan bōi no kenkyū," in *Modan gāru no kenkyū* (Tokyo: Kinseidō, 1927), reprinted in *Gendai no esupuri—Nihon no modanizumu*, no. 188, pp. 114–28.

34   *Shinseinen dokuhon zen ikkan*, ed. Shinseinen kenkyūkai (Tokyo: Sakuhinsha, 1988), p. 11. Nevertheless, many contributors to *Shinseinen* wrote about the modern boy, or chic boy, another name used to describe this new male phenomenon. See *Shinseinen*, June 1929, reprinted in *Shinseinen* (Tokyo: Hon no tomosha, 1994).

35   Kataoka Teppei, "Shinkekkon nijūsō," *Fujin kōron*, October 1928, pp. 36–40.

36   A vivid example is Kiyosawa Rei's "Modan gāru no kaibō," *Josei*, December 1927, pp. 96–103. For a related discussion, see Jay Rubin's account of Tanizaki Junichirō's *Chijin no ai (Naomi)*, which originally was published in the *Osaka Asahi* from March 1924 until June 1924 and later in *Josei* from November 1924 to June 1925. The novel was serialized in *Shufu no tomo* from January to May 1926. Jay Rubin, *Injurious to Public Morals: Writers and the Meiji State* (Seattle: University of Washington Press, 1984), pp. 236–37. (Tanizaki changed publishers because the authorities considered his subject matter unsuitable for a major newspaper's readers.)

37   Kiyosawa, "Modan gāru no kaibō," pp. 96–103.

38   Takamure Itsue, "Hasegawa Nyozekan no seitai" (1930), in *Takamure Itsue zenshū*, vol. 7 (Tokyo: Rironsha, 1967), pp. 305–6. On changing patterns of sexuality among Japanese women in the 1920s, see Donald Roden, "Taishō Culture and the Problem of Gender Ambivalence," in *Culture and Identity: Japanese Intellectuals during the Interwar Years*, ed. J. Thomas Rimer (Princeton: Princeton University Press, 1990), pp. 53–54. Jennifer Robertson deals with "the ambivalence that characterized the discourse of gender and sexuality then [from the early twentieth century] and continues to the present day, revealed in public debates about the meaning and significance of women—as revue actors, as fans, as delinquents, as wives and mothers, as workers, as consumers" in her study of the Takarazuka Revue (Takarazuka kagekidan). Jennifer Robertson, *Takarazuka: Sexual Politics and Popular Culture in Modern Japan* (Berkeley: University of California Press, 1998), p. 6. Also see Miriam Silverberg, "Advertising Every Body: Images from the Japanese Modern Years," in *Choreographing History*, ed.

Susan Leigh Foster (Bloomington: Indiana University Press, 1995), pp. 129–48.

For an overview on the subject of sexuality, see Kawamura Kunimitsu, *Sekushuariti no kindai* (Tokyo: Kōdansha, 1996); *Sekushuariti no shakaigaku, Gendai shakai gaku*, vol. 10, ed. Ueno Chizuko et al. (Tokyo: Iwanami shoten, 1996). Of particular interest in this volume are Inoue Shōichi, "Mirareru sei, Miseru sei ga dekiru made," pp. 63–76; and Muta Kazue, "Sekushuariti no hensen to kindai kokka," pp. 77–93.

39 Nii, *Kindaishin no kaibō*, p. 157.

40 On changing patterns of sexuality among young American women in the 1920s, see Cott, *The Grounding of Modern Feminism*, pp. 148–62. "Advertising and mass media took up women's heterosexuality as their own agent, blunting the Feminist point that heterosexual liberation for women intended to subvert gender hierarchy rather than to confirm it" (quoted in Cott, p. 152). Reference to similar patterns among European women can be found in Bonnie G. Smith, *Changing Lives: Women in European History since 1700* (Lexington, Mass.: University of Rochester, 1989), pp. 338–45. Helpful in forming my views was the article by Elizabeth Grosz, "Sexual Difference and the Problem of Essentialism," in *The Essential Difference*, ed. Naomi Schor and Elizabeth Weed (Bloomington: Indiana University Press, 1994), pp. 84–92.

41 "Taishō Shōwa no kokumin shisō," in *Nihon seishin kōza*, vol. 8 (Tokyo: Shinchōsha, 1934), p. 116.

42 Between 1922 and 1926 playwright and essayist Kurata Hyakuzō wrote several essays on free love and marriage, all of which were partly censored by the authorities. Iwanami shoten published them in their censored form under the title *Ippu ippu ka jiyū ren'ai ka* (Monogamy or Free Love?) in 1926.

43 Murashima Yoriyuki, *Kafe* (Tokyo: Bunka seikatsu kenkyūkai, 1929), pp. 44–45. An article featured in *Kaizō* entitled "Students and Cafés" (Gakusei to kafe), November 1934, pp. 28–35, castigates college students and the "elite" salaried class for their debauched lifestyles. Frequenting cafés and movie theaters was considered a "bourgeois" pastime. One of the most detailed accounts of Tokyo cafés and those who patronized them is Matsuzaki Tenmin, "Kafe jidai," in *Rimen anmen jitsuwa, Meiji Taishō Jitsuwa zenshū*, vol. 12 (Tokyo: Heibonsha, 1929), pp. 183–208. Also see Tsumuraya, *Kafe bunka no shogenshō*. An excellent account in English on cafés is Elise K. Tipton, "The Café: Contested Space of Modernity in Interwar Japan," in *Being Modern in Japan: Culture and Society from the 1910s to the 1930s*, ed. Elise K. Tipton and John Clark (Singapore: Australian Humanities Research Foundation, 2000), pp. 120–34. On the reviews, see Seidensticker, *Tokyo Rising*, pp. 73–87. On the invention of the café waitress, see Miriam

Silverberg, "The Café Waitress Serving Japan," in *Mirror of Modernity*, ed. Stephen Vlastos (Berkeley: University of California Press, 1998), pp. 208–25. Also see Miriam Silverberg, "Nihon no jokyū burūsu o uttata," in *Jendā no Nihonshi*, vol. 2, ed. Wakita and Hanley, pp. 585–607. See Ishikawa, *Goraku no senzen shi*, pp. 125–41; Minami, "Fūzoku no tōsei—sono hō to ronri," in *Shōwa bunka*, pp. 158–59; Nishizawa, *Zatsugaku—Kayō Shōwa shi*, pp. 262–63; Wada Hirobumi, "Dansu hōru no hikari to kage," in *Nihon no bungaku*, vol. 13 (Tokyo: Yūseidō, 1993), pp. 129–47. Nagai Yoshikazu corroborates this in his discussion of dance halls and those who patronized them. Nagai describes the attitude of the authorities toward dance halls in Nagai Yoshikazu, *Dansu monogatari: [kōsai jutsu] no yunyūshatachi* (Tokyo: Riburopōto, 1994), esp. pp. 140–215.

44 Kiyosawa, "Modan gāru no kaibō," p. 97.

45 Sawamura, "Amerikanizumu," p. 10. Harootunian notes that "film was not just a sign of capitalism; it also put on display commodity culture produced by American capitalism, lived and experienced by its principal subjects, modern men and women." *Overcome by Modernity*, p. 23.

46 Hirabayashi, "Gendai o shōchō suru mono" (*Chūō kōron*, January 1929), in *Hirabayashi zenshū*, vol. 3, p. 812.

47 Hirabayashi, "Beikoku no kikai toshite no eiga," *Hirabayashi zenshū*, vol. 2, pp. 412–13.

48 Nii Itaru, "Eiga to josei ni kindaigata" (*Kaizō*, November 1928), in *Gendai bungakuron taikei—modanizumu geijutsuha*, vol. 5 (Tokyo: Kawade shobō, 1956), pp. 109–10.

49 Murobuse Takanobu, *Gaitō no shakaigaku* (Tokyo: Inakasha, 1929), p. 82.

50 Quoted in Rayna Rapp and Ellen Ross, "The 1920s Feminism, Consumerism, and Political Backlash in the United States," in *Women in Culture and Politics*, p. 58.

51 Murayama Tomoyoshi, "Kindaishin no kyōraku seikatsu wareware to kyōraku," *Shinchō*, January 1929, p. 40.

52 Takayasu Yasuko, "Modan gāru zakkan," *Fujin kōron*, January 1927, pp. 67–68.

53 Yamakawa, "Modan gāru modan bōi" (*Keizai ōrai*, September 1927), in *Yamakawa Kikue shū*, vol. 4, p. 269.

54 Gonda Yasunosuke, "Modan seikatsu no hanran—modan seikatsu to hentai shikōse," *Kaizō*, June 1929, p. 33.

55 See Nishizawa, *Zatsugakku—Kayō Shōwa shi*, pp. 262–63; *Tokyo ero on parēdo* (Tokyo: Shōbunkaku shobō, 1931) is one example of a popular *ero* book. Also see Akita Masami, *Sei no ryōki modan* (Tokyo: Seikyūsha, 1994), esp. chapter 2. This sounds similar to the argument about cultural imperialism, which, to quote J. Tunstall, "claims that authentic, traditional and local culture in many parts of the world is being battered out of existence by the

indiscriminate dumping of large quantities of slick commercial and media products, mainly from the United States." Jeremy Tunstall, *The Media Are American: Anglo-American Media in the World* (London: Constable, 1977), p. 57.

56 Murayama, "Kindaishin no kyōraku seikatsu," pp. 38–40.

57 Chiba Kameo, *Isei o Miru* (Tokyo: Ryūmeisha, 1924), esp. "Shin jidai no igi," pp. 3–13, "Shinkō kaikyū no fujin ni atau," pp. 14–24, and "Kindai fujin no shichō to sono keikō," pp. 121–29.

58 "Zadankai," *Fujin no kuni*, p. 10.

59 Ibid., p. 9.

60 Hirabayashi, "Geijutsu-ha, puroretaria-ha oyobi kindai-ha" (*Shinchō*, May 1930), in *Hirabayashi zenshū*, vol. 2, pp. 250–51.

61 Hirabayashi Hatsunosuke, "Shakai jihyō—Shihonshugi no sentanteki shisō urutora modanizumu," *Shinchō*, February 1930.

62 Hirabayashi, "Geijutsu-ha, puroretaria-ha," in *Hirabayashi zenshū*, vol. 2, pp. 250–51.

63 "Ken'i hōkaiki no fujin—modan gāru hassei no shakateki konkyo" (*Fujin kōron*, March 1928), in *Hirabayashi zenshū*, vol. 2, p. 385.

64 Barbara Sato, "Sengojosei no yume to genjitsu—dokusha zadankai ni miru," in *Zoku Shōwa bunka—1945–1989*, pp. 84–97.

Chapter Three
Housewives as Reading Women

1 *Lady's Magazine*, February 1774, quoted in *Women's Worlds Ideology: Femininity and the Women's Magazines*, vol. 4, ed. Ros Ballester, Margaret Beetham, Elizabeth Frazer, and Sandra Hebron (London: Macmillan, 1993), p. 64.

2 See Kazumi Ishii and Nerida Jarkey, "The Housewife Is Born: The Establishment of the Notion and Identity of the *Shufu* in Modern Japan," *Japanese Studies* 22, no. 1 (2002): 35–47. According to the authors, the earliest mention of the housewife in Japan was in *Kaji Ken'yaku kun* (Tips for Economizing at Home, 1874), a journal for upper-class women that used the term to describe a wife's varied duties at home. English novels in the 1850s referred to the housewife's tasks as "her duties." The term *housewife* also was used in the Meiji period to refer to a woman who headed her own business such as an inn (*ryokan*) or rooming house (*geshuku*). In other words, the *shufu* was the female counterpart of the male *shūjin*. However, different terms were used in different areas. In downtown Tokyo (*shita machi*), for example, the term *kamisan*, which is still popular today, was more prevalent than *shufu*.

For more on the housewife, see Murakami Nobuhiko, "Katei no sei-katsu," in *Meiji joseishi—joken to ie* (Tokyo: Rironsha, 1981), pp. 233–53; Shimizu Reiko, "Shufu no jidai hajimatta" (*Fujin kōron*, April 1955), in *Shufu ronsō o yomu*, vol. 1, ed. Ueno Chizuko (Tokyo: Keisō shobō, 1994), pp. 23–33; Shimizu Michiko, " 'Jochū' imēji no henyō," pp. 159–75, and Naka-zato Hideki, "Shufu no yakuwari to kakeizan—Fujin zasshi ni miru kakei kanri," both in *Onna no bunka—Kindai Nihon bunkaron*, vol. 8, ed. Aoki, Kawamoto et al., pp. 177–99; Nomoto Kyōko, "Kaji rōdō o meguru 'shufu' to 'jochū,' " in *Onna no shakaishi, 17–20 seiki—"Ie" to jendā o kangaeru*, ed. Ōguchi Yūjirō (Tokyo: Yamakawa shuppan, 2001), pp. 311–32.

3 An article attributed to a woman contributor called Shibanoya (a pen name) informed readers that "there were no limits to a housewife's duties." See "The Housewife's Position" (Shufu no itchi), *Katei zasshi*, October 1895, reprinted in *Nihon fujin mondai shiryō shūsei, Seikatsu*, vol. 7, ed. Maruoka Hideko, pp. 92–98.

4 See "A Lady's Virtue" (Fujin no bitoku), *Katei*, February 1901, pp. 7–8. Also see "Peace in the Family Depends on the Mental Stability of the House-wife" (Ikka no heiwa wa shufu no seishin no kontei yori shozu), *Katei*, March 1901 (editorial). Even if the term *housewife* was not actually men-tioned, it was implied. Good examples are "A Lady Does Not Need Spe-cialized Study" (Fujin wa senmom no gakugeiwo narau wo yōsezu), *Fujo zasshi*, July 1891; and "Ladies and Swimming" (Fujin to kaisuihō), *Jogaku sekai*, July 1906, pp. 60–62.

5 Arase Yutaka, "Taishū shakai no keisei to tenkai," in *Nihon no shakai*, ed. Fukutake Tadashi (Tokyo: Mainichi shinbunsha, 1957), pp. 160–76.

6 On the growth of urban culture, see *Taishū bunka to masu meideiya—Kin-dai Nihon bunkaron*, vol. 7, ed. Aoki Tamotsu, Kawamoto Saburō, Tsutsui Kiyotada, Mikuriya Takashi, and Yamaori Tetsuo (Tokyo: Iwanami shoten, 1999); Arima Manabu, *Kokusaika no naka no teikoku Nihon, 1905–1924, Nihon no kindai*, vol. 4 (Tokyo: Chūō kōronsha, 1999), pp. 272–332; Itō Toshiharu, "Nihon no 1920 nendai—Tokyo o chūshin to suru toshi taishū bunka no tenkai," in *Toshi taishū bunka no seiritsu*, ed. Hirai Tadashi, Hosaka Kazuō, Kawamoto Saburō, and Yamada Takanobu (Tokyo: Yūzankaku, 1983), pp. 176–82. Also see Kuwabara Takeo, Katō Hidetoshi, and Yamada Minoru, "Jānarizumu no shisōteki no yakuwari," in *Kindai Nihon shisōshi kōza*, vol. 5, ed. Kuno Osamu and Sumiya Mikio (Tokyo: Chikuma shobō, 1960), esp. pp. 161–83.

For more on early Shōwa newspapers and the publishing boom, see Satō Takeshi, "Shinbun—kokumin dōin no mekanizumu," in *Shōwa bunka*, pp. 257–60; Ueda Yasuo, "Shuppan—Taishūka to hōkai," in *Shōwa bunka*, pp. 287–320. For a detailed view of magazines and their readers, see Naga-mine Shigetoshi, *Zasshi to dokusha no kindai* (Tokyo: Nihon editāsukūru shuppanbu, 1997). On women's journalism, *Taishōki no josei zasshi*, ed. Kindai josei bunka kenkyūkai (Tokyo: Ōzorasha, 1996); also see *Shuppan joseishi*, ed. Ikeda Emiko (Kyoto: Sekaishisōsha, 2001); Oka Mitsuo, *Fujin zasshi, jānarizumu* (Tokyo: Gendai jānarizumu shuppankai, 1981). (In spite of *Fujin sekai*'s engaging editorial policies, the magazine lacked the managing know-how to keep up with its competitors.) In English, see Rubin, *Injurious to Public Morals*, pp. 246–55. On Matsui Sumako, see Brian Powell, "Matsui Sumako: Actress and Woman," in *Modern Japan: Aspects of History, Literature and Society*, ed. W. G. Beasley (Berkeley: University of California Press, 1975), pp. 135–46; and Kano, *Acting Like a Woman in Modern Japan*, pp. 184–99.

    Kingu, the first popular magazine to become an overnight success, has attracted the attention of many scholars, both at the time and today. See, for example, Takashō Sanji, "Kingu ron," in *Sōgō jānarizumu kōza*, vol. 4 (Tokyo: Naigaisha, 1931), pp. 163–79; Kakegawa Tomiko, "Noma Seiji to Kōdansha bunka," *Shisō no kagaku*, October 1959, pp. 19–31; also Yamamoto Taketoshi, "Taishū taitōki no shuppan-o, kōkoku-o—Noma Seiji," in Yamamoto Taketoshi and Tsuganezawa Toshihiro, *Nihon no kōkokujin—jidai, hyōgen* (Tokyo: Nihon keizai shinbunsha, 1986), pp. 255–67; Satō Takumi, *"Kingu" no jidai—kokumin taishū zasshi no kōkyōsei* (Tokyo: Iwanami shoten, 2002). On the movie industry during the period, see Gonda Yasunosuke, "Minshū goraku" (*Chūgai shōgyō shinpō*, December 1923), in *Gonda Yasunosuke chosakushū*, vol. 4, pp. 72–74, 80–81; Iwasaki Akira, *Eiga ga wakakatta toki* (Tokyo: Heibonsha, 1980); Yamamoto Kikuo, *Nihon eiga ni okeru gaikoku eiga no eikyō* (Tokyo: Waseda daigaku shuppan, 1983), esp. sections 1 and 2; Makino Mamoru, "Documentation of Non-Film Material: Books, Programs, Posters, Portraits, etc.," in *Cinema no Seiki: Eiga tanjō hyakunen hyakurankai* (Tokyo: Asahi shinbunsha, 1995), pp. 136–47.

    What constitutes leisure remains a topic for debate. For an early discussion on the concept of leisure, see Kobayashi Ichizō, "Taishū gorakuron," *Kaizō*, June 1936. On the history of popular music and the record industry, see *Nihon ryūkōka shi*, Komota Nobuya et al. (Tokyo: Shakai shisōsha, 1970), pp. 36–57; and Kurata Yoshihirō, *Nihon rekōdo bunka shi* (Tokyo: Tokyo shoseki, 1979). On radio broadcasting, see *Tokyo hōsōkyoku enkaku shi* (Tokyo: Tokyo hōsōkyoku enkaku shi henshū iinkai, 1928); *Nihon hōsō shi* (Tokyo: Nihon hōsō kyōkai, 1951); Takeyama Akiko, "Hōsō," in *Shōwa bunka*, pp. 321–38; Takeyama Akiko, *Rajio no jidai: Rajio wa chanoma no shūyaku datta* (Tokyo: Sekai shisōsha, 2002).

7 Katayama Seiichi, *Kindai Nihon no joshi kyōiku* (Tokyo: Kenpakusha, 1984), esp. chapters 1–3.

8 Most readers of mass women's magazines in the 1920s would have considered themselves members of the middle class because of their educational background. Graduation from a four-year women's higher school

or normal school, also considered a high school, put young women in this category.

9 For sociologist Joke Hermes, "the gendered significance of women's magazines" is that "the repertoires offer readers a means by which to fantasize about perfect selves: the perfect cook, the up-to-date consumer or cultured person, the calm, confident realist." Joke Hermes, *Reading Women's Magazines* (Cambridge: Polity Press, 1995), p. 62.

10 See Uchida Roan, "Onna no zasshi no genzai to shōrai," in *Uchida Roan zenshū*, vol. 3 (Tokyo: Yumani shobō, 1987), p. 95. For a similar view voiced by intellectuals in the 1920s, see "Fujin zasshi wa doko e iku," *Kaizō*, March 1927, pp. 65–69. The growth of mass women's magazines is discussed in Maeda Ai, "Taishō kōki tsūzoku shōsetsu no tenkai—fujin zasshi no dokusha-sō" (*Bungaku*, July 1968), reprinted in *Maeda Ai chosakushū*, vol. 2, p. 161.

11 Uchida, "Onna no zasshi," p. 95.

12 Oka, *Fujin zasshi jānarizumu*, p. 102. Also see Shida Aiko and Yuda Yoriko in *Fujin zasshi kara mita 1930 nendai*, ed. Watashitachi no rekishi o tsuzuru kai (Tokyo: Dōjidaisha, 1987). Sandra Wilson's research also addresses the complexity of this debate. Sandra Wilson, "Women, the State and the Media in Japan in the Early 1930s: *Fujo shinbun* and the Manchurian Crisis," *Japan Forum* 7, no. 1 (1995): 87.

13 Fujitake Akira, "Taishū bunka no seiritsu," in *Kōza gendai jānarizumu*, vol. 1 (Tokyo: Jiji tsūshinsha, 1981), p. 102. Oka's and Fujitake's arguments are in keeping with the critique set forth by Matsushita Keiichi in his landmark article, "Taishū kokka no seiritsu to sono mondaisei," *Shisō*, no. 389 (November 1956). Also see *Shōhi toshite no raifu stairu, Gendai no esupuri, Seikatsu bunka shirīzu*, no. 1, ed. Fujitake Akira (Tokyo: Shibundō, 2000).

14 Saitō Michiko, "Senjika no josei no seikatsu to ishiki," in *Bunka to fashizumu*, ed. Akazawa Shirō and Kitagawa Kenzō (Tokyo: Nihon keizai hyōronsha, 1993), pp. 322–24.

15 Most Japanese intellectuals shared a view of popular culture similar to that of Theodor Adorno, who commented that because popular music (jazz included) is "patterned" and "predigested," it "serves within the psychological household of the masses to spare them the effort of that participation (even in listening or observation) without which there can be no receptivity to art." Theodor W. Adorno, "On Popular Music" (with George Simpson), *Studies in Philosophy and Social Science* (*Zeitschrift fur Sozialforschung*) 9 (1941): 17–48.

16 William H. Chafe, *The American Woman: Her Changing Social, Economic, and Political Roles, 1920–1970* (London: Oxford University Press, 1972), p. 104. Feminist Betty Friedan takes women's magazines to task for similar reasons in *The Feminine Mystique* (New York: Dell, 1963.)

17 Nancy Woloch, *Women and the American Experience* (New York: Alfred A. Knopf, 1984), p. 411.

18 Penny Tinkler, *Constructing Girlhood: Popular Magazines for Girls Growing Up in England 1920–1950* (London: Taylor and Francis, 1995), p. 134.

19 See *Nihon hōsō shi*, pp. 226–37. *Naniwabushi* are recited with the *shamisen*, a traditional musical instrument. Among the many articles on radio broadcasting published at the time are "Minshū goraku toshite no rajio," *Keizai ōrai*, January 1928, pp. 47–65; "Kyōiku toshite no rajio—kyōraku toshite no rajio," *Fujin kōron*, May 1926, pp. 32–43; and "Tokyo hōsō kyoku uramen shi," *Josei*, 1928.

20 See Oka, "Ryōsai kenbo shugi no jānarizumu," in *Fujin zasshi jānarizumu*, pp. 28–33; Haga Noboru describes *ryōsai kenbo* in its first stage as a response to Westernization during the early Meiji period when several intellectuals returned to Japan from study trips to Europe. However, he argues that the concept changed with the times and it took on conservative trappings in the 1880s. See Haga Noburu, *Ryōsai kenboron* (Tokyo: Yūzankaku, 1990), esp. pp. 5–7. Positive analyses of *ryōsai kenbo* exist in present-day scholarship. An example is Ishizuka Masahide, "Ryōsai kenbo shugi no kaimei ni yosete," *Josei kenkyū*, no. 25 (Tokyo: Kazokushi kenkyū-kai: December 1990), pp. 2–17.

Mitsuda Kyōko focuses on the government's use of *ryōsai kenbo* to create a new role for women in society in "Kindaiteki boseikan no juyō to hensei—'kyōiku suru haha oya' kara 'ryōsai kenbo' e," *Bosei o tō*, pp. 100–129; also see Wöehr, "Early Feminist Ideas on Motherhood in Japan—Challenging the Official Ideal of 'Good Wife, Wise Mother,'" *Hiroshima Journal of International Studies* 2 (1996). From the early twentieth century educators deliberated over the degree of prominence to be accorded *ryōsai kenbo* in women's education. See "Ryōsai kenbo ronsō," *Kyōiku jiron*, no. 545, October 5, 1908; and [Osaka] *Asahi shinbun*, November 7, 1908, in Kuki Yukio, Suzuki Eiichi, and Kon'no Yoshikio, *Nihon kyōiku ronsō shiroku*, vol. 1 (Tokyo: Daiichi hōki, 1980), pp. 233–52.

21 Uno, "'Good Wives and Wise Mothers' in Early Twentieth Century Japan," pp. 10–11.

22 Uchida, *Uchida Roan zenshū*, vol. 3, pp. 96–97. Also see Yamaguchi Masao's in-depth study, *Uchida Roan sanmyaku* (Tokyo: Shōbunsha, 2001) pp. 498–511.

23 Tsurumi Shunsuke, "Jānarizumu no shisō," pp. 20–22; Yamamoto, *Nihon no kōkoku-jin, jidai, hyōgen*, pp. 255–67. Regarding Noma's vision for *Kingu*, see Noma Seiji, *Watashi no hansei* (Tokyo: Chikura shobō, 1936).

24 *Shufu no tomosha no gojūnen*, p. 14.

25 Tsugawa Masashi, "Fujin zasshi no henshū," *Sōgō jānarizumu kōza*, vol. 10, 1931, pp. 56–57. (The editors were males, but some reporters were women.)

Journalist Sugimura Sojinkan notes a similar tendency in newspapers of the period. See "Nihon jānarizumu no gensei—shinbun jānarizumu," in *Sōgō jānarizumu kōza,* vol. 9, 1931, pp. 13–14; also Aono Suekichi, "Yomiuri shinbun ron," in *Sōgō jānarizumu kōza,* vol. 12, 1931, p. 17.

26 On technological advancements and the growth of mass magazines, see Sugimura, *Sōgō jānarizumu kōza,* vol. 9, pp. 17–27. For a more recent generalized study, see Suzuki Jun, "Taishū no gijutsu kakushin," in Suzuki Jun, *Shingijutsu no shakaishi,* vol. 15 (Tokyo: Chūō kōronsha, 1999), pp. 158–240.

27 *Kōto jogakkō shiryō shūsei—kōto jogakkō no kenkyū,* vol. 2, ed. Fukuda Sumiko et al. (Tokyo: Ōzorasha, 1990), appendix, p. 29.

28 See Elizabeth Knipe Mouer, "Women in Teaching," in *Women in Changing Japan,* ed. Joyce Lebra, Joy Paulson, and Elizabeth Powers (Stanford: Stanford University Press, 1976), pp. 160–61. The cost of the newspaper went from 0.28 (580) yen in 1891 to 0.50 (1,000) yen in 1915. In 1920 the cost of a morning and evening set was 1.20 (2,400) yen. See *Nedan no Meiji, Taishō, Shōwa fūzoku shi* (Tokyo: Asahi shinbunsha, 1981), p. 161.

29 "Theories of Text and Culture," in *Women's Worlds: Ideology, Femininity and the Woman's Magazine,* ed. Ros Ballaster et al., p. 14.

30 Hakubunkan's aim was to create a variety of general magazines that would appeal to different segments of society. *Taiyō* (The Sun, 1895), *Shōnen sekai,* (Youth World, 1895), and *Bungei kurabu* (Literary Club, 1895) were among the fruits of this endeavor. Early Shōwa critic Kimura Tsuneyoshi discusses Hakubunkan's contribution to late Meiji publishing in his article "Nihon zasshi hattatsu shi (2)," in *Sōgō jānarizumu kōza,* vol. 5, pp. 250–52. Of particular interest is the special issue entitled "Hakubunkan bunka," in *Hōsho gekkan,* November 1999, no. 170, ed. Suzuki Sadami et al., pp. 2–29. For an overview of Meiji, Taishō, and Shōwa publishing, see Shuppanshi kenkyūkai, "Sōgō zasshi no kenkyū (1) sōgō zasshi hyakunen shi," *Ryūdō,* July 1979, pp. 126–27.

31 *Kindai shomin seikatsu shi—ningen seken,* vol. 1, ed. Minami et al., pp. 21–25.

32 Okano Takeo, *Nihon shuppan bunkashi* (Tokyo: Hara shobō, 1981), p. 245.

33 For a discussion of *Jogaku sekai's* philosophy, see the second issue of the magazine. *Jogaku sekai,* January 1901, pp. 1–3.

34 Both *Jogaku zasshi* and *Fujo zasshi* sold for 5 sen (0.05 yen), or approximately 100 yen today.

35 Nishimura Shigeki, "Joshi no sandai iku [kyōiku] ni tsuite," *Jogaku sekai,* January 1901; Nagamawashi Tomoe, "Josei to shūyō roku," *Jogaku sekai,* January 1901; Miwata Masuko, "Jokun konseki no kan," *Jogaku sekai,* January 1905.

36 Kimura, *Sōgō jānarizumu kōza,* vol. 4, p. 253. The decline of Hakubunkan has been linked to the company's refusal to accept unsold magazines. See Hashimoto Motomu, *Nihon shuppan hanbaishi* (Tokyo: Kōdansha, 1964),

pp. 86–87; also Yamaguchi Masao, "Meiji shuppankai no hikari to yami—Hakubunkan no kōbō," in *Zasshi "Taiyō" to kokumin bunka no keisei,* ed. Suzuki Sadami (Kyoto: Shibunkaku shuppan, 2001), pp. 115–52.

37 Kimura, ibid., p. 251. The name *Jitsugyō no Nihon* (Business Japan) reflects the new importance placed on business expertise following the Sino-Japanese War (1894–95).

38 Murakami Nobuhiko, *Meiji joseishi—onna no shokugyō,* vol. 2 (Tokyo: Rironsha, 1973), pp. 315–17. Also see Anzai Jirō, "Shinbun to josei—Tokyo kakushi no katei shinbunran ni tsuite," in *Sōgō jānarizumu kōza,* vol. 3, pp. 44–45.

39 Inoue Matsuko, "Ryūkō to katei kiji ni tsuite," in *Sōgō jānarizumu kōza,* vol. 5, pp. 1–12.

40 Okano, *Nihon shuppan bunka shi,* pp. 248–49. Murai was the author of the best-selling novel *Shokudōraku.*

41 Kimura, *Sōgō jānarizumu kōza,* vol. 5, p. 253.

42 Inoue, *Sōgō jānarizumu kōza,* vol. 5, p. 7.

43 *Shufu no tomosha no gojūnen,* pp. 40–41. Although Ishikawa was known publicy as Ishikawa Takemi, the correct reading of his given name is Takeyoshi.

44 *Shokugyō fujin ni kansuru chōsa, 1922* (Tokyo: Tokyo-shi shakaikyoku, 1924). In 1925 this survey was published under the name *Fujin jiritsu no naichi* and reprinted in *Kindai fujin mondai meicho senshū zokuhen,* vol. 7 (Tokyo: Nihon tosho sentā, 1982), p. 107. Hereafter cited as *Tokyo City Office Survey of 1922.*

45 For information regarding early women's magazines in the United States, Frank Luther Mott's *A History of American Magazines,* vols. 1–5 (Cambridge: Harvard University Press, 1938–68) is still an excellent source of information. On early women's magazines in Britain, see Margaret Beetham, *A Magazine of Her Own? Domesticity and Desire in the Woman's Magazine, 1800–1914* (London: Routledge, 1996), esp. sections 3 and 4. Also see Jennifer Scanlon's exciting study on women and consumerism in the early twentieth century: *Inarticulate Longings: The Ladies' Home Journal, Gender, and the Promises of Consumer Culture* (New York: Routledge, 1995).

46 Minemura Toshio, "Kigyō fujin zasshi keitai ron," in *Sōgō jānarizumu kōza,* vol. 5, p. 26.

47 Ibid., p. 27.

48 Harrington, "Women and Higher Education in the Japanese Empire (1869–1945)," p. 170; Susan Newell, "Women Primary School Teachers and the State in Interwar Japan," in *Society and State in Interwar Japan,* ed. Elise Tipton (London: Routledge, 1997), pp. 18–21. For a discussion of the social impact of education in the Meiji period, see Carol Gluck, *Japan's Modern Myths: Ideology in the Late Meiji Period* (Princeton: Princeton University Press, 1985), pp. 163–74.

49 See "Joshi shōgakkō shūgaku ritsu" and "Joshi chūtō gakkō kōtō gakkō tō-

keihyō," in *Meiji ikō kyōiku bunka tōkei* (Tokyo: Kokuritsu kokkai toshokan chōsa rippō kōsakyoku hen, 1957); reprinted in Ōhama Tetsuya and Kumakura Isao, *Kindai Nihon no seikatsu to shakai*, pp. 72–73. On early women's higher schools, see Fukuda Sumiko et al., *Kōtō jogakkō shiryō shūsei—kōtō jogakkō no kenkyū*, pp. 3–13.

50   *Tokyo City Office Survey of 1922*; see introduction.

51   See Chimoto Akiko "Nihon ni okeru seibetsu yakuwari bungyō no keisei," in Ogino Miho et al., *Seido toshite no onna—sei, san, kazoku no hikaku shakaishi* (Tokyo: Heibonsha, 1990), p. 192. Also see Iwasaki Jirō, *Bukka no sesō hen* (Tokyo: Yomiuri shinbunsha, 1982), pp. 60–61.

52   *Shufu no tomosha no gojūnen*, p. 53.

53   See *Shufu no tomosha no gojūnen*, p. 39.

54   Hirabayashi Hatsunosuke, "Fujin zasshi kanken," *Kaizō*, March 1927, p. 70.

55   Inoue, *Sōgō jānarizumu*, vol. 5, pp. 1–2.

56   *Shufu no tomosha no gojūnen*, p. 46. (By the 1920s, however, *Shufu no tomo* had changed its editorial policy and included some articles on suffrage, for example.

57   See Hirota, *Nihon josei seikatsu shi—kindai*, vol. 4, p. 255.

58   *Fujokai* offered regular monthly question-and-answer columns that addressed readers' health problems as well as the needs of young mothers and pregnant women.

59   Nii Itaru, "Fujin zasshi ron," in *Sōgō jānarizumu kōza*, vol. 7, p. 276. Yosano Akiko expressed disapproval of women's magazines from early on. See Yosano, "Fujin zasshi no dakyōteki keikō" (January 1919), reprinted in *Teihon Yosano Akiko zenshū*, vol. 17, p. 315.

60   Yamakawa, "Fujin zasshi no hizokusei" (*Fujin to sesō*, 1937), in *Yamakawa Kikue shū*, vol. 5, p. 137.

61   "Gendai fujin zasshi ron" (*Keizai ōrai*, November 1930), in *Yamakawa Kikue shū*, vol. 5, p. 298.

62   Ibid., pp. 293–94.

63   Nii, *Sōgō jānarizumu kōza*, vol. 7, p. 275.

64   In the years 1910–19, articles featured in U.S. magazines like *Ladies' Home Journal* and *House Beautiful* introduced "minimal houses" designed to simplify women's household tasks, giving them time to leave the house, hold a job, or do volunteer work. "Rational plans, efficient technology, and easily cleaned surfaces seemed the key." See Gwendolyn Wright, "Prescribing the Model Home," in *Home: A Place in the World*, ed. Arien Mack (New York: New York University Press, 1993), p. 217.

65   *Kan'i seikatsu* (Simple Life), a magazine reflecting the ideals behind social reform advocated by Sakai Toshihiko, Ōsugi Sakae, Kōtoku Shūsui, Kamitsukasa Shōken (the magazine's publisher), and others, was published from 1906 to 1907. American writer Charles Wagner's book *The Simple Life* had already been translated into Japanese at this time. His-

torian Atina Grossmann points out that in Germany during the Weimar period, "the pivot of the new rationalized domestic culture was the 'modern superwoman'; a health- and nutrition-conscious consumer and socializer of children, gainfully employed, and a willing and active sex partner." "The New Woman and the Rationalization of Sexuality in Weimar Germany," p. 158.

66 On the *Seikatsu kaizen undō*, see *Taishō Bunka*, p. 248. *Fujokai* was one of several mass women's magazines that devoted entire issues to the Daily Life Reform Movement. For example, *Fujokai*, "Sekatsu kairyō," May 1918. Morimoto Shizuko compares Japan's situation with that in the United States in "Nichibei katei seikatsu no hikaku kenkyū—(1)," *Fujin kōron*, March 1920, pp. 53–58; and "Shakō to settai—nichibei katei seikatsu hikaku kenkyū (2)," *Fujin kōron*, May 1920, pp. 70–77. Also see "Katei seikatsu no kaizen ni chikuonki o riyō seyo—katei seikatsu kaizen no tame ni," *Fujin kōron*, July 1920, pp. 26–30; and Nishikawa Junsei, *Fujin shin undō* (Tokyo: Kōkyō shoin, 1920). For a comparative view, see Hatoyama Haruko, *Mohan katei* (Tokyo: Dai Nihon tosho, 1913), an adaptation of the English book *A Domestic Economy Reader*, a study of life reform in England.

The directive about eating white rice issued by the Ministry of Education was no doubt the result of the 1918 Rice Riots coupled with the rising cost of rice. Sukemori Kinji, one of the original members of the Daily Life Reform Organization (Seikatsu kaizen dōmeikai, 1920), discusses the problems the organization tackled in its attempt to rationalize everyday life in *Joshi shin sahō* (Tokyo: Kinkōdō, 1928), which was already in its seventieth printing. Of particular interest is the appendix "Seikatsu kaizen dōmeikai chōsa kettei jikō," pp. 1–14. New research includes Naramoto Akiko, "Seikatsu no yōfū stairu no keishiki: Taishōki ni okeru seikatsu kaizen domeikai no katsudō o chūshin toshite" (master's thesis, Seikei University, 1999); and Koyama, "Seikatsu kaizen undō ga mezasu kazokuzō, seikatsuzō," in *Katei no seisei to josei no kokuminka*, pp. 111–84. In English, see Jordan Sand, "The Cultured Life as Contested Space: Dwelling and Discourse in the 1920s," in *Being Modern in Japan*, ed. Tipton and Clark, pp. 99–101.

Harry Harootunian stresses that "the state momentarily tried to prevent consumers from being interpellated by the commodity . . ." and goes on to say that "all these new commodities pointed to the acquisition of new identities that often traversed class, gender, and sexuality, even though 'cultured living' was at first limited to the urban middle class." Harootunian, *History's Disquiet*, pp. 117–18.

67 Morishita Shizuko, "Nichibei katei seikatsu no hikaku kenkyū (1)," *Fujin kōron*, March 1920, pp. 53, 55.

68 *Shufu no tomo,* July 1918.

69 Patterns for making easy, up-to-date, economical aprons, coats, handbags, hats, and even home furnishings like fashionable pillows were regular features in mass women's magazines. See *Fujokai,* February 1920, pp. 129–35; *Fujokai,* September 1920, pp. 136–39.

70 Husbands, whose jobs took them away from the home, considered the "home" a place where they could relax. This helps explain their difficulty in perceiving the complexity of women's domestic roles.

71 Regarding the impact of photography on mass culture from the late Meiji period, see Minami, *Taishō bunka,* pp. 136–39.

72 Christopher Breward makes a similar argument in his discussion of the "promotion of fashionable femininity" in the interwar period in *The Culture of Fashion* (Manchester: Manchester University Press, 1995), pp. 199, 204–5.

73 *Shufu no tomo,* September 1918.

74 Inoue, *Sōgō jānarizumu kōza,* vol. 5, p. 202; on this same subject, see Satō Nobuko, "Fujin zasshi no henshū to kiji no torikata," in *Sōgō jānarizumu kōza,* vol. 7, p. 200.

75 The same holds true for countries other than Japan. Erika Rappaport comments that in nineteenth-century England as well as in America and France uneasiness about consumption practices and the growth of the urban translated into a fear that department stores would turn "ladies into jezebels." See Rappaport, *Shopping for Pleasure,* p. 29.

76 Regarding the newfound popularity of consumer goods, see Ogi Shinzō, Haga Tōru, and Maeda Ai, *Tokyo kūkan—1868–1930,* vol. 3: *Modan Tokyo* (Tokyo: Chikuma shobō, 1986), pp. 78–79. Also see Kayano Yatsuka, *Kindai Nihon no dezain bunka shi—1868–1926* (Tokyo: Firumu ātosha, 1992), esp. "Saisan shōhin no yōki dezain," pp. 393–408; "Modan raifu—zadankai," *Bungei shunjū,* January 1928. On the birth of the department store, see Hatsuda Tōru, *Hyakkaten no tanjō* (Tokyo: Sanseidō, 1993). Other recent scholarship is Jinno Yuki, *Shumi no tanjō: hyakkaten ga tsukutta teisto* (Tokyo: Keisō shobō, 1994); Yamamoto Taketoshi and Nishizawa Tamotsu, *Hyakka no bunka: Nihon no shōhi kakumei* (Tokyo: Sekai shisōsha, 1999). See *Mitsukoshi sanbyakunen no shōhō,* esp. pp. 160–235.

77 See Young, "Marketing the Modern," p. 55.

78 From 1918, *Shufu no tomo* regularly solicited contributions from readers about their personal problems. Murakami Nobuhiko calls this a two-sided policy. Although he believes it originated as a way for the magazine to lower its editorial expenses, he also considers it a means for "Ishikawa [Takemi] to make contact with the readers." Murakami, *Nihon no fujin mondai,* p. 124. (*Fujin sekai, Fujokai, Fujin no tomo,* and *Fujin kurabu* also allotted space for similar readers' contributions.)

79 Maeda, *Kindai dokusha no seiritsu,* p. 161.

80 "Joryū shinsaigo danwakai" (*Fujin kōron,* November 1923), in *Nihon fujin shūsei—seikatsu,* vol. 7, pp. 221–38.

81 Women's roles changed in the Meiji period as lifestyles became more afflu-ent. See "Shōwa shoki no mura ni okeru haha yakuwari kihan no henyō— zasshi *Ie no hikari* o tōshite," *Joseigaku nenpō,* no. 11, November 1990; also see *Nihon kindai shisō taikei—fūzoku. sei,* ed. Ogi Shinzō, Kumakura Isao, and Ueno Chizuko (Tokyo: Iwanami shoten, 1990), pp. 362–65.

82 *Shufu no tomo,* September 1928, quoted in Kimura Ryōko, "Fujin zasshi no jōhō kūkan to josei taishū dokushasō no seiritsu," *Shisō,* no. 812 (February 1992): 245.

83 Hirabayashi, "Fujin zasshi kanken" (*Kaizō,* March 1927), in *Hirabayashi Hat-sunosuke zenshū,* vol. 2, p. 70.

84 On April 4, 1914, the *Yomiuri* added a women's page to the newspaper. By 1921, the [Osaka] *Asahi, Kokumin, Jiji, Miyako, Hōchi,* and [Osaka] *Mainichi* had followed suit. For a more detailed discussion, see Inoue, *Sōgō jānari-zumu kōza,* vol. 5, p. 199.

85 *Kindai Nihon sōgō nenpyō* (Tokyo: Iwanami shoten, 1968), p. 214.

86 Hirabayashi, "Fujin zasshi kanken," in *Hirabayashi zenshū,* vol. 2, p. 70.

87 Ibid.

88 Gregory M. Plugfelder, " 'Smashing' Japanese-Style: Same-Sex Attach-ments in Prewar Japanese Girls' Schools" (paper prepared for the Eighth Berkshire Conference on the History of Women, Rutgers University, June 1990).

89 Honda, "Jogakusei no keifu," in *Nihon josei seikatsu shi,* pp. 187–89.

90 See Maeda, *Maeda Ai chosakushū,* vol. 2, p. 185.

91 In her chapter "Everyday Media Use," Joke Hermes remarks that "read-ing women's magazines, even if it is not important in itself, may still have its place or its importance in the structure of everyday routines, and thus lose its meaning while not disappearing entirely from readers' memories." Hermes, *Reading Women's Magazines,* p. 19.

92 See Abe Jirō, "Untenshu to hakushaku fujin no ai," in *Rekishi to jinbutsu* (Tokyo: Chūō kōronsha, April 1980), pp. 110–15; also see Murakami, "Ren'ai jiken—tenkei toshite Yoshikawa Kamako," *Taishō joseishi,* pp. 207–19.

93 Abe, *Rekishi to jinbutsu,* pp. 110–15.

94 Enchi Fumiko, *Kindai Nihon no josei shi—koi ni moe ai ni ikiru,* vol. 1 (Tokyo: Shūeisha, 1980), p. 108.

95 Ibid., pp. 112–14.

96 Ibid., p. 15. Yanagihara was best known by her pen name, Byakuren. Her given name was Akiko and Itō was her married name.

97 Yamakawa, "Yoshikawa Kamako to Kujō Takeko to Itō Byakuren" (*Onna no sekai,* June 1921), in *Yamakawa Kikue shū,* vol. 2, p. 301.

98 Henry DeWitt Smith II notes that Miyazaki was expelled from the Shinjin-kai because of his liaison with Byakuren. According to Enchi Fumiko, the general consensus was that Byakuren was influenced by the socialist lean-ings of the Shinjinkai and Miyazaki was behind her open letter to the *Tokyo Asahi*. See Henry Dewitt Smith II, *Japan's First Student Radicals* (Cambridge: Harvard University Press, 1972), p. 60; Enchi, *Kindai Nihon no joseishi, Koi ni moe ai ni ikiru*, vol. 1, pp. 28–29. See Miyazaki's open letter to the *Tokyo Asahi shinbun*, "Yōko o sukū no ga watakushi no gimu, to Miyazaki Ryū-suke," *Tokyo Asahi shinbun*, October 23, 1921, reprinted in *Taishō nyūsu jiten, Taishō 10–Taishō 11*, vol. 5, ed. Uchikawa Yoshimi et al. (Tokyo: Mainichi komyunikeishon, 1988), p. 672.

99 "Byakuren ga otto ni ketsubetsu no tegami," in *Taishō nyūsu jiten, Taishō 10–Taishō 11*, vol. 5, p. 672.

100 "Denzaemon ga Byakuren no ketsubetsujō ni hanron," *Tokyo Nichi Nichi shinbun*, October 24, 1921, in *Taishō nyūsu jiten, Taishō 10–Taishō 11*, vol. 5, p. 673. Also see *Fujin sekai*, December 1921, vol. 16, no. 12, special issue devoted to the Byakuren incident.

101 On the Hara-Ishiwara incident, see *Fujin kōron*, September 1920.

102 Oka, *Fujin zasshi jānarizmu*, pp. 68–70.

103 Journalist Sugimura Sojinkan is an exception. When he commented on the five-color sake incident, he wrote that it was ludicrous to criticize the *"atarashii onna"* for drinking a cocktail that had been especially concocted to suit women's drinking tastes the world over. Sugimura, *Jakusha no tame ni*, p. 432.

104 Yamakawa, *Yamakawa Kikue shū*, vol. 5, p. 290.

105 In their concluding remarks Rayna Rapp and Ellen Ross ("The 1920s: Femi-nism, Consumerism, and Political Backlash in the United States") assume a stance similar to that of Yamakawa: "Looking at the twenties, we were struck by the contrast between the opening up of life style opportunities for some women and the weakening of feminism as an organized, politi-cal movement to transform all of 'woman's condition'" (*Women in Culture and Politics: A Century of Change*, p. 59). Miyake Yasuko criticizes intellec-tuals like Yamakawa for harboring grandiose expectations about the fate of popular women's magazines, which she believed were read purely for entertainment and in no way reflected the intellectual level of women. Miyake Yasuko, *Gozen kuji* (Tokyo: Jitsugyō no Nihonsha, 1928), p. 39.

Chapter Four
Work for Life, for Marriage, for Love

1 Barbara Drygulski Wright, Introduction to *Women, Work, and Technology*, ed. Barbara Drygulski Wright, Myra Marx Ferree, Gail O. Mellow, Linda H.

Lewis, Maria-Luz Daza Samper, Robert Asher, and Kathleen Claspell (Ann Arbor: University of Michigan Press, 1987), p. 1.

2 "Possibilities for Becoming Professional Women [Readers' Discussion]," *Shufu no tomo,* April 1925, pp. 378–79. Also see Kawashima Yasuyoshi, *Fujin, Kateiran koto hajime* (Tokyo: Seiabo, 1996), pp. 180–208; and Miyoshi Nobuhiro, *Nihon no josei to sangyō kyōiku—Kindai sangyō shakai ni okeru josei no yakuwari* (Tokyo: Tōshindo, 2000), pp. 233–36.

3 From the early twentieth century, the concept of self-cultivation found expression in the terms *shūyō* and *kyōyō.* Some scholars have alluded to subtle differences in the two words in an attempt to explain their place in the Japanese mentality. See Karaki Junzō, *Gendaishi e no kokoromi* (Tokyo: Chikuma shobō, 1949); also see Tsutsui Kiyotada, *Nihongata "kyōyō" no unmei: Rekishi-shakaigakuteki kōsatsu* (Tokyo: Iwanami shoten, 1995), pp. 29–32; Donald Roden, *Schooldays in Imperial Japan: A Study in the Culture of a Student Elite* (Berkeley: University of California Press, 1975), pp. 1–9, 45–53.

In historical references to the terms *shūyō* and *kyōyō, shūyō* is linked mainly to the emergence of a strong sense of national consciousness apparent until the late Meiji period (Karaki, pp. 17–25), while *kyōyō* acquired its significance with Taishō period intellectualism and individualism. In comparing the two terms, Tsutsui argues that originally *shūyō* and *kyōyō* were identical, with the emphasis on character building (*jinkaku kōjō*); the distinction between the two emerged clearly in the 1920s. At that time, *shūyō* fit the ideal for self-cultivation prevalent especially among middle-class people, while *kyōyō* embodied the ethical principles that regulated the ideals of a particular group of higher-school (*kyūsei kōkō*) students (equivalent to first- and second-year university students) (see Tsutsui, pp. 29–32). In my view, however, the separation of the terms from a sociohistorical standpoint does not necessarily reflect a complete break in the two concepts.

4 Tazaki Nobuyoshi, "Josei rōdō no shoruikei," in *Nihon josei seikatsu shi—kindai,* vol. 4, ed. Joseishi sōgō kenkyūkai (Tokyo: Tokyo daigaku shuppankai, 1990), p. 185.

5 Okuda Akiko, "Shokugyō fujin no tanjō," in *Mainoritii toshite no joseishi,* ed. Okuda Akiko (Tokyo: Keisō shobō, 1997), p. 239; Yamakawa Kikue, "Gendai shokugyō fujin ron" (*Chūō kōron,* January 1929), in *Nihon fujin mondai shiryō shūsei—shisō,* vol. 8, ed. Maruoka Hideko (Tokyo: Domesu shuppan, 1976), pp. 334–35; Oku Mumeo, "Fujin rōdō kumia undō" (1925), reprinted in *Kindai fujin mondai meicho senshū,* vol. 6 (Tokyo: Nihon tosho sentā, 1982), pp. 463–66.

6 *Fujin nenkan* (1936), reprinted in *Fujin nenkan,* vol. 2 (Tokyo: Nihon tosho sentā, 1981), p. 70.

7 Kawasaki Natsu, "Chinōteki shokugyō," in *Shokugyōfujin o kokorozasu hito no tami";* reprinted in *Kindai fujin mondai meicho senshū,* vol. 10, pp. 59–131.

8 Ibid., pp. 71, 76; "Tokyo ni okeru fujin shokugyō," in *Fujin jiritsu no michi*, vol. 7 of *Kindai fujin mondai meicho senshū*, pp. 10–14.

9 For a broad sampling of salaries, see Kawazaki, "Chinōteki shokugyō," pp. 65–66, 74, 78, 82–83, 109, 112, 114, 118, 119–20, 122, 127–28, 134, 139, 142, 145, 151, 167, 173, 186, 190, 193–94, 196, 198, 200, 202, 204.

10 Shimoda Utako, "Women's Higher-School Graduates in the Home," *Fujokai*, March 1924, advertisement, p. 12.

11 For a sampling of readers' comments, see *Fujokai*, February 1924, pp. 270–72; *Fujokai*, March 1924, p. 290; *Fujin kōron*, July 1925, pp. 329–33.

12 Kawashima Yasuyoshi, *Fujin, Kateiran koto hajime* (Tokyo: Seiabō, 1996).

13 Readers' Column, *Fujokai*, February 1924, p. 270.

14 *Fujin kōron no gojūnen*, p. 27.

15 "Zadankai," *Gendai no esupuri, Nihon modanizumu*, no. 188, pp. 92–93.

16 Murakami, *Nihon no fujin mondai*, p. 67; Yamakawa, "Fujin no shokugyō mondai," *Kokka gakkai zasshi*, February 1919; *Yamakawa Kikue shū*, vol. 2, p. 17.

17 Ōkōchi, *Nihonteki chūsan kaikyū*, pp. 91–107. Also see Okuda, *Mainoritii toshite no joseishi, Kindai o yomikaeru*, vol. 1, pp. 238–39.

18 Sakurai Heigorō, "Modan gāru to shokugyō fujin," *Josei*, August 1927; also see "Zadankai," in *Gendai no esupuri, Nihon modanizumu*, no. 188, p. 90. While Maeda Hajime's book was not intended as an academic study (Maeda Hajime, *Shokugyō fujin monogatari* [Tokyo: Toyō keizai shuppanbu, 1929], p. 26), he stresses the newness of the term *professional working woman* (*shokugyō fujin*). Maeda includes the dancer, café hostess, and street girl in his definition of the modern girl.

19 Kitazawa Shūichi, "Shoppu gāru," *Kaizō*, April 1925, pp. 172–73.

20 Ibid., p. 177.

21 Oku Mumeo, "Shokugyō fujin no shinshutsu," in *Fujin kōron daigaku: Fujin shokugyōhen* (Tokyo: Chūō kōronsha, 1931), p. 12.

22 Murakami, *Taishōki no shokugyō fujin*, p. 168. Okamoto Ippei's series of cartoons of a female bus conductor corroborates Murakami's statement. See *Ippei zenshū*, vol. 6 (Tokyo: Senshinsha, 1928), pp. 153–54; also see Masaki Tomohiko, *Basu shasho no jidai* (Tokyo: Gendai shokan, 1992), pp. 21–44.

23 *Tokyo nichi nichi shinbun*, April 18, 1930; Konno Minako, *OL no sōzō—Imi sekai toshite no jendā* (Tokyo: Keisō shobō, 2000), pp. 26–46.

24 See Abe Tsunehisa and Satō Yoshimari, *Nihon kindai joseishi—tsūshi to shiryō* (Tokyo: Fuyo shobō, 2000), pp. 40–44; Saitō Minako, *Modan gāru-ron*, pp. 72–131. For a discussion in English of women factory workers and their working conditions during the years 1910–19 and the 1920s, see Barbara Molony, "Activism among Women in the Taishō Cotton Textile Industry," in *Recreating Japanese Women*, pp. 224, 232–35. For a comparison with women factory workers in the United States, see *America's Working Women: A Documentary History, 1600 to the Present*, ed. Rosalyn Baxandall,

Linda Gordon, and Susan Reverby (New York: Vintage Books, 1976), pp. 156–59; also see Sheilah Rowbotham, *Hidden from History: Rediscovering Women in History from the Seventeenth Century to the Present* (New York: Vintage Books, 1976), pp. 29, 33.

25 Yoshizawa Natsuko, "Sei no daburu. standādo o meguru tandādo—'heibon' ni okeru (chosha) no sekushuariti," *Onna no bunka—Kindai Nihon bunkaron*, vol. 8, pp. 204–6.

26 1922 Tokyo City Office Survey, p. 132.

27 Yamamuro Gunpei, "Shokugyō ni jūji suru fujin ni teisō mondai" (Regarding the Question of Virtue among Working Women, *Shufu no tomo*, March 1918, pp. 16–17.

28 Kaetsu Takako, "Soto ni tsutomuru wakaki fujin no kakugo," *Shufu no tomo*, March 1918, p. 14.

29 *Shokugyō zukushi—gendai manga taikan*, vol. 8 (Tokyo: Chūō bijutsusha, 1928), pp. 135, 169, 205; and *Onna no sekai—Gendai manga taikan*, vol. 9 (Tokyo: Chūō bijutsu sha, 1928), p. 50. On the same subject, see Takahashi Keiji, *Nihon seiseikatsushi* (Tokyo: Shunjūsha, 1931), pp. 324–25.

30 *Kokumin shinbun*, July 24, 1924.

31 Kitamura, *Hyōhi wa ugoku*, p. 124. For an assessment of sexual harassment in the workplace, see Iwao Sumiko, *The Japanese Woman: Traditional Image and Changing Reality* (New York: Free Press, 1993), pp. 204–6.

32 *Kindai Nihon no joseishi*, vol. 1, p. 135.

33 Murakami, *Taishōki no shoku gyō fujin*, p. 167.

34 Kitamura, *Hyōhi wa ugoku*, p. 123.

35 Figures reported by the Police Department censor; see Yamakawa, "Gendai shokugyō fujin ron," in *Nihon fujin mondai shiryō shūsei—Shichō*, vol. 8, p. 336.

36 See Ichikawa Kōichi, "Taishū kayō—[Tokyo kōshinkyoku] kara [Oyama no sugi no ko] made," in *Shōwa bunka*, ed. Minami, pp. 472–75; also see Nishizawa, *Kayō Shōwa shi*, pp. 184–88. An 1875 engraving made in the United States depicts a similar scene of a group of coquettish office ladies reading magazines and doing no work. See *America's Working Women*, ed. Baxandall et al., p. 234.

37 Tago Kazutami, "Fujin honrai no mokuteki to fujin no shokugyō," *Fujin kōron*, March 1919, pp. 16–17.

38 Ishikawa Takemi, "Marriage or Work," *Shufu no tomo*, April 1925, p. 1.

39 On the "tea pourer," see "Josei no nōryoku o saikentō" (Rethinking a Woman's Ability), *Fujin Kōron*, July 1957, pp. 92–101; Susan J. Pharr, *Losing Face: Status Politics in Japan* (Berkeley: University of California Press, 1990), pp. 59–73.

40 Yamada Waka, "Shufu no chikara," *Shōwa fujin dokuhon, katei hen*, no. 23, 1927; reprinted in *Nihon fujin mondai shiryō shūsei-Seikatsu*, vol. 7, p. 280.

Yamada received approximately 780 letters a day for her column "*Josei sōdan*," primarily from concerned housewives, working women, and students.

41 See Hiratsuka Raichō, "Nora san ni" (*Seitō,* January 1912), in *Hiratsuka Raichō chosakushū,* vol. 1, pp. 79–85; Ikuta Chōkō and Honma Hisao, *Shikai mondai jyūnikō* (Tokyo: Shinchōsha, 1919), pp. 314–20; Suzuki Bunshirō, *Fujin mondai no hanashi: Asahi jōshiki kōza,* vol. 9 (Tokyo: Asahi shinbunsha, 1929), pp. 98–105; Kiyosawa Rei, "Gendai no shokugyō fujin no sho mondai," pp. 55–57.

42 Sakurai, "Modan gāru to shokugyō fujin," *Josei,* August 1927, p. 171.

43 See Kathleen S. Uno, "Women and the Changes in the Household Division of Labor," p. 27, and Anne Walthall, "The Life Cycle of Farm Women in Tokugawa Japan," p. 57, both in *Recreating Japanese Women.* Also see E. Patricia Tsurumi, *Factory Girls: Women in the Thread Mills of Meiji Japan* (Princeton: Princeton University Press, 1990), p. 24. Suzuki, *Fujin mondai no hanashi,* esp. "Fujin no rōdo oyobi shokugyō mondai," p. 220. For a comparative discussion of the factory worker and the women's higher-school graduate, see Kimura Kyoko, "Jogakusei to jokō," *Onna no bunka, Kindai Nihon bunkaron,* vol. 8, esp. pp. 80–91.

44 For a comprehensive discussion of the "new" middle class, refer to Ōkōchi, *Nihonteki chūsan kaikyū;* Itō, "Zōdai suru shinchūsan kaikyū," *Taishō bunka,* pp. 183–95; also see Terade Kōji, *Seikatsu bunkaron e no shōtai* (Tokyo: Shibundō, 1994), section 4, pp. 184–201; David R. Ambaras, "Social Knowledge, Cultural Capital, and the New Middle Class in Japan, 1895–1912," *Journal of Japanese Studies* 24, no. 1 (1998): 1–33.

45 Terade, *Seikatsu bunkaron,* p. 183; Nii Itaru, "Sararīman ron," *Chūō kōron,* December 1928, pp. 43–44; Earl H. Kinmonth, *The Self-Made Man in Meiji Japanese Thought: From Samurai to Salary Man* (Berkeley: University of California Press, 1981), pp. 289–91.

46 *Nihon ryūkōka shi,* p. 240.

47 Itō, *Taishō bunka,* ed. Minami, pp. 186–87. According to Fukutake Tadashi's explanation of the class structure in the prewar period, in spite of the demise of the four-class system in the Meiji period, status consciousness continued and was an important factor encouraging the growth of the economy. Fukutake describes a "link" between the ruling upper classes and the "medium and small sized entrepreneurs as the owners of small factories and large stores, who, with medium- and small-sized landowners, formed a small middle class directly above the peasants, laborers, small merchants, and artisans. The new middle class of public officials, white-collar workers in large enterprises, teachers and other professional workers was not only smaller in number than the old middle class but also fully incorporated into the overall structure of social stratification. In fact,

the new middle class played the role of intermediary between the ruling class and the old middle class." Tadashi Fukutake, *Japanese Society Today*, 2d ed. (Tokyo: University of Tokyo Press, 1981), p. 8. Also see Peter Duus, *The Rise of Modern Japan* (Boston: Houghton Mifflin, 1976), pp. 148–50.

48 *Tokyo City Office Survey of 1922*. See introduction.

49 *Fujin shokugyō sensen no tenbō* (Tokyo: Tokyo shiyakusho, 1932), p. 81. This survey was conducted in 1931 and published in 1932. Hereafter cited as *Tokyo City Office Survey of 1931*.

50 *Kyūshoku fujin no kankyō chōsa* (Tokyo: Tokyo-fu gakumubu shakaika, 1931), pp. 1, 39.

51 *Meiji Taishō kokumu sōran* (Tokyo: Tōyō keizai shinpōsha, 1927), pp. 677–78.

52 "Shokugyō fujin no shūshoku daiichinichi no nikki," *Shufu no tomo*, May 1926, p. 138.

53 Ōbayashi Munetsugu, "Jokyū no shakaiteki kōsatsu," *Chūō kōron*, April 1932, p. 153.

54 Honda Tōru, "Shokugyō fujin to shūshoku nan," *Fujin kōron*, March 1930, p. 97.

55 "Kawazaki Natsu, "Chinōteki shokugyō," in Kawazaki Natsu, *Shokygyō fujin o kokorozasu hito no tame ni* (1932), reprinted in *Kindai fujin mondai meicho senshū*, vol. 10, pp. 63–204.

56 Masaki, *Basu shashō no jidai* (Tokyo: Gendai shokan, 1992), p. 22.

57 William H. Chafe describes a situation in the United States in the late 1920s where white-collar work, particularly the expansion of clerical jobs, offered an "outlet for middle-class and upper-class girls to find positions consistent with their social status." See *The American Woman*, p. 56.

58 *Habits of the Heart: Individualism and Commitment in American Life*, Robert N. Bellah et al. (Berkeley: University of California Press, 1985), p. 119. According to historian Nancy Woloch, with the emergence of a middle class in the early nineteenth century in the United States, the " 'home' came to function as a retreat from the 'world.' " The middle-class women "assumed a distinctive role" and entered into a "bargain based on mutual gain" in which men "had the opportunity to rise in the world, women had the opportunity to rise in the home." Note the similarities with Alexis de Tocqueville, *Democracy in America*, vol. 2, pp. 221–22. The reality was that "middle-class women and those who aspired to that status were only remote beneficiaries of the middle class bargain." Woloch, *Women and the American Experience*, p. 74.

59 Margit Nagy, "Middle-Class Working Women," in *Recreating Japanese Women*, p. 204.

60 Tazaki, *Nihon josei seikatsu shi*, vol. 4, p. 185.

61 *Tokyo City Office Survey of 1922*, pp. 48–49; *Tokyo City Office Survey of 1931*, pp. 32–35.

62 Hashimoto Noriko claims that employers considered women's salaries as "supplements" rather than as remuneration that would allow total economic independence. Hashimoto Noriko, *Danjo kyōgakusei no shiteki kenkyū* (Tokyo: Otsuki shoten, 1992), p. 170.

63 Murakami, *Nihon no fujin mondai*, pp. 69–71.

64 Kitaya Michiko, "Shūshoku sannenkan ni kurushiku soshite tanoshii seikatsu," *Shufu no tomo*, March 1923, pp. 187–88.

65 *Tokyo City Office Survey of 1931*, pp. 65–68.

66 Murakami, *Nihon no fujin mondai*, pp. 65–66.

67 Ibid. Also see Oku Mumeo, "Shokugyō fujin undō no shōten," *Fujin kōron*, January 1927, pp. 42–43; and Oku Mumeo, "Shokugyō fujin no shinshutsu," in *Fujin kōron daigaku: Fujin shokugyōhen*, 1931, p. 16. Historian Narita Ryūichi comments that Oku hoped that housewives felt a social responsibility just as they felt a responsibility to be "good wives" to their men. See Narita Ryūichi, "Women in the Motherland: Oku Mumeo through Wartime and Postwar," in *Total War and Modernization*, ed. Yasushi Yamanouchi, J. Victor Koschmann, and Ryūichi Narita (Ithaca: Cornell University Press, 1998), p. 143.

68 From the early years of Meiji, "supplementing the family income" was the major factor placing women in factories. Okuda Akiko, Preface to *Onna to otoko no jikū*, in Okuda Akiko et al. (Tokyo: Fujiwara shoten, 1995), p. 18.

69 A multiplicity of spiritual and moral claims that focused on what an ideal life ought to be like were manifested in trends referred to variously as culturalism (*kyōyōshugi*), humanism (*jindōshugi*), and personalism (*jinkakushugi*). These also were associated with aspects of Taishō-period "democracy." For a growing number of intellectuals, self-cultivation provided a compelling philosophical question. See Takeuchi Yō, *Risshin shusse to Nihonjin* (Tokyo: Nippon hōsō shuppan kyōkai, January 1996), p. 162; also see Rimer, preface to *Culture and Identity*, pp. x–xi; Gluck, *Japan's Modern Myths*, p. 276.

70 Sukegawa Koreyoshi, "Taishōki kyōyō-ha to hihyō no dōkō," in *Nihon bungaku zenshū*, vol. 5 (Tokyo: Gakutōsha, 1978), pp. 443–45; also see Stephen W. Kohl, "Abe Jirō and the Diary of Santarō," and Rimer, "Kurata Hyakuzō and the Origins of Love and Understanding," both in *Culture and Identity*, pp. 7–21 and 22–36.

71 Kohl, "Abe Jirō and the Diary of Santarō," pp. 8–9.

72 Kagawa Toyohiko's best-selling novel *Shisen o koete*, part of a trilogy published in October 1920, sold more than 600,000 copies. See Okano, *Nihon shuppan bunka shi*, pp. 321–22.

73 *Tokyo City Office Survey of 1922*, pp. 109–14. Also see Maeda, *Maeda Ai chosakushū*, vol. 2, pp. 188–90. Masuda Giichi, editor in chief of Jitsugyō no Nihon's *Fujin sekai*, emphasizes the benefits derived from reading in his

book *Fujin to shūyō* (Tokyo: Jitsugyō no Nihonsha, 1928), pp. 281–90. Masuda wrote a monthly column for *Fujin sekai* devoted to self-cultivation.

74 Miyake Yasuko, "Shokugyō to kekkon mondai," *Shufu no tomo*, April 1925, pp. 28–29.

75 All of the above examples are found in the *Tokyo City Office Survey of 1922*, pp. 109–14.

76 Kawai Michiko, "Shokugyō fujin no jikaku to shūyō—atarashiki jidai no wakaki shokugyō fujin no ayumu beki michi," *Shufu no tomo*, June 1924, pp. 4–10.

77 Mori Ritsuko, "Reimei jidai no Nihon josei," in *Tokyo City Office Survey of 1931*, p. 48.

78 Chiba, *Isei o miru*, p. 387.

79 Hatoyama Haruko, *Fujin seikatsu no kaizen* (Tokyo: Senshindō, 1920), pp. 19, 27, 281.

80 Ibid., pp. 281–82.

81 Miura Ryōko, "Jogakkō sotsugyōgo no yuki michi," *Shufu no tomo*, May 1922, pp. 34–35.

82 Maeda, *Maeda Ai chosakushū*, vol. 2, p. 191.

83 *Tokyo City Office Survey of 1922*, p. 93.

84 Ibid., p. 96.

85 Ibid., p. 102.

86 Sukegawa, *Nihon bungaku zenshū*, vol. 5, p. 448.

87 "Shijō kurabu," *Shufu no tomo*, April 1920, p. 179.

88 Ibid., October 1919, p. 155.

89 Ibid., February 1922, p. 154. Also see Kimura, "Fujin zasshi no jōhō kūkan," pp. 238–39.

90 "Kakushu shokugyō fujin no shūnyū to shoku o eru made no keiken," *Shufu no tomo*, March 1923, pp. 184–88.

91 "Atarashii fujin no shokugyō—jidōsha no onna untenshu," *Shufu no tomo*, March 1923, pp. 181–83.

92 "Shokugyō fujin no seikatsu nikki—aru hi no nikki," *Shufu no tomo*, June–August 1923.

93 "Jogakude no wakai fujin no ayumu beki shokugyō no michi—shōrai yūbō naru fujin no shokugyō wa nanika," *Shufu no tomo*, April 1923, p. 213.

94 "Shokugyō fujin wa ikaniseba seikō suruka," *Shufu no tomo*, April 1923, p. 221.

95 Tsutsui Kiyotada, "Kindai Nihon no kyōyōshugi to shūyōshugi," *Shisō*, no. 812 (February 1992): 159.

96 Following World War II, the founder of Panasonic Electric Company, Matsushita Kōnosuke, started the magazine *PHP* (*Peace, Happiness, and Prosperity*), in which he connects self-cultivation (*shūyō*) with getting ahead in the world (*shusse*).

97   "Daiissen ni hataraku onna no hitobito," *Fujin kōron,* January 1926, p. 116.
98   Murakami, *Taishōki no shokugyō fujin,* pp. 71–72.
99   *Ie no hikari,* June 1935, quoted in Itagaki Kuniko, *Shōwa senzen—senchūki no nōson seikatsu* (Tokyo: Sanrei shobō, 1992), pp. 122–24.
100 Ibid., p. 148.
101 Ibid.
102 *Tokyo Asahi shinbun,* June 19, 1932.
103 *Tokyo City Office Survey of 1922,* p. 43; and *Tokyo City Office Survey of 1931,* pp. 73, 77.
104 In contrast to Murakami Nobuhiko's claim that at approximately this same time, 45 percent of the working women in the United States were twenty-five years of age or younger (*Taishōki no shokugyō fujin,* pp. 63–64), the 1936 Gallup poll reported that 82 percent of Americans were opposed to women working after marriage. For the American perspective, see *America's Working Women,* ed. Baxandall et al., pp. 215–16; and Sara M. Evans, *Born for Liberty—A History of Women in America* (New York: Free Press, 1989), pp. 156–60. Regarding the restructuring of the labor force in the United States, see Robert L. Daniel, *American Women in the Twentieth Century: The Festival of Light* (New York: Harcourt Brace Jovanovich, 1987), pp. 73–75.
105 *Tokyo City Office Survey of 1931,* p. 310.
106 Murakami, *Taishōki no shokugyō fujin,* p. 66. In *Women and the American Experience* Nancy Woloch remarks: "The final message by the middle-class wife of the 1920s was the need for adjustment. Women's magazines advised her not to reject femininity but to enjoy it, to approach domesticity with a positive outlook" (p. 411). In their case, however, it was the feminists who fought back and voiced their opposition.
107 See Yamada, *Nihon fujin mondai shiryō shūsei-seikatsu,* vol. 7, pp. 278–80.
108 Tago Kazutami, "Wakaki fujin no nayami," *Fujokai,* May 1922, p. 15.
109 On the same subject, see Linda J. Nicholson, *Gender and History: The Limits of Social Theory in the Age of the Family* (New York: Columbia University Press, 1986), pp. 96–100.
110 Tago, *Fujokai,* May 1922, p. 15.
111 Shimada Tomiko, "Jiga no mezame to sekai e no kaigan," in *Josei kaihō no shisō to kōdō,* pp. 192–93. U.S. Judge Ben H. Lindsey's *The Companionate Marriage,* which was translated into Japanese in 1930, offered hope to intellectuals like Hirabayshi Hatsunosuke for alternative relationships. "Lindsey hanji," in *Yūai kekkon,* trans. Harada Mamoru (Tokyo: Chūō kōronsha, 1930).
112 For a male's point of view on marriage, see Sharon H. Nolte, *Liberalism in Modern Japan: Ishibashi Tanzan and His Teachers, 1905–1960* (Berkeley: University of California Press, 1987), pp. 95–97.

113 Inoue Teruko, "Ren'ai kan to kekkon kan no keifu," in *Josei gaku to sono shūhen* (Tokyo: Keisō shobō, 1980), pp. 4–8.

114 Yamawaki Gen, "Musume chūshin no jiyū kekkon nare," *Fujin kōron,* July 1919, p. 30.

115 See Rimer, "Kurata Hyakuzō and the Origins of Love and Understanding," in *Culture and Identity,* pp. 29–31. Between 1922 and 1926 Kurata wrote several essays on the subject of free love and marriage, all of which underwent some form of censorship. These essays were published in book form under the title *Ippu ippu ka jiyū ren'ai ka* (Monogamy or Free Love?) (Tokyo: Iwanami shoten, 1926).

116 See Kuriyagawa Hakuson, "Ren'ai to jinsei," *Fujin kōron,* June 1922, pp. 25–31; Kagawa Toyohiko, "Ren'ai to tamashii no shikkan," *Fujin kōron,* January 1928, pp. 13–16.

117 Chiba Kameo, "Utsuri yuku teisō kannen," *Fujokai,* January 1927, pp. 13–14.

118 Tada Yōko, "Ren'ai nan," *Fujin kōron,* October 1928, p. 40.

119 Ibid., p. 42.

120 Ibid.

121 Yamada Waka, *Josei sōdan,* ed. Tokyo Asahi shinbunsha (Tokyo: Kimura shobō, 1932); reprinted in *Kindai fujin mondai meicho senshū,* vol. 8: *Shakai mondai hen* (Tokyo: Nihon tosho sentā, 1983), pp. 188–89.

122 Miki Tomiko, "Entōi fujin ga ryōen o eta uchiake banashi (2)—imōto nimo saki o kosareta watakushi ga ryōen o eta keiken," *Shufu no tomo,* March 1930, p. 136.

123 Noda Eiko, "Watakushi no eranda risō no otto," *Shufu no tomo,* April 1925, pp. 48–49, 54–55.

124 Ozaki Chiyoko, "Musume o kekkon saseta oya no keiken," *Fujin kōron,* October 1928, p. 72.

125 "Gendai no musume no chōsho," *Shufu no tomo,* February 1926, p. 15.

126 Ibuka Hanako, "Fujin no hanmon sōdan," *Shufu no tomo,* July 1930, pp. 55–56.

127 Toda Midori, "Ren'ai kekkon ni shippai shita keiken," *Shufu no tomo,* October 1928, pp. 171–72.

128 Anonymous, "Tsuma no himitsu," *Fujin kōron,* October 1928, pp. 86–87.

129 The intensity of intellectuals' concern with self-cultivation was actually due to their dissatisfaction with Meiji modernization and its emphasis on technological development and the aggrandizement of the state to the exclusion of the individual. The masses did not enter into the intellectuals' perspective.

130 All of the above comments are found in the *Tokyo City Office Survey of 1922,* pp. 128–32.

131 *Tokyo City Office Survey of 1922,* pp. 128–32.

Chapter Five
Hard Days Ahead: Women on the Move

1 The groundwork for a "new" middle-class woman's status was laid in the Meiji period. Acquiring an education in the limited number of secondary schools established for women was more highly valued than property, monetary wealth, or a devotion to career goals.

2 Yosano, "Fujin kaizō to kōtō kyōiku" (1915), in *Teihon Yosano Akiko zenshū*, vol. 15, pp. 182–83.

3 Itō Sō, *Taishū bunka*, p. 240.

4 Yamaguchi Masao adds a new application to modern life by his positioning of local cities. See Yamaguchi Masao, *"Zasetsu" no Shōwa shi* (Tokyo: Iwanami shoten, 1995), pp. 396–97.

5 Yamakawa, "Keihintsuki tokkahin toshite no onna" (*Fujin kōron*, January 1928), in *Yamakaw a Kikue shū*, vol. 5, pp. 5–6.

6 Haga Noboru, "Senka no naka de," in *Ryūkō sesō kindaishi—ryūkō to sesō*, ed. Wakamori Tarō (Tokyo: Yūzankaku, 1970), pp. 230–31. Lively discussions also appeared in women's magazines. See, for example, "Shokugyō to seikatsu—YWCA yūshiki fujinbu ni oite" (Women and Work—YWCA-Educated Women Speak), *Fujin no tomo*, March 1937, pp. 146–51; "Sensō ga okottara fujin wa nani o nasu bekika?" (The Responsibility of Women If War Breaks Out), *Shufu no tomo*, August 1937, pp. 94–109; " 'Tokyo' o kataru—zadankai" (Talking about "Tokyo"—Panel Discussion), *Fujin no tomo*, May 1937, pp. 66–83; "Korekara no fufu—korekara no kekkon" (Marriage in the Future—Married Couples in the Future), *Shufu no tomo*, April 1938, pp. 260–81; "Senji no mohanteki na katei keizaiei no jikken" (Real-Life Models for Home Management during Wartime), *Shufu no tomo*, September 1939, pp. 168–71.

7 Hashikawa Bunzō, "Shōwa jūnendai no shisī," in *Kindai Nihon shisōshi*, ed. Ienaga Saburō (Tokyo: Chikuma shobō, 1959), pp. 285–86.

8 *Shōwa 11 nenban fujin nenkan* (Tokyo: Tokyo rengō fujinkai shuppanbu, 1935; reprint, Tokyo: Nihon tosho sentā, 1988), pp. 70–71.

9 On working women and the war effort, see Louise Young, *Japan's Total Empire: Manchuria and the Culture of Wartime Imperialism* (Berkeley: University of California Press, 1998), pp. 172–74. Most women's magazines of the period carried articles on this topic. See "Josei keizai chishiki—senji seikatsu no nayami to kaiketsu" (What Women Know about the Economy—Solving Troubles Related to Wartime Life), *Fujin kōron*, July 1931, pp. 256–78; "Fujin no chikara de jūgo wa katashi" (Women's Power Strengthens the Home Front), *Shufu no tomo*, August 1938, pp. 56–57; "Senji kyoku wa fujin ni nani o yōkyū shite iru ka—zadankai" (What Was Required of Women during Wartime—Panel Discussion), *Fujin kurabu*, February 1940,

pp. 78–85. Also see *Onna to sensō,* ed. Tokyo rekishigaku kagaku kenkyūkai (Tokyo: Shōwa shuppan, 1991); and Orii Miyako and Iwai Sachiko, "Sensō to onna no nichijō seikatsu," in *Nihon josei seikatsushi—kindai,* vol. 4, ed. Joseishi sōgo kenkyukai (Tokyo: Tokyo daigaku shuppan, 1990); Nakajima Kuni, "Jidai o miru kindai," particularly "Sensō to josei," in *Nihon josei no rekishi—bunka to shisō* (Tokyo: Kadokawa shoten, 1993), pp. 223–34; Nakajima Kuni, "Kokkateki bosei—Senjika no joseikan," in *Onna no imēji, Kōza joseigaku,* vol. 1, ed. Joseigaku kenkyūkai hen (Tokyo: Keisō shobō, 1984), pp. 235–63.

A study that makes use of the visual to analyze the role of women during the war period is art historian Wakakuwa Midori's *Sensō ga tsukuru joseizō* (Tokyo: Keisō shobō, 1995). For a well-documented study on women in wartime, see Kondō Kazuko, "Onna to sensō—bosei, katei, kokka," in *Onna to otoko no jikū, Nihon joseishi saikō—kindai,* vol. 5, ed. Okuda Akiko (Tokyo: Fujiwara shoten, 1995), pp. 481–515. Narita Ryūichi provides an alternative approach to this subject in "Women in the Motherland: Oku Mumeo through Wartime and Postwar," in *Total War and "Modernization,"* ed. Yasushi Yamanouchi, J. Victor Koschmann, and Ryūichi Narita (Ithaca: Cornell University East Asia Series, 1998), pp. 137–58. The contributors to this series shed light on the role of the nation-state in mobilization policies. Their stance negates the view that "different societies" are the "inescapable result of their divergent cultural traditions" (p. viii).

10   All of these quotes appear in "Shokugyō sensen de katsuyaku suru Osaka fujin no zadankai" (Osaka Women's Views regarding the Job "Front"— Panel Discussion, *Shufu no tomo,* April 1938, pp. 428–29.

11   "Jyūgo no sangyō fujin senshi no aikoku zadankai" (Patriotic Women "Warriors" [working women] Talk about the Home Front), *Shufu no tomo,* September 1939, p. 81.

12   Kawasaki Natsuko, "Shokugyō fujin no teinensei" (Retirement Age for Working Women), *Fujin kōron,* March 1939.

13   *Shōwa 13 nenban fujin nenkan* (Tokyo: Tokyo rengō fujinkai, 1937), p. 160. For articles appearing in women's magazines, see, for example, "Fujin no tairiku shinshutsu annai" (A Guide for Women Going to the Continent), *Shufu no tomo,* September 1939, pp. 208–9; "Kōku musume bakari no aozora zadankai" (Air Girls' Roundtable Discussion), *Shufu no tomo,* September 1939, pp. 274–79.

14   "Tokyo, Osaka shokygyō fujin no shūshoku an'nai" (A Guide for Professional Working Women in Tokyo and Osaka), *Shufu no tomo,* March 1938, p. 541.

15   "Shokugyō fujin toshite donna josei o motomeruka," *Fujin kōron,* March 1938, 259.

16   Shimoda Jirō, *Joshi shūshinsho,* vol. 4 (Tokyo: Tokyo kaiseikan, 1927), pp. 93,

101; *Fujin no yowatari no hiketsu senkajō* (Tokyo: Shufu no tomosha, 1932); Soma Kokukō, *Fūfu kyōiku* (Tokyo: Shufu no tomosha, 1941).

17 "Shokygyō fujin toshite donna josei o motomeruka," *Fujin kōron*, March 1938, pp. 259, 263.

18 Minami, "Fūzoku no tōsei—sono hō to ronri," in *Shōwa bunka: 1925–1945*, ed. Minami, pp. 158–59; Wakakuwa, *Sensō ga tsukuru joseizō*. Wakakura draws attention to the covers of women's magazines to show the manipulation of women during wartime.

19 For a discussion of government control on the media in English, see Gregory J. Kasza, *The State and the Mass Media in Japan: 1918–1945* (Berkeley: University of California Press, 1988), esp. pp. 28–101. On press coverage and the conversion of popular entertainment, see Young, *Japan's Total Empire*, pp. 81–86. For a discussion of women's magazines during the war, see *Sensō to josei zasshi—1931–1945*, ed. Kindaishi josei bunkashi kenkyūkai (Tokyo: Domesu shuppan, 2001).

20 Orii and Iwai, "Sensō to onna no nichijō seikatsu," p. 207.

21 "Jihenka ni ryōen o eru hiketsu," *Shufu no tomo*, September 1940, p. 92.

22 Itō Yasuko, "Haisen zengo ni okeru seikatsu ishiki no henyō," in *Nihon josei seikatsu shi*, vol. 5 (Tokyo: Tokyo daigaku shuppankai, 1990), p. 30.

23 Ōwaki Masako, "Hōritsu ni okeru joseikan," in *Onna no imēji*, vol. 1, ed. Joseigaku kenkyūkai, pp. 102–28; Sally Ann Hastings, "Women Legislators in the Postwar Diet," in *Re-imagining Japanese Women*, ed. and intro. Anne E. Imamura (Berkeley: University of California Press, 1996), pp. 271–82; also see Susan J. Pharr, *Political Women in Japan: The Search for a Place in Political Life* (Berkeley: University of California Press, 1981), p. 23.

24 On the Occupation reforms, see *Sengo fujin mondai shi: kyōdō tōgi*, ed. Ichibangase Yasuko (Tokyo: Domesu shuppan, 1971). Of importance here are "Fujin no hōritsuteki chii no henka," chapter 1, section 2; and "Fujin sanseiken no kōsei," section 3. For more on this topic, see Nishi Kiyoko, *Senryōka no Nihon fujin seisaku—sono rekishi to shōgen* (Tokyo: Domesu shuppan, 1985), esp. "Fujin seisaku no kaikaku hajimaru," pp. 17–53. Of particular significance is jurist Wagatsuma Sakae's book, *Atarashii ie no rinri—kaisei minpō yowa* (Tokyo: Gakushū shoin, 1949), which was intended to explain the Occupation reforms to women in easily comprehensible Japanese. Another landmark study is Kawashima Takeyoshi, *Nihon shakai no kazokuteki kōsei* (Tokyo: Nihon hyōronsha, 1950).

25 Shigemitsu Aoi and Hirabayashi Taiko, "Dokuritsu Nihon no fujin ni nozomu," *Shufu no tomo*, July 1952, p. 58.

26 Ibid., pp. 27–28.

27 See Hastings, "Women Legislators in the Postwar Diet," pp. 272–76; also Pharr, *Political Women in Japan*, p. 35.

28 Pharr, *Political Women in Japan*, p. 35.

29 "Ren'ai to kekkon," in *Gendai josei kōza,* vol. 2, Kamei Katsuichirō et al. (Tokyo: Kadokawa shoten, 1955).

30 "Furoku," in *Gendai josei kōza,* vol. 2, p. 4.

31 Ibid., p. 8.

32 "Osaka musume ren'ai to kekkon o kataru," *Shufu no tomo,* July 1949, pp. 35–37.

33 Ibid.

34 "Furoku," p. 3.

35 "Kekkon ka shokugyō ka—sanjū musume-san bakari no uchiake zadankai," *Shufu no tomo,* February 1950, p. 155.

36 Ibid., p. 159.

37 Mishima Yukio, "Donna josei ni miryoku ga aruka—dokushin ninki mono no zadankai," *Shufu no tomo,* October 1948, p. 106. See, for example, Nomura Masaichi, "Koi no michi no magarikata—Shōwa no danjo kōsai," in *Shōwa no sesōshi,* ed. Ishige Naomichi (Tokyo: Domesu shuppan, 1993), pp. 145–54.

38 Ishikawa Hiroyoshi, "Denka to joseitachi," in *Yoka no sengo shi,* ed. Ishikawa Hiroyoshi (Tokyo: Tokyo shoseki, 1979), pp. 110–11.

39 Itō, *Nihon josei seikatsu shi,* pp. 27–28.

Bibliography

Abe Jirō. "Untenshu to hakushaku fujin no ai." In *Rekishi to jinbutsu,* 110–15. Tokyo: Chūō kōronsha, 1980.

Abe Tsunehisa and Satō Yoshimari. *Nihon kindai joseishi—tsūshi to shiryō.* Tokyo: Fuyō shobō, 2000.

Adamson, Walter L. "Modernism and Fascism: The Politics of Culture in Italy." *American Historical Review* 195, no. 2 (1990): 359–90.

Akita Masami. *Sei no ryōki modan.* Tokyo: Seikyūsha, 1994.

Allen, Frederick Lewis. *Only Yesterday: An Informal History of the 1920's.* New York: Harper and Row, 1931.

Ambaras, David R. "Social Knowledge, Cultural Capital, and the New Middle Class in Japan, 1895–1912." *Journal of Japanese Studies* 24, no. 1 (1998): 1–33.

Ando Kōsei. *Ginza saiken.* 1931. Tokyo: Chūō kōronsha, 1977.

Aoki Tamotsu, Kawamoto Saburō, Tsutsui Kiyotada, Mikuriya Takashi, and Yamaori Tetsuo. *Onna no bunka.* Vol. 8 of *Kindai Nihon bunkaron.* Tokyo: Iwanami shoten, 2000.

———, eds. *Taishū bunka to masu meideiya.* Vol. 7 of *Kindai Nihon bunkaron.* Tokyo: Iwanami shoten, 1999.

Arase Yutaka. "Taishū shakai no keisei to tenkai." In *Nihon no shakai,* ed. Fukutake Tadashi, 160–76. Tokyo: Mainichi shinbunsha, 1957.

Arima Manabu. *"Kokusaika" no naka no teikoku Nihon, 1905–1924.* Vol. 4 of *Nihon no kindai.* Tokyo: Chūō kōronsha, 1999.

Asahi shinbun shōshi. Tokyo: Asahi shinbunsha, 1951.

Ballester, Ros, Margaret Beetham, Elizabeth Frazer, and Sandra Hebron, eds. *Women's Worlds Ideology: Femininity and the Women's Magazines.* Vol. 4. London: Macmillan, 1993.

Banno Junji. *Takei Nihon no rekishi.* Vol. 13 of *Kindai Nihon no shuppatsu.* Tokyo: Shōgakkan, 1989.

Barshay, Andrew E. "Imagining Democracy in Postwar Japan: Reflections on Maruyama Masao and Modernism." *Journal of Japanese Studies* 18, no. 2 (1992): 365–406.

Baudrillard, Jean. "The System of Objects." 1968. Reprinted in *Jean Baudril-*

lard: Selected Writings, ed. Mark Poster, 10–28. Stanford: Stanford University Press, 1988.

Baxandall, Rosalyn, Linda Gordon, and Susan Reverby. *America's Working Women: A Documentary History, 1600 to the Present.* New York: Vintage Books, 1976.

Bebel, August, *Fujinron.* Trans. Yamakawa Kikue. Tokyo: Arusu, 1923.

Beetham, Margaret. *A Magazine of Her Own? Domesticity and Desire in the Woman's Magazine, 1800–1914.* London: Routledge, 1996.

Bell, Daniel. *The Cultural Contradictions of Capitalism.* New York: Basic Books, 1978.

———. *The End of Ideology.* Cambridge: Harvard University Press, 1988.

Bellah, Robert N., et al. *Habits of the Heart: Individualism and Commitment in American Life.* Berkeley: University of California Press, 1985.

Benjamin, Walter. *Illuminations: Essays and Reflections.* Ed. and intro. Hannah Arendt. New York: Shocken Books, 1969.

Bernstein, Gail Lee, ed. *Recreating Japanese Women, 1600–1945.* Berkeley: University of California Press, 1991.

Bethel, Diane. "Visions of a Humane Society: Feminist Thought in Taishō Japan." *Feminist International*, no. 2 (1980): 158–60.

Birnbaum, Phyllis. *Modern Girls, Shining Stars, the Skies of Tokyo: Five Japanese Women.* New York: Columbia University Press, 1999.

Boorstin, Daniel J. *The Americans: The Democratic Experience.* New York: Vintage Books, 1974.

Brady, Malcolm, and James McFarlane, eds. *Modernism 1890–1930.* London: Penguin Books, 1976.

Braisted, William Reynolds. *Meiroku Zasshi: Journal of the Japanese Enlightenment.* Tokyo: University of Tokyo Press, 1976.

Brandon, Ruth. *The New Women and the Old Men: Love, Sex and the Woman Question.* New York: W. W. Norton, 1990.

Breward, Christopher. *The Culture of Fashion.* Manchester: Manchester University Press, 1995.

Brown, Dorothy M. *Setting a Course: American Women in the 1920s.* Boston: Twayne Publishers, 1987.

Butler, Judith. *Gender Trouble: Feminism and the Subversion of Identity.* New York: Routledge, 1990.

Calinescu, Matei. *The Five Faces of Modernity: Modernism, Avant-Garde, Decadence, Kitsch, Postmodernism.* Durham: Duke University Press, 1987.

Cantor, Norman, and Michael Wetham, eds. *The History of Popular Culture.* New York: Macmillan, 1968.

Chafe, William H. *The American Woman: Her Changing Social, Economic, and Political Roles, 1920–1970.* London: Oxford University Press, 1972.

Chiba Kameo. *Isei o Miru.* Tokyo: Ryūmeisha, 1924.

Chino Yōichi. *Kindai Nihon fujin kyōikushi—taiseinai fujin dantai no keisei katei o chūshin ni.* Tokyo: Domesu shuppan, 1979.

Cott, Nancy F. *The Grounding of Modern Feminism.* New Haven: Yale University Press, 1987.

———. "The Modern Woman of the 1920s, American Style." In *A History of Women.* Vol. 5: *Toward a Cultural Identity in the Twentieth Century,* ed. Françoise Thébaud, 77–91. Cambridge: Belknap Press of Harvard University Press, 1994.

Curti, Lidia. "What Is Real and What Is Not: Female Fabulations in Cultural Analysis." In *Cultural Studies,* ed. Lawrence Grossberg, Cary Nelson, and Paula Treichler, 134–53. New York: Routledge, 1992.

Daniel, Robert L. *American Women in the Twentieth Century: The Festival of Light.* New York: Harcourt Brace Jovanovich, 1987.

Davis, Natalie Zemon. *The Return of Martin Guerre.* Cambridge: Harvard University Press, 1983.

Day, Dorothy. *Setting a Course: American Women in the 1920s.* Boston: G. K. Hall, 1987.

de Grazia, Victoria, with Ellen Furlough, eds. *The Sex of Things: Gender and Consumption in Historical Perspective.* Berkeley: University of California Press, 1996.

Doak, Kevin Michael. *Dreams of Difference: The Japan Romantic School and the Crisis of Modernity.* Berkeley: University of California Press, 1994.

Doke, S. "The Reconstruction of Tokyo." In *The Japan Year Book: Earthquake Edition 1924–25,* no. 18, 87–109. Tokyo: Eibun Nihon nenkansha, 1924.

Dore, Ronald P. *Education in Tokugawa Japan.* Berkeley: University of California Press, 1965.

Douglas, Ann. *The Feminization of American Culture.* New York: Anchor Press Doubleday, 1988.

Duus, Peter. *The Rise of Modern Japan.* Boston: Houghton Mifflin, 1976.

———, ed. *Cambridge History of Japan.* Vol. 6: *The Twentieth Century.* Cambridge: Cambridge University Press, 1988.

Enchi Fumiko, ed. *Kindai Nihon no josei shi.* Vol. 1: *Koi ni moe ai ni ikiru.* Tokyo: Shūeisha, 1980.

Evans, Sara M. *Born for Liberty—A History of Women in America.* New York: Free Press, 1989.

Ewen, Stewart, and Elizabeth Ewen. *Channels of Desire: Mass Images and the Shaping of American Consciousness.* Minneapolis: University of Minnesota Press, 1999.

Eysteinsson, Astradur. *The Concept of Modernism.* Ithaca: Cornell University Press, 1990.

Fletcher, Miles. *The Search for a New Order: Intellectuals and Fascism in Prewar Japan.* Chapel Hill: University of North Carolina Press, 1982.

Friedan, Betty. *The Feminine Mystique.* New York: Dell, 1963.

Fujimori Terunobu. *Kenchiku tantei no bōken.* Tokyo: Chikuma shobō, 1986.

Fujin kōron no gojūnen. Tokyo: Chūō kōronsha, 1965.

Fujin nenkan. Vol. 2. Tokyo: Nihon tosho sentā, 1981.

Fujin shokugyō sensen no tenbō. Tokyo: Tokyo shiyakusho, 1932.

Fujita Yoshimi. *Meiji jogakkō no sekai.* Tokyo: Seieisha, 1984.

Fujitake Akira. "Taishū shakai no seiritsu." In *Kōza gendai jānarizumu,* vol. 1. Tokyo: Jiji tsūshinsha, 1981.

———, ed. *Shōhi toshite no raifu stairu, Gendai no esupuri. Seikatsu bunka shirīzu.* No. 1. Tokyo: Shibundō, 2000.

Fukawa Kiyoshi. *Kindai Nihon—Josei rinri shisō no nagare.* Tokyo: Ōtsuki shoten, 2000.

Fukuda Sumiko et al. *Kōtō jogakkō shiryō shūsei—kōtō jogakkō no kenkyū.* Tokyo: Ozorasha, 1990.

Fukutake, Tadashi. *Japanese Society Today.* 2d ed. Tokyo: University of Tokyo Press, 1981.

Fukuzawa Yukichi. *Fukuzawa Yukichi on Japanese Women: Selected Works.* Trans. and ed. Eiichi Kiyoka. Tokyo: University of Tokyo Press, 1988.

Furukawa Sachiko. "Bē-beru no fujin kaihōron." In *Nyūmon josei kaihōron,* ed. Ichibangase Yasuko, 62–94. Tokyo: Aki shobō, 1975.

Gardner, Vivien, and Susan Rutherford, eds. *The New Woman and Her Sisters: Feminism and Theater 1850–1914.* Ann Arbor: University of Michigan Press, 1992.

Garon, Sheldon. *Molding Japanese Minds: The State in Everyday Life.* Princeton: Princeton University Press, 1997.

Gendai manga taikan. Vols. 8–9. Tokyo: Chūō bijutsu sha, 1928.

Gendai ryūkōgo jiten. Tokyo: Tokyodō shuppan, 1974.

Giddens, Anthony. *The Consequences of Modernity.* Stanford: Stanford University Press, 1990.

Glennie, Paul. "Consumption within Historical Studies." In *Acknowledging Consumption,* ed. Daniel Miller, 164–203. London: Routledge, 1995.

Gluck, Carol. *Japan's Modern Myths Ideology in the Late Meiji Period.* Princeton: Princeton University Press, 1985.

Gluck, Carol, and Stephen R. Graubard, eds. *Showa: The Japan of Hirohito.* New York: W. W. Norton, 1992.

Gonda Yasunosuke. *Gonda Yasunosuke chosakushū.* Vol. 4. Tokyo: Bunwa shobō, 1975.

Grossberg, Lawrence, Ellen D. Wartella, and Charles Whitney. *Media Making: Mass Media in a Popular Culture.* Thousand Oaks, Calif.: Sage Publications, 1998.

Grossmann, Atina. "Girlkultur or Thoroughly Rationalized Female: A New Woman in Weimar Germany?" In *Women in Culture and Politics: A Century of*

Change, ed. Judith Friedlander, Blanche Wiesen Cook, Alice Kessler-Harris, and Carroll Smith-Rosenberg, 62–80. Bloomington: Indiana University Press, 1986.

————. "The New Woman and the Rationalization of Sexuality in Weimar Germany." In *Powers of Desire: The Politics of Sexuality,* ed. Ann Snitow, Christine Stansell, and Sharon Thompson, 153–71. New York: Monthly Review Press, 1983.

Grosz, Elizabeth. "Sexual Difference and the Problem of Essentialism." In *The Essential Difference,* ed. Naomi Schor and Elizabeth Weed, 82–97. Bloomington: Indiana University Press, 1994.

Haga Noboru. *Ryōsai kenboron.* Tokyo: Yūzankaku, 1990.

Hall, Stuart. "The Meaning of New Times." In *Stuart Hall: Critical Dialogues in Cultural Studies,* ed. David Morley and Kuan-Hsing, 223–37. London: Routledge, 1996.

Hamada Shirō. *Hyakkaten issekiwa.* Tokyo: Nihon denpō tsūshinsha, 1927.

Hanes, Jeffrey E. "Masu karuchyā/sabu karuchāzu/popyura karuchā." In *Toshi no kūkan toshi no shintai, 21 seiki no toshi shakaigaku,* vol. 4, ed. Yoshimi Shunya, 91–136. Tokyo: Keisō shobō, 1996.

Hani Motoko. *Hani Motoko chosakushū.* Vol. 1. Tokyo: Fujin no tomosha, 1928.

Harootunian, Harry. *History's Disquiet: Modernity, Cultural Practice, and the Question of Everyday Life.* New York: Columbia University Press, 2000.

————. "Overcome by Modernity: Fantasizing Everyday Life and the Discourse of the Social in Interwar Japan." In *parallax,* issue 2, *Theory/Practice,* 77–88. Leeds, U.K.: Wild Pansy Press/University of Leeds, 1996.

————. *Overcome by Modernity—History, Culture, and Community in Interwar Japan.* Princeton: Princeton University Press, 2000.

Harrington, Ann M. "Women and Higher Education in the Japanese Empire (1869–1945)." *Journal of Asian History* 21, no. 2 (1987): 169–86.

Hasegawa Izumi et al. *Kindai bungei hyōronshū.* Tokyo: Ōfusha, 1965.

Hashikawa Bunzō. "Shōwa jūnendai no shisō." In *Kindai Nihon shisōshi kōza— rekishiteki gaikan,* vol. 1, ed. Ienaga Saburō, 280–96. Tokyo: Chikuma shobō, 1959.

Hashimoto Motomu. *Nihon shuppan hanbaishi.* Tokyo: Kōdansha, 1964.

Hashimoto Noriko. *Danjo kyōgakusei no shiteki kenkyū.* Tokyo: Ōtsuki shoten, 1992.

Hastings, Sally Ann. "Women Legislators in the Postwar Diet." In *Re-imagining Japanese Women,* ed. and intro. Anne E. Imamura, 271–82. Berkeley: University of California Press, 1996.

Hatoyama Haruko. *Fujin seikatsu no kaizen.* Tokyo: Senshindō, 1920.

————. *Mohan katei.* Tokyo: Dai Nihon tosho, 1913.

Hatsuda Tōru. *Hyakkaten no tanjō.* Tokyo: Sanseidō, 1993.

Hermes, Joke. *Reading Women's Magazines.* Cambridge: Polity Press, 1995.

Hidaka Rokurō. "Kikai jidai ni okeru ningen no mondai." In *Gendai ideorogī*, 121–47. Tokyo: Keisō shobō, 1960.

Hirabayashi Hatsunosuke. *Hirabayashi Hatsunosuke bungei hyōron zenshū*. Vols. 1–3. Tokyo: Bunsendō, 1975.

Hirai Tadashi. *Berlin 1923–1945*. Tokyo: Serika shobō, 1981.

Hirai Tadashi et al. *Toshi taishū bunka no seiritsu*. Tokyo: Yūhikaku, 1983.

Hirata Yumi. *Josei hyōgen no Meiji-shi*. Tokyo: Iwanami shoten, 1999.

Hiratsuka Matsunori. *Joshi kyōikushi—jinbutsu chūshin ni*. Tokyo: Teikoku chihō gyosei gakkai, 1965.

Hiratsuka Raichō. *Genshi josei wa taiyō de atta. Hiratsuka Raichō jiden*. Vols. 1–2. Tokyo: Ōtsuki shoten, 1971.

——. *Hiratsuka Raichō chosakushū*. 10 vols. Tokyo: Ōtsuki shoten, 1983.

Hobsbawm, Eric. *The Age of Empire: 1875–1914*. New York: Vintage Books, 1987.

Honda Masuko. *Jogakusei no keifu—saishoku sareru Meiji*. Tokyo: Seidosha, 1990.

Honma Nagayo and Kamei Shunsuke. *Amerika no taishū bunka*. Tokyo: Kenkyūsha, 1975.

Horiba Kiyoko. *Seitō no jidai—Hiratsuka Raichō to atarashii onnatachi*. Tokyo: Iwanami shoten, 1988.

Horiuchi Fumiko. *Modan gāru no koi—Horiuchi Keizō to watashi*. Tokyo: Sōshisha, 1987.

Horkheimer, Max, and Theodor W. Adorno. *Dialectic of Enlightenment*. 1944. Reprint. New York: Continuum, 1993.

Hoston, Germaine A. *Marxism and the Crisis of Development in Prewar Japan*. Princeton: Princeton University Press, 1986.

Huyssen, Andreas. *After the Great Divide: Modernism, Mass Culture, Postmodernism*. Bloomington: Indiana University Press, 1986.

Ibsen, Henrik. *A Doll's House*. New York: Dover Publications, 1992.

Ichibangase Yasuko, ed. *Sengo fujin mondai shi: kyōdō tōgi*. Tokyo: Domesu shuppan, 1971.

Ide Fumiko. *Hiratsuka Raichō—kindai to shinpi*. Tokyo: Shinchōsha, 1987.

Ikeda Emiko, ed. *Shuppan joseishi*. Kyoto: Sekaishisōsha, 2001.

Ikimatsu Keizō. *Gendai Nihon shisō shi*. Vol. 4: *Taishōki no shisō to bunka*. Tokyo: Aoki shoten, 1971.

——. Vol. 3. *Kindai Nihon shisō shi*. Tokyo: Aoki shoten, 1956.

Ikuta Chōkō and Honma Hisao. *Shakai mondai jūniko*. Tokyo: Shinchōsha, 1919.

Inaba Michio. "Taishū bunka." In *Taishū shakai*, vol. 7, ed. Fukutake Tadashi, 165–80. Tokyo: Tokyo daigaku shuppankai, 1957.

Inoue Kiyoshi. *Nihon Joseishi*. Tokyo: San'i chi shobō, 1948.

Inoue Teruko. *Josei gaku to sono shūhen*. Tokyo: Keisō shobō, 1980.

Ishigaki Ayako. *Onna wa jiyū de aru*. Tokyo: Bungei shunjū, 1955.

Ishii Kazumi and Nerida Jarkey. "The Housewife Is Born: The Establishment of the Notion and Identity of the *Shufu* in Modern Japan." *Japanese Studies* 22, no. 1 (2002): 35–47.

Ishikawa Hiroyoshi, ed. *Goraku no senzen shi*. Tokyo: Tokyo shoseki, 1981.

————, ed. *Yoka no sengo shi*. Tokyo: Tokyo shoseki, 1979.

Ishizuka Masahide. "Ryōsai kenbo shugi no kaimei ni yosete." *Josei kenkyū*, no. 25 (December 1990): 2–17.

Itagaki Kuniko. *Shōwa senzen—senchūki no nōson seikatsu*. Tokyo: Sanrei shobō, 1992.

Itagaki Takaho et al. *Kikaibi no tanjō*. Tokyo: Tenjinsha, 1930.

Itō Toshiharu. "Nihon no 1920 nendai—Tokyo o chūshin to suru toshi taishū bunka no tenkai." In *Toshi taishū bunka no seiritsu*, ed. Hirai Tadashi, Hosaka Kazuō, Kawamoto Saburō, and Yamada Takanobu, 176–204. Tokyo: Yūzankaku, 1983.

Ivy, Marilyn. "Formations of Mass Culture." In *Postwar Japan as History*, ed. Andrew Gordon, 239–58. Berkeley: University of California Press, 1993.

Iwao, Sumiko. *The Japanese Woman: Traditional Image and Changing Reality*. New York: Free Press, 1993.

Iwasaki Akira. *Eiga ga wakakata toki*. Tokyo: Heibonsha, 1980.

Iwasaki Jirō. *Bukka no sesō hen*. Tokyo: Yomiuri shinbunsha, 1982.

Izeki Jūjirō. *Wanamēkā hōten*. Tokyo: Jitsugyō no Nihon sha, 1926.

Jinno Yuki. *Shumi no tanjō: hyakkaten ga tsukutta teisuto*. Tokyo: Keisō shobō, 1994.

Joseishi sōgō kenkyūkai, ed. *Nihon josei seikatsushi*. Vols. 3–5. Tokyo: Tokyo daigaku shuppankai, 1982.

Kakegawa Tomiko. "Noma Seiji to Kōdansha bunka." *Shisō no kagaku* (October 1959): 19–31.

Kamei Katsuichirō et al. *Gendai josei kōza*. Vol. 2. Tokyo: Kadokawa shoten, 1955.

Kanda Michiko. "Fujinron no hensen—josei no chii kōjō o motomete." In *Gendai no esupuri—fujinron*, ed. Matsubara Jirō and Kanda Michiko, 15–27. Tokyo: Shibundō, 1972.

Kaneko Sachiko. *Kindai Nihon joseiron no keifu*. Tokyo: Fuji shuppan, 1999.

Kano, Ayako. *Acting Like a Woman in Modern Japan: Theater, Gender, and Nationalism*. New York: Palgrave, 2001.

Kanō Masanao and Horiba Kiyoko. *Takamure Itsue*. Tokyo: Asahi shinbunsha, 1985.

Kanō Mikiyo. *Jiga no kanata e—kindai o koeru feminizumu*. Tokyo: Shakai hyōronsha, 1990.

Karaki Junzō. *Gendaishi e no kokoromi*. Tokyo: Chikuma shobō, 1949.

Kasza, Gregory J. *The State and the Mass Media in Japan: 1918–1945*. Berkeley: University of California Press, 1988.

Katayama Seiichi. *Kindai Nihon no Joshi kyōiku*. Tokyo: Kenpakusha, 1984.

Katō Hidetoshi et al. *Meiji Taishō Shōwa sesōshi*. Tokyo: Shakai shisōsha, 1967.

Katō Saburō. *Māsharu Fīrudo to sekai ichi no daishōten*. Tokyo: Kaizōsha, 1929.

Katori Shunsuke. *Modan gāru: Takehisa Chieko to iu joyū ga ita*. Tokyo: Chikuma shobō, 1996.

Kawamoto Saburō. "Shoshimin eiga no 'tanoshii wagaya.' " In *Taishū bunka to masu meideiya*, vol. 7 of *Kindai Nihon bunkaron*, ed. Aoki Tamotsu et al., 1–17. Tokyo: Iwanami shoten, 1999.

Kawamura Kunimitsu. *Sekushuariti no kindai*. Tokyo: Kōdansha, 1996.

Kawashima Takeyoshi. *Nihon shakai no kazokuteki kōsei*. Tokyo: Nihon hyōron-sha, 1950.

Kawashima Yasuyoshi. *Fujin, Kateiran koto hajime*. Tokyo: Seiabō, 1996.

Kayano Yatsuka. *Kindai Nihon no dezain bunka shi, 1868–1926*. Tokyo: Firumu ātosha, 1992.

Kayser, Rudolf. "Amerikanismus." *Vossiche Zeitung*, no. 458, September 27, 1925. Reprint, "Americanism," in *The Weimar Republic Sourcebook*, ed. Anton Kaes, Martin Jay, and Edward Dimendberg, 395–97. Berkeley: University of California Press, 1994.

Keene, Donald. *Dawn to the West: Japanese Literature in the Modern Era*. New York: Henry Holt, 1984.

Key, Ellen. *Ren'ai to kekkon*. Trans. Harada Minoru. Tokyo: Shueikaku, 1913.

Kikuchi Kan. *Ren'ai kekkon no sho*. Tokyo: Modan Nihonsha, 1935.

Kimura Kyōko. "Fujin zasshi no jōhō kūkan to josei taishū dokushasō no seiritsu." *Shisō*, no. 812 (February 1992): 231–52.

Kimura Shōhachi. *Zuihitsu josei sandai*. Tokyo: Kawade shobō, 1956.

Kindai josei bunkashi kenkyūkai, ed. *Sensō to josei zasshi, 1931–1945*. Tokyo: Domesu shuppan, 2001.

———, ed. *Taishōki no josei zasshi*. Ōzorasha, 1996.

Kindai Nihon sōgō nenpyō. Tokyo: Iwanami shoten, 1968.

Kinmonth, Earl H. *The Self-Made Man in Meiji Japanese Thought: From Samurai to Salary Man*. Berkeley: University of California Press, 1981.

Kitada Akihiro. *Kōkoku no tanjō*. Tokyo: Iwanami shoten, 2000.

Kitamura Kaneko. *Hyōhi wa ugoku*. Tokyo: Heibonsha, 1930.

Kiyonaga Takashi. *Ryōsai kenbo no tanjō*. Tokyo: Chikuma shobō, 1995.

Kiyosawa Rei. "Gendai no shokugyō fujin no sho mondai." In *Fujin kōron daigaku: Fujin shokugyōhen*, 55–57. Tokyo: Chūō kōronsha, 1931.

Kōchi Nobuko, ed. *Shiryō bosei hogo ronsō*. Tokyo: Domesu shuppan, 1984.

Kokubo Sakura. "Shōwa shoki no mura ni okeru haha yakuwari kihan no hen'yō—zasshi *Ie no hikari* o tōshite." *Joseigaku nenpō*, no. 11 (November 1990).

Komota Nobuo et al. *Nihon ryūkōka shi*. Tokyo: Shakai shisōsha, 1970.

Kon Wajirō. *Kōgenkau*. 1927. In *Kon Wajirō shū*, vol. 1. Tokyo: Domesu shuppan, 1971.

————. *Kōgenkau nyūmon*. Ed. Fujimori Terunobu. Tokyo: Chikuma shobō, 1987.

————, ed. *Shinpan dai Tokyo an'nai*. Chūō kōronsha, 1929.

Konno Kenzō. *Puroretaria ren'aikan*. Tokyo: Sekaisha, 1930.

Konno Minako. *OL no sōzo—Imi sekai toshite no jendā*. Tokyo: Keisō shobō, 2000.

Koshō Yukiko, ed. *Shiryō Joseishi ronsō*. No. 3. Tokyo: Domesu shuppan, 1987.

Koyama Shizuko. *Katei no seisei to josei no kokuminka*. Tokyo: Keisō shobō, 1999.

————. *Ryōsai kenbo to iu kihan*. Tokyo: Keisō shobō, 1991.

Koyasu Nobukuni. *Kindai chi no arukeorojī*. Tokyo: Iwanami shoten, 1996.

Kuki Yukio, Suzuki Eiichi, and Kon'no Yoshikio. *Nihon kyōiku ronsō shiroku*. Vol. 1. Tokyo: Daiichi hōki, 1980.

Kurahara Korehito. "Teikokushugi to geijutsu" (1930). In *Kurahara Korehito hyōronshū*, 50–52. Tokyo: Shin Nippon shuppansha, 1967.

Kurata Yoshihiro. *Nihon rekōdo bunka shi*. Tokyo: Tokyo shoseki, 1979.

Kuwabara Takeo. "Taishō gojūnen" (1962). In *Kuwabara Takeo shū*, vol. 6, 298–322. Tokyo: Iwanami shoten, 1980.

Kuwabara Takeo, Katō Hidetoshi, and Yamada Minoru. "Jānarizumu no shisōteki yakuwari." In *Kindai nihon shisōshi kōza*, vol. 5: *Chishikijin no seisei to yakuwari*, ed. Kuno Osamu and Sumiya Mikio, 161–83. Tokyo: Chikuma shobō, 1960.

Kyūshoku fujin no kankyō chōsa. Tokyo: Tokyo-fu gakumubu shakaika, 1931.

Leach, William. *Land of Desire: Merchants, Power, and the Rise of a New American Culture*. New York: Vintage Books, 1993.

Levine, Lawrence W. "AHR Forum the Folklore of Industrial Society: Popular Culture and Its Audiences." *American Historical Review* 197, no. 5 (1992): 1369–99.

Mackie, Vera. *Creating Socialist Women in Japan: Gender Labour and Activism, 1900–1937*. Cambridge: Cambridge University Press, 1997.

Maeda Ai. *Maeda Ai chosakushū*. Vol. 2. Tokyo: Chikuma shobō, 1989.

Maeda Hajime. *Shokugyō fujin monogatari*. Tokyo: Toyō keizai shuppanbu, 1929.

Martin, Biddy. *Woman and Modernity: The (Life)styles of Lou Andreas-Salome*. Ithaca: Cornell University Press, 1991.

Marx, Karl. *Capital: A Theory of Political Economy*. Reprint. New York: Vintage Books, 1977.

Masaki Tomohiko. *Basi shashō no jidai*. Tokyo: Gendai shokan, 1992.

Masuda Giichi. *Fujin to shūyō*. Tokyo: Jitsugyō no Nihonsha, 1928.

Matsubara Jirō and Kanda Michiko, eds. *Gendai no esupuri—fujinron*. Tokyo: Shibundō, 1972.

Matsumoto Sannosuke. *Meiji seishin no kōzo*. Tokyo: Nippon hōsō shuppan kyōkai, 1981.

Matsushita Keiichi. *Gendai Seiji no jōken*. Tokyo: Chūo kōronsha, 1959.

Matsuzaki Tenmin. *Ginza.* 1927. Reprint. Tokyo: Shinsensha, 1986.

———. "Kafe jidai." In *Rimen anmen jitsuwa,* vol. 12: *Meiji Taishō jitsuwa zenshū,* 183–208.

Meiji Taishō kokumu sōran. Tokyo: Tōyō keizai shinpōsha, 1927.

Miki Kiyoshi. "Fuan no shisō to sono chōkō." 1933. In *Gendai bungakuron taikei,* vol. 5. Tokyo: Kawade shobō, 1954.

Mills, C. W. *The Power Elite.* New York: Oxford University Press, 1956.

Minami Hiroshi. "Masu komyunikēshon no seiritsu." In *Nihon fūzoku shi,* vol. 11, 15–27. Tokyo: Yūzankaku shuppan, 1959.

———, ed. *Gendai no esupuri.* No. 188: *Nihon modanizumu.* Tokyo: Shibundō kōbundō, 1983.

———, ed. *Nihon modanizumu no kenkyū—shisō, seikatsu, bunka.* Tokyo: Burēn shuppan, 1982.

———, ed. *Shōwa bunka, 1921–1945.* Tokyo: Keisō shobō, 1987.

———, ed. *Taishō bunka.* Tokyo: Keisō shobō, 1965.

Minami Hiroshi et al. *Kindai shomin seikatsu shi.* Vols. 1–10. Tokyo: San'ichi shobō, 1984–88.

Mitsuda Kiyoko. "Kindaiteki boseikan no juyū to henka—'kyōiku suru ha-haoya' kara 'ryōsai kenbo' e." In *Bosei o tō,* vol. 2: *Rekishiteki hensen,* ed. Wakita Haruko. Kyoto: Jinbun shoin, 1985.

Miyake Yasuko. *Gozen kuji.* Tokyo: Jitsugyō no Nihonsha, 1928.

Miyoshi Nobuhiro. *Nihon no josei to sangyō kyōiku—Kindai sangyō shakai ni okeru josei no yakuwari.* Tokyo: Tōshindō, 2000.

Mott, Frank Luther. *A History of American Magazines.* Vols. 1–5. Cambridge: Harvard University Press, 1938–68.

Mouer, Elizabeth Knipe. "Women in Teaching." In *Women in Changing Japan,* ed. Joyce Lebra, Joy Paulson, and Elizabeth Powers, 157–90. Stanford: Stanford University Press, 1976.

Mumford, Lewis. *Technics and Civilization.* 1934. Reprint. New York: Harcourt Brace Jovanovich, 1967.

Murakami Nobuhiko. "Joseishi kenkyū no kadai to tenbō." *Shisō,* no. 549 (March 1970): 83–95.

———. *Meiji joseishi.* Vol. 2: *Onna no shokugyō.* Tokyo: Rironsha, 1973.

———. *Nihon no fujin mondai.* Tokyo: Iwanami shinsho, 1978.

———. *Onna no fūzoku shi.* Tokyo: Daviddo sha, 1957.

———. *Taishō joseishi.* Vols. 1–3. Tokyo: Rironsha, 1982.

———. *Taishōki no shokugyō fujin.* Tokyo: Domesu shuppan, 1983.

Murashima Yoriyuki. *Kafe.* Tokyo: Bunka seikatsu kenkyūkai, 1929.

Murata Noro. *Nihon ren'ai shi.* Tokyo: Shūeikaku, 1925.

Murobuse Takanobu. *Chūkankaikyū no shakaigaku.* Tokyo: Nihon hyōronsha, 1932.

———. *Gaitō no shakaigaku.* Tokyo: Inakasha, 1929.

————. *Josei no sōzō.* Tokyo: Hihyōsha, 1925.

Muta Kazue. *Senryaku toshite no kazoku.* Tokyo: Shinyōsha, 1996.

Nagai Yoshikazu. *Dansu monogatari: [kōsai jutsu] no yunyūshatachi.* Tokyo: Riburopōto, 1994.

Nagamine Shigetoshi. *Zasshi to dokusha no kindai.* Tokyo: Nihon editāsukūru shuppanbu, 1997.

Najita Tetsuo and H. D. Harootunian. "The Debate on Modernity." In *Cambridge History of Japan,* vol. 6: *The Twentieth Century,* ed. Peter Duus, 758–68. Cambridge: Cambridge University Press, 1988.

Nakajima Kenzō. *Shōwa jidai.* Tokyo: Iwanami shinsho, 1957.

Nakamura Mitsuo. *Fūzoku shōsetsu ron.* Tokyo: Kawade shobō, 1950.

Narita Ryūichi. "Women in the Motherland: Oku Mumeo through Wartime and Postwar." In *Total War and Modernization,* ed. Yasushi Yamanouchi, J. Victor Koschmann, and Ryūichi Narita, 137–58. Ithaca: Cornell University Press, 1998.

Naruse Jinzō. *Naruse Jinzō chosakushū.* Vol. 2. Tokyo: Nihon joshi daigaku, 1956.

Natsume Sōseki. "Gendai Nihon no kaika." In Natsume Sōseki, *Watashi no kojinshugi,* 37–66. Tokyo: Kōdansha, 1988.

Nedan no Meiji, Taishō, Shōwa fūzoku shi. Tokyo: Asahi shinbunsha, 1981.

Newell, Susan. "Women Primary School Teachers and the State in Interwar Japan." In *Society and State in Interwar Japan,* ed. Elise Tipton, 17–41. London: Routledge, 1997.

Nicholson, Linda J. *Gender and History: The Limits of Social Theory in the Age of the Family.* New York: Columbia University Press, 1986.

Nihon fujin mondai shiryō shūsei. Vols. 1–4. Tokyo: Domesu shuppan, 1977.

Nihon fūzokushi gakkai, ed. *Nihon fūzokushi jiten.* Tokyo: Kōbundō, 1979.

Nihon hōsō shi. Tokyo: Nihon hōsō kyōkai, 1951.

Nii Itaru. "Eiga to josei ni kindaigata." 1928. In *Gendai bungakuron taikei— modanizumu geijutsuha,* 109–10. Tokyo: Kawade shobō, 1956.

————. *Gendai ryōki sentan zukan.* Tokyo: Shinchōsha, 1931.

————. *Kindaishin no kaibō.* Tokyo: Ijōsha, 1925.

Nishi Kiyoko. *Senryōka no Nihon fujin seisaku—sono rekishi to shōgen.* Tokyo: Domesu shuppan, 1985.

Nishikawa Junsei. *Fujin shin undō.* Tokyo: Kōkyō shoin, 1920.

Nishikawa Yūko. *Kindai kokka to kazoku moderu.* Tokyo: Yoshikawa kōbunkan, 2000.

Nishimura Isaku. *Ai to hangyaku—Bunka gakuin no gojūnen, Bunka gakuin shi hensanshitsu.* Tokyo: Bunka gakuin shuppanbu, 1971.

————. *Ware ni eki ari.* Tokyo: Kigensha, 1960.

Nishizawa Sō. *Zatsugaku—Kayō Shōwa shi.* Tokyo: Mainichi shinbunsha, 1980.

Nolletti, Arthur Jr. "Ozu's *Tokyo Story* and the 'Recasting' of McCarey's *Make*

Way for Tomorrow." In *Ozu's Tokyo Story,* ed. David Desser, 25–34. Cambridge: Cambridge University Press, 1997.

Nolte, Sharon H. *Liberalism in Modern Japan: Ishibashi Tanzan and His Teachers, 1905–1960.* Berkeley: University of California Press, 1987.

Noma Seiji. *Watashi no hansei.* Tokyo: Chikura shobō, 1936.

Nomoto Kyōko. "Kaji rōdō o meguru 'shufu' to 'jochū.' " In *Onna no sha-kaishi, 17–20 seiki—"Ie" to jendā o kangaeru,* ed. Ōguchi Yūjirō, 311–32. Tokyo: Yamakawa shuppansha, 2001.

Nomura Masaichi. "Koi no michi no magarikata—Shōwa no danjo kōsai." In *Shōwa no sesōshi,* ed. Ishige Naomichi. Tokyo: Domesu shuppan, 1993.

Odagiri Hideo. *Ko no jikaku—taishū no jidai no hajimari no naka de.* Tokyo: Shakai hyōronsha, 1990.

Ogi Shinzō, Haga Tōru, and Maeda Ai. *Tokyo kūkan, 1868–1930.* Vol. 3 of *Modan Tokyo.* Tokyo: Chikuma shobō, 1986.

Ogi Shinzō, Kumakara Isao, and Ueno Chizuko, eds. *Nihon kindai shisō taikei—fūzoku, sei.* Tokyo: Iwanami shoten, 1990.

Ogino Miho et al. *Seido toshite no onna—sei, san, kazoku no hikaku shakaishi.* Tokyo: Heibonsha, 1990.

Ōhama Tetsuya and Kumakura Isao. *Kindai Nihon no seikatsu to shakai.* Tokyo: Hōsō daigaku kyōiku shinkōkai, 1989.

Ohmann, Richard. *Selling Culture: Magazines, Markets, and Class at the Turn of the Century.* London: Verso, 1996.

Oka Mitsuo. *Fujin zasshi jānarizumu.* Tokyo: Gendai jānarizumu shuppankai, 1981.

Oka Yoshitake. "Generational Conflict after the Russo-Japanese War." Trans. and adapted by J. Victor Koschmann. In *Conflict in Japanese History: The Neglected Tradition,* 198–200. Princeton: Princeton University Press, 1982.

———. "Nichiro sensō-go ni okeru atarashii sedai no seichō—1905–1914." *Shisō,* no. 512 (February–March 1967): 1–2.

Okamoto Ippei. *Ippei zenshū.* Vol. 6. Tokyo: Senshinsha, 1928.

Okano Takeo. *Nihon shuppan bunkashi.* Tokyo: Hara shobō, 1981.

Ōkōchi Kazuo. *Nihonteki chūsan kaikyū.* Tokyo: Bungei shunjūshinsha, 1960.

Ōkoshi Aiko. *Kindai Nihon no jendā.* Tokyo: San'i chi shobō, 1997.

Ōkubo Hokushū. *Modan gāru hiwa.* Tokyo: Nishōdo, 1927.

Okuda Atsuko, ed. *Onna to otoko no jikū—Nihon joseishi saikō.* Vols. 1–6. Tokyo: Fujiwara shoten, 1995–96.

Ōtake Hideo. "Taishū shakairon no tōjō to henyō." In *UP,* no. 282. Tokyo: Tokyo daigaku shuppankai, 1996.

Ouditt, Sharon. *Fighting Forces, Writing Women: Identity and Ideology in the First World War.* London: Routledge, 1994.

Ōya Sōichi. *Ōya Sōichi zenshū.* Vol. 2. Tokyo: Eichōsha, 1982.

Ozu Yasujirō. *Ozu Yasujirō sakuhinshū.* Vol. 4. Tokyo: Rippū shobō, 1984.

Pflugfelder, Gregory M. " 'Smashing' Japanese-Style: Same-Sex Attachments in Prewar Japanese Girls' Schools." Paper prepared for the Eighth Berkshire Conference on the History of Women, Rutgers University, June 1990.

Pharr, Susan. *Losing Face: Status Politics in Japan.* Berkeley: University of California Press, 1990.

————. *Political Women in Japan: The Search for a Place in Political Life.* Berkeley: University of California Press, 1981.

Powell, Brian. "Matsui Sumako: Actress and Woman." In *Modern Japan: Aspects of History, Literature and Society,* ed. W. G. Beasley, 135–46. Berkeley: University of California Press, 1975.

Rabson, Steve. "Yosano Akiko on War: To Give One's Life or Not—a Question of Which War." *Journal of the Association of Teachers of Japanese* 25, no. 1 (1991): 45–74.

Raddeker, Helene Bowen. *Treacherous Women of Imperial Japan: Patriarchal Fictions, Patricidal Fantasies.* London: Routledge, 1997.

Rapp, Rayna, and Ellen Ross. "The 1920s Feminism, Consumerism, and Political Backlash in the United States." In *Women in Culture and Politics: A Century of Change,* ed. Judith Friedlander. Bloomington: Indiana University Press, 1986.

Rappaport, Erika Diane. *Shopping for Pleasure: Women in the Making of London's West End.* Princeton: Princeton University Press, 2000.

Riesman, David. *The Lonely Crowd.* New Haven: Yale University Press, 1959.

Rimer, J. Thomas, ed. *Culture and Identity: Japanese Intellectuals during the Interwar Years.* Princeton: Princeton University Press, 1990.

Robertson, Jennifer. *Takarazuka: Sexual Politics and Popular Culture in Modern Japan.* Berkeley: University of California Press, 1998.

Rodd, Laurel Rasplica. "Yosano Akiko and the Bunka gakuin: Educating Free Individuals." *Journal of the Association of Teachers of Japanese* 21, no. 1 (1991): 75–89.

Roden, Donald. *Schooldays in Imperial Japan: A Study in the Culture of the Student Elite.* Berkeley: University of California Press, 1975.

Rosenberg, Bernard, and David Manning White, eds. *Mass Culture: The Popular Arts in America.* New York: Free Press, 1957.

Rowbotham, Sheilah. *Hidden from History: Rediscovering Women in History from the Seventeenth Century to the Present.* New York: Vintage Books, 1976.

Rubin, Jay. *Injurious to Public Morals: Writers and the Meiji State.* Seattle: University of Washington Press, 1984.

Rubinger, Richard. "Who Can't Read and Write? Illiteracy in Meiji Japan." *Monumenta Nipponica* 55, no. 2 (2000): 163–99.

Ryū Kaori. *Danpatsu.* Tokyo: Asahi shinbunsha, 1990.

Saijō Yaso. *Uta no jijoden.* Tokyo: Seikatsu hyakka kankōkai, 1956.

Saitō Michiko. *Hani Motoko—shōgai to shisō.* Tokyo: Domesu shuppan, 1988.

———. "Senjika no josei no seikatsu to ishiki." In *Bunka to fashizumu,* ed. Akazawa Shirō and Kitagawa Kenzō, 285–326. Tokyo: Nihon keizai hyōronsha, 1993.

Saitō Minako. *Modan gāru ron: Onna no ko ni wa shusse no michi ga futatsu aru.* Tokyo: Magajin hausu, 2000.

Sakai Toshihiko. *Sakai Toshihiko josei ronshū.* Ed. Suzuki Yūko. Tokyo: San'ichi shobō, 1983.

Sakata Minoru. "Taishō kara Shōwa e." In *Shakai shinrishi—Shōwa jidai o megutte,* ed. Minami Hiroshi, 39–56. Tokyo: Seishin shobō, 1965.

Sand, Jordan. "The Cultured Life as Contested Space: Dwelling and Discourse in the 1920s." In *Being Modern in Japan: Culture and Society from the 1910s to the 1930s,* ed. Elise K. Tipton and John Clark, 99–136. Singapore: Australian Humanities Research Foundation, 2000.

Sanyū shinbunsha, ed. *Mitsukoshi sanbyakunen no shōhō: Sono hatten no monogatari.* Tokyo: Hyōgensha, 1972.

Sasaki Hideaki. *"Atarashii Onna" no tōrai—Hiratsuka Raichō to Sōseki.* Nagoya: Nagoya Daigaku Shuppankai, 1994.

Sasaki Kuni. *Sekensō ningensō.* Tokyo: Meiji insatsu, 1927.

Sato, Barbara Hamill. "The Moga Sensation: Perceptions of the Modan Gāru in Japanese Intellectual Circles during the 1920s." *Gender and History* 5, no. 3 (1993): 361–81.

———. "Sengo josei no yume to genjitsu—dokusha zadankai ni miru." In *Zoku Shōwa bunka—1945–1989,* ed. Minami Hiroshi. Tokyo: Keisō shobō, 1990.

———. " 'Sōgōka sareta' zasshi ni okeru jendā—no hyōshō—Taiyō 'Kateiran' o megutte." In *Nihon kenkyū,* no. 17, 273–83. Tokyo: Kadokawa shoten, 1997.

———. "Sōkan 'kinji no fujin mondai' to katei no rinen." In *Zasshi "Taiyō" to kokumin bunka no keisei,* ed. Sadami Suzuki, 554–67. Kyoto: Shibunkaku shuppan, 2001.

Scanlon, Jennifer. *Inarticulate Longings: The Ladies' Home Journal, Gender, and the Promises of Consumer Culture.* New York: Routledge, 1995.

Schrader, Barbel, and Jurgen Schebera. *The "Golden" Twenties: Art and Literature in the Weimar Republic.* New Haven: Yale University Press, 1990.

Scott, Joan Wallach. *Gender and the Politics of History.* New York: Columbia University Press, 1988.

Sechiyama Kaku. *Higashi Ajia no kafuchōsei—jendā no hikaku shakaigaku.* Tokyo: Keisō shobō, 1996.

Seidensticker, Edward. *Tokyo Rising: The City since the Great Earthquake.* New York: Alfred A. Knopf, 1990.

Sekii Mitsuo, ed. *Shiryō shihon bunka no modanizumu—Bungaku jidai no shosō.* Tokyo: Yumani shobō, 1997.

Shimoda Utako. *Kōsetu sōsho.* Vol. 5. Tokyo: Jissen jogakkō shuppanbu, 1933.

————. *Nihon no josei.* Tokyo: Jitsugyō no Nihonsha, 1912.

Shin feminizumu hihyō no kai, ed. *"Seitō" o yomu.* Tokyo: Gakugei shorin, 1987.

Shinozuka Eiko. *Josei to kazoku — Kindai no jitsuzō.* Vol. 8: *Nijū seiki no Nihon.* Tokyo: Yomiuri shinbunsha, 1995.

Shinseinen kenkyūkai, ed. *Shinseinen dokuhon zen ikkan.* Tokyo: Sakuhinsha, 1988.

Shokugyō fujin ni kansuru chōsa, 1922. Tokyo: Tokyo-shi shakaikyoku, 1924. Reprint, *Fujin jiritsu no michi,* in *Kindai fujin mondai meicho senshū zokuhen,* vol. 7. Tokyo: Nihon tosho sentā, 1982.

Showalter, Elaine. *Sexual Anarchy: Gender and Culture at the Fin de Siècle.* New York: Viking Penguin, 1990.

Shufu no tomosha no gojūnen. Tokyo: Shufu no tomosha, 1967.

Shuppanshi kenkyūkai. "Sōgō zasshi no kenkyū — sōgō zasshi hyakunen shi." *Ryūdō* (July 1979): 118–43.

Sievers, Sharon L. *Flowers in Salt.* Stanford: Stanford University Press, 1983.

Silberman, Bernard S., and H. D. Harootunian, eds. *Japan in Crisis: Essays on Taishō Democracy.* Princeton: Princeton University Press, 1974.

Silverberg, Miriam. "Advertising Every Body: Images from the Japanese Modern Years." In *Choreographing History,* ed. Susan Leigh Foster, 129–48. Bloomington: Indiana University Press, 1995.

————. "The Café Waitress Serving Japan." In *Mirror of Modernity,* ed. Stephen Vlastos, 208–25. Berkeley: University of California Press, 1998.

————. "Constructing a New Cultural History of Prewar Japan." In *Japan in the World. boundary 2* 18, no. 3 (1991): 129–48.

————. "The Modern Girl as Militant." In *Recreating Japanese Women, 1600–1945,* ed. Gail Lee Bernstein, 239–66. Berkeley: University of California Press, 1991.

Smith, Bonnie G. *Changing Lives: Women in European History since 1700.* Lexington, Mass.: University of Rochester, 1989.

Smith, Henry D. II. "The Edo-Tokyo Transition: In Search of Common Ground." In *Japan in Transition from Tokugawa to Meiji,* ed. Marius B. Jansen and Gilbert Rozman, 347–74. Princeton: Princeton University Press, 1986.

————. *Japan's First Student Radicals.* Cambridge: Harvard University Press, 1972.

Snitow, Ann, Christine Stansell, and Sharon Thompson, eds. *Powers of Desire: The Politics of Sexuality.* New York: Monthly Review Press, 1983.

Sōgō jānarizumu kōza. Vols. 7–12. Tokyo: Naigaisha, 1931–32.

Sonoda Hidehiro. "Kindai Nihon no bunka to chūryū kaikyū. In *Toshi bunka,* vol. 2 of *Kindai Nihon bunkaron,* ed. Aoki Tamotsu et al., 99–116. Tokyo: Iwanami shoten, 1999.

Sugimura Sojinkan. *Jakusha no tame ni.* Tokyo: Shiseidō shoten, 1916.

Sukegawa Koreyoshi. "Taishōki kyōyō-ha to hihyō no dōkō." In *Nihon bungaku zenshū*, vol. 5. Tokyo: Gakutōsha, 1978.

Sukemori Kingo. *Joshi shinsahō*. Tokyo: Kinkōdō, 1928.

Sumiya Mikio. "Kokumin teki vijon no tōgō to bunkai." In *Kindai Nihon shisōhi kōza—shidōsha to taishū*, vol. 5. Tokyo: Chikuma shobō, 1960.

Suzuki Bunshirō. *Fujin mondai no hanashi: Asahi joshiki kōza*. Vol. 9. Tokyo: Asahi shinbunsha, 1929.

Suzuki Sadami. *Modan toshi no hyōgen: jiko, gensō, josei*. Kyoto: Hakuchisha, 1992.

———, ed. *Modan gāru no yūwaku—Modan toshi bungaku*. Vol. 2. Tokyo: Heibonsha, 1989.

Suzuki Sadami et al. "Hakubunkan bunka." *Hōsho gekkan*, no. 170 (November 1999): 2–29.

Taishō daishinsai dai kasai. Tokyo: Dainihon yūbenkai—kōdansha, 1923.

Takahashi Akira. "Toshika to kikai bunmei." In *Kindai Nihon shisōshi kōza*, vol. 6, ed. Odagiri Hideo, 173–230. Tokyo: Chikuma shobō, 1960.

Takahashi Keiji. *Nihon seiseikatsushi*. Tokyo: Shunjūsha, 1931.

Takamure Itsue. *Takamure Itsue zenshū*, vol. 7. Tokyo: Rironsha, 1967.

Takasu Yoshijiro. "Taishō, Shōwa no kokumin shisō." In *Nihon seishin kōza*, vol. 8. Tokyo: Shinchōsha, 1934.

Takemura Tamio. *Taishō bunka*. Tokyo: Kōdansha, 1980.

Takeuchi Yō. *Taishū modanizumu no yume no ato*. Tokyo: Shinyōsha, 2001.

Takita Keiko. " 'Shinseinen' no jidai to Amerika—aru Nihon modanizumu no tanjō." *Tokyo daigaku hikaku bungaku kai—hikaku bungaku kenkyū*, no. 56 (December 1989): 60–80.

Tanaka Sumiko, ed. *Josei kaihō no shisō to kōdō—senzen hen*. Tokyo: Jiji tsūshin, 1975.

Tanizaki Junichirō. *Naomi*. Trans. Anthony H. Chambers. New York: North Point Press, 1999.

Terade Kōji. *Seikatsu bunkaron e no shōtai*. Tokyo: Shibundō, 1994.

Tinkler, Penny. *Constructing Girlhood: Popular Magazines for Girls Growing Up in England, 1920–1950*. London: Taylor and Francis, 1995.

Tipton, Elise K. "The Café: Contested Space of Modernity in Interwar Japan." In *Being Modern in Japan: Culture and Society from the 1910s to the 1930s*, ed. Elise K. Tipton and John Clark, 120–34. Singapore: Australian Humanities Research Foundation, 2000.

Tocqueville, Alexis de. *Democracy in America*. Vol. 2. New York: Vintage Books, 1945.

Tokutomi Soho. *Dairoku nichiyō kōdan*. Tokyo: Minyūsha, 1905.

Tokyo ero on parēdo. Tokyo: Shōbunkaku shobō, 1931.

Tokyo hōsōkyoku enkaku shi. Tokyo: Tokyo hōsōkyoku enkaku shi henshū iinkai, 1928.

Tokyo shi shakaikyoku, ed. *Fujin jiritsu no michi.* In *Kindai fujin mondai meicho zenshū zokuhen*, vol. 7. Tokyo: Nihon tosho sentā, 1982.

Tomotsugu Jutarō. *Mezurashii saiban jitsuwa.* Tokyo: Hōrei bunka kyōkai, 1932.

Tsudajuku rokujūnenshi. Tokyo: Tsudajuku daigaku shuppan, 1960.

Tsukamoto Shūko. "Yosano Akiko, Hiratsuka Raichō, Yamakawa Kikue no bosei hogo ronsō." In *Nyūmon josei kaihōron*, ed. Ichibangase Yasuko, 223–55. Tokyo: Aki shobō, 1975.

Tsumuraya Hiroshi. *Kafe bunka no shogenshō.* Tokyo: Shakai gaitōsha, 1928.

Tsurumi, E. Patricia. *Factory Girls: Women in the Thread Mills of Meiji Japan.* Princeton: Princeton University Press, 1990.

Tsurumi Shunsuke. "Taishōki no bunka." In *Tsurumi Shunsuke shū—gendai Nihon shisōshi*, vol. 5, 411–13. Tokyo: Chikuma shobō, 1991.

Tsutsui Kiyotada. "Kindai Nihon no kyōyōshugi to shūyōshugi." *Shisō*, no. 812 (February 1992): 151–74.

———. *Nihongata "kyōyō" no unmei: Rekishi-shakaigakuteki kōsatsu.* Tokyo: Iwanami shoten, 1995.

Tunstall, Jeremy. *The Media Are American: Anglo-American Media in the World.* London: Constable, 1977.

Uchida Roan. "Onna no zasshi no genzai to shōrai." In *Uchida Roan zenshū*, vol. 3, 95–97. Tokyo: Yumani shobō, 1987.

Uchikawa Yoshimi, Matsushima Eiichi, et al. *Taishō nyūsu jiten.* Vol. 5: *Taishō 10–Taishō 11.* Tokyo: Mainichi komyunikēshon, 1988.

Ueno Chizuko. *Kindai kazoku no seiritsu to shūen.* Tokyo: Iwanami shoten, 1994.

———, ed. *Shufu ronsō o yomu.* Vol. 1. Tokyo: Keisō shobō, 1994.

Ueno Chizuko et al. *Sekushuariti no shakaigaku.* Vol. 10: *Gendai shakai gaku.* Tokyo: Iwanami shoten, 1996.

Unno Hiroshi. *Modan toshi Tokyo: Nihon no senkyūhyaku nijū nendai.* Tokyo: Sanyōsha, 1983.

Uno, Kathleen. "Good Wives and Wise Mothers in Early Twentieth Century Japan." Paper presented at a joint meeting of the Pacific Coast Branch of the American Historical Association and the Western Association of Women Historians, San Francisco, California, August 11, 1988.

———. "The Origins of 'Good Wife, Wise Mother' in Modern Japan." In *Japanische Frauengeschichte(n)*, ed. Erich Pauer and Regine Mathias, 31–47. Marburg: Forderverein Marburger Japan-Reihe, 1995.

———. "Women and the Changes in the Household Division of Labor." In *Recreating Japanese Women*, ed. Gail Lee Bernstein, 17–41. Berkeley: University of California Press, 1991.

Wada Hirobumi. "Dansu hōru no hikari to kage." In *Nihon no bungaku*, vol. 13, 129–47. Tokyo: Yūseidō, 1993.

Wada Yōichi, ed. *Shinbun gaku o manabu hito no tame ni.* Tokyo: Sekai shisōsha, 1980.

Wagatsuma Sakae. *Atarashii ie no rinri—kaisei minpō yowa.* Tokyo: Gakushū shoin, 1949.

Wakamori Tarō. *Nihon no joseishi.* Vol. 4: *Atarashisa o motomete.* Tokyo: Shūeisha, 1966.

———. *Ryūkō sesō kindaishi—ryūkō to sesō.* Tokyo: Yūzankaku, 1970.

———. *Taishū bunka no jidai—zusetsu.* Vol. 8 of *Nihon rekishi.* Tokyo: Chūō kōronsha, 1961.

Wakita Haruko, ed. *Bosei o tō—rekishiteki hensen.* Vol. 2. Kyoto: Jinbun shoin, 1985.

Wakita Haruko and Susan B. Hanley, eds. *Jendā no Nihonshi.* Vols. 1–2. Tokyo: Tokyo daigaku shuppankai, 1994.

Watashitachi no rekishi o tsuzuru kai, ed. *Fujin zasshi kara mita 1930 nendai.* Tokyo: Dōjidaisha, 1987.

Williams, Raymond. *Communications.* London: Penguin Books, 1962.

———. *The Politics of Modernism: Against the New Conformists,* ed. and intro. Tony Pinkney. London: Verso, 1995.

Williams, Rosalind H. *Dream World: Mass Consumption in Late Nineteenth-Century France.* Berkeley: University of California Press, 1992.

Wilson, Sandra. "Women, the State and the Media in Japan in the Early 1930s: *Fujo shinbun* and the Manchurian Crisis." *Japan Forum* 7, no. 1 (1995): 87–106.

Wöhr, Ulrike. "Early Feminist Ideas on Motherhood in Japan: Challenging the Official Ideal of 'Good Wife, Wise Mother.' " *Hiroshima Journal of International Studies* 2 (1996).

———. "Mo hitotsu no *Seitō*—onnatachi no rentai o mezashita zasshi *Shinjin fujin.*" In *Nihon joseishi saikō-kindai,* vol. 5, ed. Okuda Akiko, 312–34. Tokyo: Fujiwara shoten, 1995.

Wollstonecraft, Mary. "Of the Pernicious Effects Which Arise from the Unnatural Distinctions Established in Society." In *A Vindication of the Rights of Woman* (1792), ed. Carol H. Posyon, 140–50. New York: W. W. Norton, 1988.

Woloch, Nancy. *Women and the American Experience.* New York: Alfred A. Knopf, 1984.

Wright, Barbara Drygulski. Introduction to *Women, Work, and Technology,* ed. Barbara Drygulski Wright, Myra Marx Ferree, Gail O. Mellow, Linda H. Lewis, Maria-Luz Daza Samper, Robert Asher, and Kathleen Claspell. Ann Arbor: University of Michigan Press, 1987.

Wright, Gwendolyn. "Prescribing the Model Home." In *Home: A Place in the World,* ed. Arien Mack. New York: New York University Press, 1993.

Yamada Keiko. "Atarashii Onna." In *Onna no imēji,* vol. 1 of *Kōza joseigaku,* ed. Joseigaku Kenkyūkai, 210–34. Tokyo: Keisō shobō, 1984.

Yamada Masahiro. *Kindai kazoku no yukue—Kazoku to aijō no paradokusu.* Tokyo: Shinyōsha, 1994.

Yamada Waka. *Josei sōdan*. Ed. Tokyo Asahi shinbunsha. Tokyo: Kimura shobō, 1932. Reprint, *Kindai fujin mondai meicho zenshū*. Vol. 8: *Shakai mondai hen*. Tokyo: Nihon tosho sentā, 1983.

Yamada Yoshie, Torii Toshiko, Yoshizawa Chieko, and Nakai Yoshiko. " 'Seitō' ni kakawatta hitobito." In *Taishōki no josei zasshi*, ed. Kindai josei bunkashi kenkyūkai, 149–281. Tokyo: Ozorasha, 1996.

Yamaguchi Masao. "Meiji shuppankai no hikari to yami—Hakubunkan no kōbō." In *Zasshi "Taiyō" to kokumin bunka no keisei*, ed. Suzuki Sadami, 115–52. Kyoto: Shibunkaku shuppan, 2001.

———. *Uchida Roan Sanmyaku*. Tokyo: Shōbunsha, 2001.

———. *"Zasetsu" no Shōwa shi*. Tokyo: Iwanami shoten, 1995.

Yamakawa Kikue. *Yamakawa Kikue shū*. Vols. 1–4. Tokyo: Iwanami shoten, 1982.

Yamamoto Akira. *Fūzoku no ronri*. Tokyo: Weekend Books, 1979.

Yamamoto Kikuo. *Nihon eiga ni okeru gaikoku eiga no eikyō—hikaku eiga shi kenkyū*. Tokyo: Waseda daigaku shuppanbu, 1983.

Yamamoto Taketoshi. *Shinbun to minshū—Nihon gata shinbun no keisei katei*. Tokyo: Kinokuniya shoten, 1978.

Yamamoto Taketoshi and Nishizawa Tamotsu, eds. *Nihon no hyakkaten no bunka: Nihon no shōhi kakumei*. Tokyo: Sekai shisōsha, 1999.

Yamamoto Taketoshi and Tsuganezawa Toshihiro. *Nihon no kōkoku—hito, jidai, hyōgen*. Tokyo: Nihon keizai shinbunsha, 1986.

Yamazaki Masakazu. *Fukigen no jidai*. Tokyo: Kōdansha, 1986.

Yanagi Yōko. *Fasshonka shakaishi—haikara kara modan made*. Tokyo: Gyōsei, 1987.

Yanagida Izumi, Katsumoto Seiichirō, and Ino Kenji. *Taishō bungaku shi— zadankai*. Tokyo: Iwanami shoten, 1965.

Yanagita Kunio. *Meiji Taishō shi—sesōhen*. Tokyo: Heibonsha, 1967.

Yasumaru Yoshio. *"Hōhō" toshite no shisōshi*. Tokyo: Azekura shobō, 1996.

Yoneda Sayoko. "Shufu to shokugyō fujin." In *Iwanami kōza*, vol. 18 of *Nihon tsūshi*, ed. Asao Nagahiro, Amino Yoshihiko, Ishii Susumu, Kanō Masanao, Hayakawa Shōhachi, and Yasumaru Yoshio, 169–203. Tokyo: Iwanami shoten, 1994.

Yosano Akiko. *Teihon Yosano Akiko zenshū*. Vol. 20. Tokyo: Kōdansha, 1980.

Yoshimi Shun'ya. "Amerikanaizēshon to bunka no seijigaku." In *Gendai shakai no shakaigaku*, vol. 1 of *Gendai shakaigaku*, ed. Mita Munesuke, Inoue Shun, Ueno Chizuko, Ōsawa Masachi, and Yoshimi Shun'ya, 157–231. Tokyo: Iwanami shoten, 1997.

———. "Taishū bunka ron—komyunikēshon toshite no taishū bunka." In *Shinbungaku hyōron*, no. 39 (April 1990): 78–86.

———. *Toshi no doramutorugi—Tokyo/sakariba mo shakaishi*. Tokyo: Kōbundō, 1987.

Young, Louise. *Japan's Total Empire: Manchuria and the Culture of Wartime Imperialism*. Berkeley: University of California Press, 1998.

———. "Marketing the Modern: Department Stores, Consumer Culture, and the New Middle Class in Interwar Japan." In *International Labor and Working-Class History*, no. 55, 52–70. New York: International Labor and Working Class History, 1999.

Magazines

Bungei shunjū, 1923–36
Chūō kōron, 1913–36
Fujin kōron, 1916–44, 1952–62
Fujin kurabu, 1920–45
Fujin no kuni, 1925–26
Fujin no tomo, 1920–30
Fujin sekai, 1908–30
Fujo zasshi, 1891–92
Fujokai, 1910–43
Ie no hikari, 1925–38
Jogaku sekai, 1901–25
Jogaku zasshi, 1885–1904. Reprint. Tokyo: Rinsen shoten, 1984.
Josei, 1922–28
Josei kaizō, 1922–23
Kaizō, 1919–38
Katei, 1901–2
Katei zasshi. Reprint. Tokyo: Ryūkei shosha, 1982.
Modan Nippon, 1930–32
Seitō, 1911–16
Shincho, 1920–32
Shufu no tomo, 1917–45
Taiyō, 1900–1922

Newspapers

Kokumin shinbun, 1910–34
Tokyo Asahi shinbun, 1918–33
Tokyo nichin nichi shinbun, 1920–31
Yomiruri shinbun, 1900–1935

Index

Cott, Nancy, 186n. 40
Culture: America and, 31–32, 38–39, 72–73, 187n. 55; consumerism, 34–38, 49–51, 178nn. 88, 92, and 93; music, 35, 80, 126, 128, 189n. 6; popular, 18–19, 38, 42, 84, 178n. 92, 191n. 15; speed *(speedo/sokudo)*, 38–39. *See also* Film; Magazines, women's
Curti, Lidia, 165n. 4

Daily Life Reform Movement (Seikatsu kaizen undō), 102–3, 195n. 65, 196n. 66
Davis, Natalie Zemon, 167n. 20
Day, Dorothy, 169n. 7
De Gracia, Victoria, 13
Department stores, 29; in America, 177n. 79; escapism and, 16; in Germany, 35; Mitsukoshi (department store), 27–28; modern girl in, 46, 121, 122, 157; modernity and, 105. *See also* Magazines, women's
A Doll's House (Ibsen), 14–15, 27
Domesticity: changes in, 102–3, 195n. 65, 196n. 66, 197n. 70; efficiency and, 39, 178n. 93; food preparation, 102–3; gender roles in, 24, 106, 173n. 36, 197n. 70; Nora in *A Doll's House* (Ibsen), 14–15, 27; and the professional working woman, 127; "protection of motherhood debate" *(bosei hogo ronsō)*, 23–25, 172n. 34, 173n. 36; technology and, 39, 43, 163; women's magazines and, 85–86, 88–89, 93, 106. *See also* Housewives *(shufu)*
Dore, R. H., 36

Earthquake (Kantō daishinsai, 1923), 8, 19, 32–34, 45, 178n. 92, 180n. 110
Ebina Danjō, 110
Economics: Daily Life Reform Movement (Seikatsu kaizen undō), 102–3, 195n. 65, 196n. 66; and disposable income, 30, 36, 174n. 55; and household management, 100–102, 136, 195n. 64; of the leisure class *(yūkan kaikyū)*, 37; and outside employment and marriage, 133, 135–37; in post–World War I era, 30, 174n. 55; and professional working woman, 128–29; and purchase price of magazines, 92, 96; and women's independence, 132–34

Education: alternative, 40–41, 180n. 105; and coeducational schools, 124; employment opportunities and, 116, 138–40; and "good wife and wise mother" *(ryōsai kenbo)*, 5–6, 20, 86, 153, 167n. 21, 192n. 20; higher education, 25–26, 89–91, 129–30; and independence, 40–41, 180n. 105; marriage and, 41, 146, 180n. 105; of the new woman *(atarashii onna)*, 14, 19–20; of the professional working woman, 128–29, 203n. 47; and reading, 14, 35–36, 90, 134–38, 205n. 73; self-determination and, 200n. 3; women's magazines and, 19, 80, 82, 91–94, 96, 106–7
Employment: and class, 115–16; discrimination in, 21–23; discussions of in magazines, 117–18; and economic independence, 24, 74, 131–34; education and, 129–30, 155; of factory workers, 119, 123, 201n. 24, 205n. 68; and gender-differentiated labor, 142, 207n. 106; of *gāru* ("such-and-such" girl), 119, 120–24; lifestyle changes and, 150–51; of middle-class women, 115, 139–40; motherhood and, 24; for rural women, 139–40, 154; and salaried class *(shin chūkan sō)*, 37; as self-advancement, 129–30, 154–55, 204nn. 57 and 58; as self-cultivation, 135; social class and, 128–32, 203n. 47, 204n. 57; as social experience, 136; statistics on women, 115–16, 129–30; wages, 96, 116–17; war and, 124–25, 156–57, 209n. 9; and the woman problem *(fujin mondai)*, 142; and women as objects of sexual curiosity, 119–26, 157–59; and workplace relationships, 158–59. *See also* Professional working woman *(shokugyō fujin)*
Enchi Fumiko, 110, 199n. 98
Europe, 8, 30, 31–32, 38

Family: children's education and, 19–20; and collective family services, 39, 179n. 98; family system

234 *Index*

Kurata Hyakuzō, 134, 144, 186n. 42, 208n. 115
Kurishima Sumiko, 110
Kuriyagawa Hakuson, 144
Kuwabara Takeo, 28, 30

Leisure, 103, 105, 163
Literacy and reading, 14, 35–36, 90, 134–38, 205n. 73
Locke, John, 173n. 36
Lukács, Georg, 23

Mackie, Vera, 172n. 27
Maeda Ai, 108
Maeda Hajime, 201n. 18
Magazines, women's: advertisements in, 83, 85, 88, 98; as community forum, 82, 108–9, 116–17; confessional articles *(kokuhaku kiji)* in, 81, 82, 105–8, 113, 197n. 78; current events in, 98–99; editorial policies of, 80–81, 87–88, 189n. 6; education and, 80, 82, 91–94, 96, 106–7; family articles *(katei kiji)* in, 81, 97, 100; "good wife and wise mother" *(ryōsai kenbo)* in, 86, 192n. 20; gossip columns in, 109–10; intellectuals on, 79, 82–84, 86–87, 100–103; job opportunities discussed in, 138–39; on love marriages, 147–48, 162; the modern girl in, 54–55, 56, 57–60, 63, 88–89, 183n. 12; photography in, 104–5; practical articles *(jitsuyō kiji)* in, 100–101; readers' letters in, 106–8, 117–18, 137, 138, 144–45; rural women and, 81, 106, 139–40, 154, 190n. 8; self-cultivation articles *(shūyō)* in, 81, 115, 137–38, 147–49, 200n. 3; sensationalism in, 36, 63, 68, 72, 109–11; social class and, 23–24, 80–82, 90–91, 190n. 8; state censorship of, 107; traditional image of women in, 84–85, 88–89; trendy articles *(ryukō kiji)* in, 81, 97, 99, 103–5; and women journalists, 125–26
Marriage: employment and, 136, 141–42, 158, 207n. 106; gender roles in, 14–16, 19–21, 24–25, 169n. 8, 173n. 36; and husband selection, 142–46; love marriages, 147–48, 155, 161–

62; and Meiji Civil Code, 2, 15–16, 169n. 8; and the new woman, 14–16, 19–21, 169n. 8, 184n. 29; parents and, 146–48, 153, 158–59, 161–62; patriotism and, 159; professional working woman and, 126–27, 135; self-cultivation and, 135–36, 141, 143–46; sexual freedom and, 39–40, 61–63, 184n. 29; and stereotype of single women, 3; women's education and, 41, 180n. 105; in women's magazines, 93–94, 109–11, 117, 147–48, 162; and workplace relationships, 158–59; World War II and, 162. *See also* Gender roles; Sex and sexuality
Maruyama Masao, 5
Marx, Eleanor, 14
Marxism, 21, 22, 25, 156, 175n. 62
Massification *(taishūka)*, 30, 42–43, 82, 180n. 110
Masuda Giichi, 205n. 73
Matsui Sumako, 15, 80
Matsushita Keiichi, 180n. 110
Mechanization *(kikaika)*, 31, 33, 39, 179n. 101
Meiji Civil Code: family in, 40, 73, 79, 159; marriage, 2, 15, 169n. 8; women's magazines and, 85–86; women's status in, 1–2, 15–16, 22, 79, 169n. 8
Meiji period: education in, 90–92, 209n. 1; and *Fujin sekai* (Women's World) magazine, 93–94; "good wife and wise mother" *(ryōsai kenbo)* in, 86, 192n. 20; housewives in, 79, 188n. 2; industrialization *(kindai)* during, 7; magazines in, 91–92; and women's employment, 133
Middle class: education and, 58, 129–30, 204n. 57; and leisure, 103; as magazine readers, 17, 36, 81–82, 190n. 8; and "protection of motherhood debate" *(bosei hogo ronsō, 23–25, 172n. 34, 173n. 36; self-advancement of, 129–30, 204nn. 57 and 58; self-cultivation and, 134, 135, 200n. 3, 205n. 69; sexuality of, 119–20, 204nn. 57 and 58; social activism of, 152–53, 155–56; war and, 18–19, 23–24, 30, 162, 174n. 55; in work force, 115,

Shimanaka Yūsaku, 106
Shimoda Utako, 20, 23, 79
Shufu no tomo (Housewife's Companion) magazine: confessional articles *(kokuhaku kiji)* in, 105–6, 197n. 78; current events in, 98–99; intellectuals on, 84; marketing of, 94, 97–100; on marriage, 159; practical articles *(jitsuyō kiji)* in, 100–101; readers' letters in, 117, 137, 138; self-cultivation and, 137, 138; traditional image of women in, 84–85; and women's wartime employment, 156–57, 209n. 9
Sievers, Sharon, 171n. 21, 172n. 27
Silverberg, Miriam, 181n. 3, 186n. 43
Smith, Bonnie, 186n. 40
Smith, Henry DeWitt, 199n. 98
Social activism, 20–23, 59, 152–53, 155–56
Social class: consumerism and, 30; and employment, 115–16, 129–32, 203n. 47, 204n. 57; friendships and, 108; and magazine readership, 23–24, 80–82, 90–91, 190n. 8; *modanizumu* (modernism) and, 37; modern girl and, 48, 72; people's history *(minshū-shi)* and, 5–6, 166n. 10; upper-class women, 79, 110–11; and women's history, 4–6; and women's magazines, 80–82, 90–91, 190n. 8; working class women, 5
Social girl *(shakai josei)*, 59
Socialism, 21–23
Soeta Azenbō, 128, 129
"A Solution to the Woman Problem" (Fujin mondai no kaiketsu), 22
Speed (speedo/sokudo), 38–39
Sugimura Sojinkan, 199n. 103
Sukegawa Koreyoshi, 205n. 70
Sukemori Kinji, 196n. 66
Suzuki Bunshirō, 55–56
Suzuki Sadami, 181n. 3
Swanson, Gloria, 51

Tada Michitaro, 180n. 110
Tago Kazutami, 142–43
Takahashi Akira, 178n. 92
Takamure Itsue, 57, 58, 59, 67, 185n. 38
Takasu Yoshijirō, 38
Takeuchi Yō, 205n. 69

Tanaka Sumiko, 4
Tanizaki Junichirō *(Naomi)*, 35, 46, 181n. 2
Technology, 1, 33, 38, 39, 43, 74, 163, 180n. 110
Techow, Herman, 2
Tetsuo Najita, 178n. 88
Tinkler, Penny, 84
Tokutomi Sohō, 18
Tokyo: cafés, 69, 186n. 43; cultural changes in, 33–34, 176n. 70; Ginza, 49–50, 62, 63, 182n. 5; Great Kantō Earthquake and, 33–34, 45; middle-class women in, 18; movie theaters, 79–80; rural women in, 28, 139–40, 154
Tokyo City Employment Bureau for Women (Tokyo-shi fujin shoku-gyō shōkaijo), 115, 156
Tokyo City Office Survey (1922, 1931), 96, 131, 132, 133–35, 141–42
"Tokyo Marching Song" (Tokyo kō-shinkyoku), 35, 80, 126
Tokyo Story (Tokyo monogatari), 2–4
Tomi *(Tokyo Story)*, 3
Trendy articles *(ryūko kiji)*, 81, 97, 99, 103–5
Tsuda Umeko, 20
Tsugawa Masashi, 87
Tsuji Jun, 143
Tsurumi Shunsuke, 180n. 110
Tsutsui Kiyotada, 200n. 3
Tunstall, Jeremy, 187n. 55

Uchida Roan, 83, 86
Unno Hiroshi, 176n. 70
Uno, Kathleen, 167n. 21
Urban women: consciousness of, 43; cultural changes and, 18–19, 33–34, 176n. 70; as magazine readers, 81, 190n. 8

Wagner, Charles, 195n. 65
Wakakuwa Midori, 209n. 9, 211n. 18
Wakamori Tarō, 30, 42
Wakita Haruko, 6
Westernization: America and, 31, 38–39, 67, 68, 72, 73, 186n. 40, 187n. 55; clothing and, 51, 55, 63, 104; Europe and, 8, 30, 31–32, 38; of hairstyles,

Barbara Sato is Professor of History at Seikei University in Tokyo, Japan.

Library of Congress Cataloging-in-Publication Data

Sato, Barbara.
The new Japanese woman : modernity, media, and women in interwar Japan /
Barbara Sato.
p. cm. — (Asia-Pacific)
Includes bibliographical references and index.
ISBN 0-8223-3008-3 (cloth : alk. paper) — ISBN 0-8223-3044-X (pbk. : alk. paper)
1. Women—Japan—History—20th century.   2. Sex role—Japan—History—20th
century.   3. Feminism—Japan—History—20th century.   4. Social change—
Japan—History—20th century.   5. Japan—Social conditions—20th century.
I. Title.   II. Series: Asia-Pacific.
HQ1762.S353   2003
305.4'0952'0904—dc21   2002015237